Good Times

Clay Lindsay
A Good Man from Mason, Texas

The People, Places and Events
that Shaped His Life

Deloris Haley Lindsay

DEDICATION

I dedicated this book to my husband, Alva Clay Lindsay.

I had been divorced for several years and was perfectly content with my life. I was not looking for another husband. My mother met Clay at his place of business. She said, "I found someone you need to meet. I've checked him out, and no one has anything bad to say about him." Mom did not give up. She continued to sing his praises.

A few months and a couple of phone calls later, we met. The AT&T Christmas Party was to be a dinner and dance. I needed a date, so I called this man I had never met and asked him if he would like to go to dinner and a dance. He said, "Yes."

Because of a twist of fate, our first meeting was at my mother's house, just as she wanted. We went to the party. One song we danced to was "For the Good Times" by Ray Price. That became our song. Less than a year later, on Oct. 30, 1971, I married that handsome, hard-working, honest, fun-loving, mischievous, unassuming, well-respected, witty, 49-year-old bachelor.

When I asked him why he never married before, he said, "I guess I was just waiting for you."

Clay died June 14, 2020, a few months before our 49th wedding anniversary. I am glad you waited for me, Clay. Thank you for the "Good Times."

Table of Contents

ACKNOWLEDGMENTS

In the early 1990s, about 9 p.m., my phone rang. A man said, "This is Jack Lindsay, and I'm trying to locate Clay Lindsay." My response, "The only Jack Lindsay I know has been dead for years. Who are you, and what do you want?"

Jack Alan Lindsay explained that he was researching the Lindsay family and that his grandfather and Clay's grandfather were brothers. That was the beginning of our lifetime friendship with Jack Alan and Peggy Bue Lindsay. Yes, Jack and Peggy Lindsay. They have the same names as Clay's brother and one of his sisters.

The information they shared formed the foundation of the family research that I have continued for over twenty years.

After Clay's death, I asked family and friends to share their memories of him. I included some family history and shared it with those attending his memorial service. The project grew and grew, took on a life of its own, and it became this book.

Clay's nieces and nephews were an invaluable source of information about his former life. Family archives, letters, news clippings, ancestry and census records, Clay's stories, and his WWII diary supplied much information.

My friends, Kathleen F. Roe and Patricia Crisler, my cousin, Marvetta Mayo, my daughter, Alica Kay Lindsay, and my sister, Pamela Haley Bruce, proofread many chapters. Thank you for your suggestions and encouragement.

Our friend, Milton Bailey, shared stories of his experiences as a lifelong cowboy and manager of large sheep, goat, and cattle ranches and what it means to "work sheep."

A big thank you to Clay's 2nd-cousin, Charles A. Kettner, Ph.D. Charles is the editor of "Die Kettner Briefe: The Kettner Letters: A Firsthand Account of a German Immigrant in the Texas Hill Country (1850-1875)." He shared information about self-publishing and information about Clay's great-grandfather, Franz (Francis) Kettner.

Many thanks to our nephew, Coby James of Gulf Coast Imaging Studios Texas City, Texas, for processing the photos.

My sincere thanks and deepest appreciation go to Rory and Kristi Glasgow. When I asked for someone to help format this book, Mr. Glasgow graciously volunteered. "Good Times" would not have been published without you.

INTRODUCTION

Most people don't become interested in family history until the people they should have listened to are gone. I listened to my grandmother, and I developed an interest in family history from her shared stories. My ancestors are not just names on a page. To me, they are real people. They lived and loved, and they are the reason that I exist.

When my husband, Alva Clay Lindsay, died, I wanted to share a few stories about his life so that future generations would know him. I included his ancestors because they made him the exceptional man that he was. I included personal stories and stories from family and friends because they knew him best.

When you finish reading "Good Times," start your family history journey. It will be important to someone you love.

1

James Buchanan Lindsay

James Buchanan Lindsay, Alva Clay Lindsay's 2nd-great-grandfather, was born March 29, 1813, in Lincoln, Tennessee. The 1840 census lists James, his wife, Martha, and four children living in Jackson, Alabama. His father, John, and several other family members also lived in Jackson.

In the 1840s, James, his wife, children, and father John, moved to Titus County Texas. Alva Clay Lindsay's great-grandfather, John Allen Lindsay, was James and Martha's oldest son.

Titus County is in northeastern Texas, one county removed from the state's northern boundary and two counties removed from the state's eastern boundary. Mount Pleasant is the county seat and the county's largest town. It is located sixty miles southwest of Texarkana and 105 miles northeast of Dallas.

Titus County comprises 412 square miles of the East Texas timberlands, which is heavily forested with a great variety of softwoods and hardwoods, especially pine, cypress, and oak.

The earliest Anglo settler in what is now Titus County is said to have been Kendall Lewis, who moved into the county in 1835 with his wife, probably a Creek Indian.

Lewis's land grant, patented February 1842, is said to have been the first land surveyed in the County. The family settled on Swauano Creek and remained in the County until problems with Indians caused the Lewis family to leave the State in 1846.

During the early 1840s, settlement of the area proceeded rapidly. In 1846, the First Legislature of Texas established Titus County, which included present-day Morris and Franklin counties. Titus County was named for Andrew Jackson Titus, an early Red River County settler. Mount Pleasant was established as the County seat.

The State Census of 1847 lists the population of Titus County as over 2,500. Titus County's economy was based on agriculture. Corn was the most important food crop. Cotton was the most important cash crop.

In 1850, 3,750 people lived in the county. The 269 farms produced 66,000 bushels of corn and 292 bales of cotton. County farmers also reported 6,838 cattle, 1,014 sheep, and 12,315 hogs that year.

The Lindsay, Allen, Coots, Smith families, and Thomas Stanley Milligan lived in the same community. These families would become intertwined.

Margaret (Peggy) Allen, Hugh Joseph Allen's oldest daughter, was born in Smithville, DeKalb, Tenn., Aug. 9, 1821. Margaret was 18 when she married Andrew Jackson Coots Aug. 19, 1839. They had seven children before he died 10 years later: Dec. 19, 1849.

On Jan. 9, 1851, Margaret Allen Coots married James A. Smith. He died Dec. 17, 1851. Margaret was pregnant. Their child was born in 1852. Margaret Allen Coots Smith, twice widowed, had eight children, the oldest 11 years old and the youngest an infant.

1852 was not a good year for the Lindsay family. James' wife Martha died leaving him a widower with four children: Elizabeth 15, John 14, William 12, and Thomas 10.

James Buchanan Lindsay and Margaret (Peggy) Allen Coots Smith married Sept. 12, 1852. Together, they raised their combined families plus four daughters while they lived in Mason, Texas.

On Aug. 25, 1860, when the census was taken, the family lived north of town. James was 47; Margaret was 39. Six children lived in the household; Monroe Coots 17, Martha Coots 15, James Smith 8, and three little girls: Mary 5, Catherine 2, and Alameda who was three months old.

The same census shows that John Allen Lindsay, age 22, was married to 17-year-old Matilda Ellen Milligan, the daughter of Thomas Stanley Milligan.

John Allen and Matilda Ellen Milligan Lindsay had 12 children, two sons, and 10 daughters. Alva James (A. J. or Al) Lindsay, their oldest son, was Alva Clay Lindsay's great-grandfather.

John Allen died Oct. 01, 1891. He is buried in the Lindsay Family Cemetery on the Lindsay Ranch, five miles north of Mason on U.S. Highway 87.

John's brother, William M. Lindsay, married Julia Anolio Hendricks. William died Oct. 13, 1897. Their brother, Thomas D. Lindsay, never married. He died Texas, Feb. 21, 1917. All three brothers died in Mason, Texas.

James' oldest daughter, Elizabeth, married C. L. D. Adams. After his death, she married George B. Burns. Elizabeth died Sept. 1, 1891, in Mason. They are also buried in the Lindsay Family Cemetery.

The following obituary was printed in the Mason News Saturday, May 25, 1886:

Mrs. Margaret Lindsay

"Mrs. Margaret Lindsay departed the life at 9 o'clock p.m., May 10, 1886, in the 65th year of her age.

She died at the residence of her niece, Mrs. Bird, five miles north of Mason, Texas. She was buried in the Crosby Cemetery in the presence of a large concourse of relatives and friends, the Rev. Mr. Leaton officiating. For three months, Mrs. Lindsay had been sick nigh onto death, most of this time being spent at the residence and under the tender care of her devoted daughter, Mrs. T. R. Cox, the faithful wife of Mason's long-standing and worthy chief magistrate.

It must be a sweet consolation to the many relatives and friends of the deceased to know that in her painful and long-continued sickness, she had every attention that loving sons and daughters and other relatives could bestow and that she died in the full faith of a bright beyond.

Mrs. Lindsay was born in Tennessee, and when yet a mere girl espoused the cause of Christ and identified herself with the Primitive Baptist Church of which she remained a consistent member to the day of her death. Her father, the Rev. Mr. Allen, moved with his family to Titus County, Texas, where Miss Margaret was united in marriage with Mr. Coots, who died, leaving her with six children, one of whom, George, preceded his mother to the great unknown by only a few days, from the residence of our same worthy townsman, T. R. Cox, Esq., leaving a large family and many relatives and friends to mourn his loss.

After the death of Mr. Coots, the elder, his widow, was united in marriage with Mr. Smith, who died leaving her one child, Mr. James A. Smith of Peter's Prairie, Mason County, a good citizen and a great consolation to his mother in her declining years.

After the death of Mr. Smith, his widow was united in marriage with Mr. James B. Lindsay, the father, of a former marriage, of our fellow citizens John A. and Thomas D. Lindsay.

Thirty years ago, Mrs. Lindsay moved with her third and last husband from Titus to Mason County. At that time, this was a vast howling wilderness, with no church or school or mill within a hundred miles of where Mason now stands; but Mrs. Lindsay, through all the dark hours incident to the raising of a large family, fourteen children, in such a wilderness, not only never forgot her early Christian training, but so far succeeded in impressing the great practical principals of the Christian religion upon her offspring that of all her fourteen children, forty grandchildren, and ten great-grandchildren, not one of them was ever arraigned before any court of justice, even on a charge of a misdemeanor and perhaps there is not one of them living today who could not look the world square in the face and truthfully say "I owe no bank." The fundamental principles of her religion were: "Be honest, owe no man, love one another."

Mr. Lindsay died in 1874 in Colorado, where they had gone in 1870 for the benefit of his health. After this sad event, she returned and spent most of her time with her son, James, here in Mason County.

Mrs. Platt, nee Lindsay, of Austin, who was with her mother in her last sickness, is the only surviving child of seven by her mother's third marriage. Only three of the children of the first or Coots marriage remain - Mrs. T. R. Cox of Mason, Mrs. C. S. Cox of Weed, New Mexico, and Mr. M. J. Coots of Walsenburg, Colorado.

Mrs. Margaret Lindsay was emphatically a frontier Christian woman who lived and died, was loved and respected by all who know her. How many of us could say with Mrs. Lindsay? "Should the Death Angel knock at my door tonight, I am ready."

Note: The above was taken verbatim from the "Mason News" of May 15, 1886. by Peggy L. Lindsay, wife and associate researcher and compiler of the Lindsay Family Genealogy, Jack A. Lindsay, Rt. 2 Box 580 Liberty Hill, Texas 78642 (20 February 1992 JAL) copied August 14, 1999, by Deloris Haley Lindsay.

Why did Margaret and James go to Colorado? Who went with them? We can find Margaret nor James in the 1870 census. However, Margaret's son, Monroe Jackson Coots, age 27, is living on the Huerfano River and Tributaries, Huerfano, Colorado Territory, United States. The Census Post Office: Butte Valley.

Some of the Caveness family also traveled from Mason to Colorado. Monroe Jackson Coots and Mary Ellen Caveness married in Colorado on May 4, 1872. They had several sons and daughters before Monroe died Dec. 23, 1892.

Family information states that James died Aug. 17, 1873, in Butte Valley, Huerfano, Colorado, at 60 years of age. Margaret returned to Texas. Census records show the Coots family in Walsenburg, Colorado, for many years. Some stayed there, while others moved to New Mexico and back to Texas.

The Lindsay family and their relatives were traveling people!

2
Hugh Joseph Allen, Sr.

Hugh Joseph Allen, Sr. was born in Pitt, Stokes, North Carolina, May 21, 1801, to Hezekiah Allen and Martha Elizabeth Fereby Lawson. He married Caroline Matilda Frazier in Tennessee in 1819-1820. They had 13 children before Caroline died Dec. 6, 1867. Hugh married Elizabeth Mescal Dec. 11, 1870, in Burnet County, Texas. He was still living in Burnet County when he married Mary Edwards, Jan. 13, 1878.

Hugh Joseph Allen, Sr. wrote a letter to his son, Hugh Joseph Allen, Jr. in 1886. He wrote that he did not expect to live long. He said that he was almost blind and crippled. He died Sept. 5, 1886 in Red Rock or Bastrop, Texas, at the age of 85. Mr. Allen's burial place is not known. Some information states that he is buried in High Grove Cemetery in Bastrop, Texas but a search did not find his grave; other information has suggested that he bought two plots in the Old Burnet Cemetery.

Hugh Joseph Allen, Sr. accomplished a lot and traveled many miles in his 85 years. He traveled from North Carolina to Texas and then he continued traveling all over the settled areas of the state. Mr. Allen lived a full life, as you will learn when you read his story.

Hugh and Caroline were living in Tennessee when their first child, Margaret, was born in 1821. Over the next few years, their family continued to grow as did their property. Some of the land surveys of property belonging to Mr. Allen are:

- ALLEN, Hugh-16A survey on Jones Fork of Caney Fork Begin E50P S50P W50P N50P Entry 309 24 Aug 1824. SCC Wm Austin & Hardy Allen.
- Tennessee. 1826 - 9 Nov; (Smith Co., TN Surveys Bk 1 p217)
- 1839 -June 18 -DeKalb Co, TN Deed Book A p 310

It is not known why they left Tennessee and traveled to Texas. It was a long, difficult journey for the family of seven. When they arrived in Titus County in 1838-39, the family had four daughters, Margaret, Mahala, Martha, Caroline and one son James Madison Allen.

Some of the Allen's neighbors in Titus County were James Buchanan Lindsay and his family and Thomas Milligan. Hugh's oldest daughter, Margaret, would later become the wife of Mr. Lindsay. Her sister, Mahala, married Thomas Milligan. We will learn more about Margaret and Mahala as they and their children become members of the Lindsay family.

Hugh Allen received a land grant in Red River Co, Texas; 1200 or 1600 acres, situated in Titus and Cass Counties in 1838. No one knows how long they stayed in that area but nine years later, in 1847, the family was living in Bexar Co, Texas in on Cibolo Creek, two miles from Selma, Texas.

A notice from the Postmaster in Clarksville, Texas, dated April 21, 1849, reads: "A list of letters remaining in the Post office at Clarksville, Texas, which if not taken out by the 30th of June next, will be forwarded to the Post office Department as dead letters." There are approximately 200 names listed. It is signed by John A. Bagby P. M. April 1, 1849. Two of the people listed are Allen, Hugh and Allen, Mrs. A. (I wonder if those letters are still in the dead letter department?)

Clarksville, the county seat of Red River County, is fifty-eight miles northwest of Texarkana near the center of the county. It was incorporated by an act of the Texas Congress in 1837. From the late 1830s until the Civil War, Clarksville was the most important trading center in Northwest Texas. Steamboats brought goods from New Orleans by way of the Red River and delivered them to Rowland's Landing fifteen miles to the north. A post office opened in 1846, and in 1848 semi-weekly mail service was instituted between Clarksville and Natchitoches, Louisiana.

The Allen family were living on Cibolo Creek in Bexar Co, Texas in 1847. Cibolo Creek was called "Xoloton" by the early Coahuiltecan Indians of the area and "Bata Coniquiyoqui" by Tonkawa Indians. During the expedition of the Marqués de San Miguel de Aguayo in 1721 the stream was named "Río Cibolo."

In 1768 the Marqués de Rubí included Cibolo Creek in his list of potential sites for posts to solidify the Spanish hold on Texas. In the late 1840s and early 1850s the communities of Schertz, Sutherland Springs, Cibolo, Boerne, La Vernia, and Bulverde were established along the creek.

The Allen family were still living on Cibolo Creek at the time of the 1850 census. They were a family of nine. The children that had come to Texas with them were living elsewhere except for James Monroe Allen who was 18 years old when the census was taken. The other children living with them, all two years apart, were: Hugh Jr.; Mary; Elizabeth; Daniel; Sarah and little Rebecca who was only 2 years old. The census also shows that the Allen, Greenwood and Turner families were next-door-neighbors. The interaction between these families will be seen later in the story.

The 1860 census shows the Allen family living in Selma, Texas, Bexar County. At that time, only Daniel, Sarah and Rebecca were living with their parents, Hugh and Caroline. Daniel Parker Allen saw service as a member of the Confederate States Army during the American Civil War. Two young men named Daniel P. Allen enlisted in the CSA in April 1862 in Clarksville, TX. One of these men was Hugh Allen's son.

The first Daniel P. Allen enlisted April 1, 1862, for 18 months. Comm. Off: Sanders, V. P., Capt., Co. A. 15th Regt., TC. Col. Geo. H. Sweet Comdg., CSA. His age was not listed.

The second Daniel P. Allen was 21 years old when he enlisted April 21, 1862. This is the right age for our Daniel. Com. Off: Johnson, John, Captain. Co. A. 15th Reg. TC, Col. Geo. H. Sweet Comdg. Comdg., CSA. This young man enlisted for 12 mos.; reenlisted for war Mar. 6, 1864, near Dalton, Ga.

Daniel Parker Allen married 20-year-old Margaret Matilda "Milly" Wooten, who was born Mississippi. They were wed May 25, 1868, at Wolf's Crossing in Llano, Texas. Daniel's family moved back and forth between Llano County and Camp San Saba. Their first child, William, was born at Camp San Saba Feb. 25, 1869.

On August 11, 1870, when the census was taken, Daniel, Matilda, their one-year-old son William, Daniel's 70-year-old father Hugh Allen and 6-year-old nephew, Hugh Thomas Saunders, Rebecca's son, were living together in the Sandie Mountain Area of Llano County, Texas.

Their second child, Gracie, was also born at Camp San Saba Jan. 21, 1872. The family must have settled in the Wolf's Creek area in Llano County because that is where their other children were born in 1873, 1874 and 1875.

There is no record of Daniel's death, but Matilda is listed in the 1880 census as a 31-year-old widow. She is living with her widowed father, W. E. Wooten and her four children at Camp San Saba in McCullough County, Texas. At this time, Hugh Joseph Allen, Sr. is living in Burnet, Texas with his wife Mary. He is sick and suffering from a "nervous affection" according to the census. He is living next door to his son Hugh Joseph Allen, Jr.

From: Frontier Times Magazine: Vol 10, #6, Mar-1933, Early History of Camp San Saba:

Camp San Saba was the largest town and principal settlement in McCulloch County until after the organization of the county and establishment of Brady as the county seat in 1876.

The road leading from Fort Mason is said to have been established in 1850 by direction of Col. Harvey of the Second U. S. Dragoons, and Camp Colorado, on Jim Ned Creek about nine miles east of where Coleman, Texas now stands, which was established by Major Van Dorn of the Second Cavalry in 1856 crossed the San Saba River at a point known as the Hardee of Camp Colorado Crossing.

The name Hardee was evidently after William Joseph Hardee, an officer who served with distinction in the Mexican War and who entered the Confederate Army in the Civil War, with the rank of colonel and was promoted to lieutenant general. He was at one time commandant of West Point Military Academy and was also author of Hardee's Tactics, the standard military tactics manual during the Civil War period.

In the southern part of McCulloch County is the beautiful San Saba River. This was Comanche country. They made their winter camp among the granite rocks near the head of a creek that bears the name of their formidable old chief, Chief Ketemoczy, from whose name comes the more abbreviated name Katemcy.

Among the cliffs and deep little gorges of these granite rocks the old chief and his tribe would spend the winter, and then in the springtime move to more pleasant quarters down on the San Saba, near the present village of Camp San Saba.

It was at or near this spot that John O. von Meusebach, the founder of Fredericksburg and commissioner general of the Adelsverein, also known as the German Emigration Company, met with a large band of Comanche warriors and their chiefs in the early part of 1847.

After being in council with them for several days he arranged for another meeting at the next full moon at which time he again met with them at a point evidently several miles below, and made a treaty allowing the Germans to survey and explore the whole San Saba country.

The territory was surveyed in 1847 under the supervision of John J, Giddings. This land is part of the Fisher and Miller grant by President Sam Houston to them in 1843; they ceded or sold their rights to the Adelseverin or German Emigration Company. Part of the Lindsay Ranch is on the Fisher and Miller grant.

Hugh Allen, Alva Clay Lindsay's 3rd great-grandfather, was the first white settler in the Katemcy Creek area, McCulloch County, just a few miles north of Mason. For a living, he hunted, killed and skinned the Texas Longhorn cattle. A century later, Alva Clay Lindsay and his father, John Alva Lindsay, also lived on Katemcy Creek.

In the early part of the Civil War companies of state troops known variously as rangers, mounted volunteers, etc., were organized all over the state. The ones in this part of the state were a part of Col. J. E. McCord's regiment.

One or more of these companies had a camp on the San Saba River about a mile or a mile and a half south and east of the Hardee crossing above referred to, near another crossing known as the Flat Rock crossing. They were quartered in log cabins and a few tents.

It was from this camp of rangers that the town of Camp San Saba took its name. It is said that the first soldiers to occupy the camp were members of Capt. McMillan's company of San Saba and among the members of that company is said to have been W. W. Brooks, Mart Bolt, "Doc" Hansford, the company physician, W. L. Hays, Tom Fry, Dick Nelson, Tom Forker and others. This great article is excellent genealogy and history of the area.

Further mentions of some of Alva Clay Lindsay's relatives are R. Caveness, Farrier. Capt. O'Brien's Company, Enlisted men: W. W., Caveness, S., Caveness, William, Crosby, J., Coots, J. B., Lindsay, T. D., Lindsay, C. C., Turner, and Geo. Gamel; These men were from the counties of McCulloch, Mason, San Saba, Llano, Burnet and possibly one or two from Blanco. Hugh Allen: Katemcy Creek, the old Fisher and Miller map published in 1855 has it Katemsey's Creek; Tecumseh Creek.

William R. Turner and his family moved to the Hugh Allen place on Feb. 12, 1861, according to a member of the family. Several families moved into the county about 1862, there was quite a settlement on Lost Creek a few miles east of Camp San Saba. These early settlers lived in log or picket houses, some with puncheon floors, and some with flag-stone floors.

William R. Turner, mentioned above, was the first to build a stone house. This residence was quite large, and, having several children, his home must have been the social center of the time. Judge Woodall is said to have taught school in Camp

San Saba at a very early day, as did Miss Moss and Miss Allen; Camp meetings were held in the early days.

A Masonic lodge was organized at or near Camp San Saba in 1864 thought to have been principally among the members of the "ranger" camp. This lodge later became McCulloch Lodge No. 273 A. F. & A. M., and was moved to Mason, Texas, and the Masonic Lodge at that place still retains the same name and number.

Just after the Civil War, several people moved into the country up and down the river and started cattle ranches.

Frontier Times Magazine, Vol 9, #4, Pg. 170-171 published this letter from Mrs. Maddux:

We are in receipt. of a letter from a real Texas mother, Mrs. Mattie A. Maddux, 922 West 9th Street, Dallas, Texas, who has been a regular reader of Frontier Times for the past six or seven years, and which we are glad to publish for the good information it contains.

Mrs. Maddox is a daughter of William Greenwood, who settled in Mason County in the early fifties, and was one of the prominent citizens of that section for many years. The letter follows:

Dear Mr. Hunter: An article in the November number of your magazine gives Mr. Turner credit for being the oldest settler at Camp San Saba.

His grandfather settled near that place in the latter '5Os. He moved to that county from near San Antonio and lived there several years. He was also my grandfather, and when I was a child, I spent many pleasant hours in the old log house built by Grandfather Allen.

One Christmas my father's family went to visit them, and when we arrived my grandmother had a big fat turkey roasting before the big log fire. There was also another settler at the time grandfather lived there by the name of Rumsey, or Ramsey. I remember going fishing with a pin hook in a little branch near the home. It had no name that I can remember.

I also remember that we went to a bluff where the bees were coming out of a hole, and Jack Couch was suspended by a rope, and he took out the honey if there was any. One night one of my uncles and this man Couch thought they would go out and get a turkey. It wasn't long until they heard a turkey gobble. They went toward where the call seemed to come from. Presently the air was full of arrows, and my uncle was shot in the back.

Soon afterward my grandfather Hugh Allen, left that county. Then Mr. Bill Turner moved there. I do not know whether he occupied the house grandfather built, but I am inclined to think he did. I once knew all these people. I never was at Camp San Saba. It was a household word for several years. I thought you might want to keep the record straight is why I am sending you this note.

Albert Turner is younger than myself, and I remember quite well when they moved to that county. They spent the night in my father's home. I expect I enjoy your magazine more than any of your readers. As soon as the postman delivers the little yellow back magazine I repair to my room and read every page before closing it. I am eighty-one years old today and am getting pretty feeble.

The following letter from Hugh Allen to Governor Runnels will give you a glimpse of what life was like on the Texas frontier.

TAKEN FROM TEXAS INDIAN PAPERS 1846-1859, pgs. 308-309-310

No 203 LETTER FROM HUGH ALLEN TO H dated NOV. 21, 1858

SAN SABA RIVER BELKNAP CROSSING 18 MILES NORTH OF FT. MASON, TEXAS
GOV RUNNELS MY DEAR SIR
I WISH TO INFORM YOU THE CONDITION THAT I AM PLAICED (PLACED) IN ON THE ACCOUNT OF NO PROTECTION NOR SECURITY OF LIFE OR PROPERTY. I HAVE LIVED 20 YEARSE ON THE FRONTEERS OF TEXAS AND THIS IS THE FIRST TIME I EVER MARKED PAPER ON THE ACCOUNT OF INDIANS DEPREDATION, BUT THO TROUBLED OFTEN BY THEM LAST MARCH THE 27 AT LATE DUSK MY SONE WAS SHOT WITH AN ARROW SLIGHTY IN ONE MILE OF MY HOUSE THAT KNIGHT AT 12oc

I REPORTED TO MAJOR THOMAS COMMANDER AT FT. MASON REQUESTED MEN TO BE AT MY HOUSE BY SUNRIZE NEXT MORNING THE DISTANCE OF 18 MILES AT 12oc SARGENT NcNELTY CAME WITH 10 MEN WENT TO THE SAN SABA RIVER IN 400 YARDS OF THE PLACE THE DEPRECATION WAS COMMITTED THERE THEY FISHED AND WALLOWED ABOUT UNTIL PAST 2oc

THEN THEY WENT TO THE PLACE THARE WE FOUND THREE ARROWS SHOT INTO A LOG MOCKESON TRACKS AND HORSE TRACKS THEY THEN FOLLOWED THE TRAIL ABOUT 2 MILES AND RETURNED BACK AND THERE CAME A RAIN THEY THEN RETURNED TO FT. MASON AND I UNDERSTAND REPORTED THEY FOLLOWED THE TRAIL 15 MILES AND THE RAIN DESTROYED THE TRAIL THAT WAS PARTE OF G. COMPANY 2CAY.

AND ON THE 27 OF OCT LAST THE INDIANS CAME AND STOLE THE LAST HORSE WE HAD AND KILLED WHAT BEEF THEY WANTED AND DROVE OFF THE NEXT MORNING I SENT MY SONE TO FT. MASON LIEUTENANT SHAFFER OF B COMP WAS IN COMMAND HE SAID TO MY SONE THAT IT WAS NOT THE INDIANS IT WAS WHITE MEN SO RECEIVED NO HELP.

THREE DAYS AFTERWARDS A GOVERNMENT TRAIN COMING FROM FT. CHADBOURNE CAME WITH WHITE BLANKETS LIKE THE RESERVE INDIANS GETS OF GOVERNMENT

THE REASON THE CITISONS DO NOT CALL ON THE MILITARY FORCES WHEN THEY CALL, THEY ARE HERD AND HERD NO GOOD IS DONE.

THE REPORT OF MANY TO THE WAR DEPARTMENT THAT IT IS WHITE MEN HAS COST MANEY A WOMAN AND CHILDS LIFE AND NOW THE WOODS ARE FULL OF INDIANS SINE IN ONE MILE OF MY HOUSE I DARE NOT TO LEAVE MY HOUSE TO DO ONE MILE ON ANEY BUSINESS FOR FEAR MY FAMILY IS MURDERED BEFORE I CAN GET BACK.

I PAY MY TAXES AS OTHER CITISONS FOR PROTECTION AND HAS CALLED TO GET IT NOW MY DEAR SIR. I CALL ON YOU FOR SOME PROTECTION IN SOME WAY THE IDEY OF WAITING INTIL WE SEE WHAT EFECT THIS LARGE CAMPEIGN WILL HAVE. I THINK EVER SINCE VAN DORN ROUTED THEM AND DISMOUNTED SO MANEY THEY HAVE BIN DOWN TO GET MORE HORSES AND I THINK HE WILL DRIVE THEM DOWN ON US SO NO MORE AT PRESENT BUT IT REMAINS YOURS, ETC HUGH ALLEN SEN ENDORSED HUGH ALLEN NOVR 21

In April 1859 Hugh moved his family back to Cibolo creek. He had previously sold that property to William Turner, husband of his daughter, Martha Ann. He and William Turner traded the Cibolo Creek for the Katemcy Creek property. William Turner moved his family onto the Katemcy property sometime after Oct. 12, 1860, when he purchased it from Hugh Allen.

Much has been written about that property in the Handbook of McCulloch County History, Volume 1 and published by Pioneer Book Publishers.

The original stone floor of Hugh's cabin can still be seen today. The property is now called Wau-Ban-See. The original building built by William Turner is still there today and was a historical site until closed by the present owners. The spring located at this ranch house was a long-ago meeting place for Indians. The name, Wau-Ban-See, is an Indian name meaning "Earth Mirrored in the Water."

Alva Clay Lindsay's 3rd great-grandfather, Hugh Joseph Allen, Sr. was a remarkable man.

Mr. Allen's daughter, Mahayla, married Thomas Stanley Milligan, the first sheriff of Mason County, who was kill by Indians in 1860. Their daughter, Matilda Ellen Milligan, married John Allen Lindsay, they were Clay's great grandparents.

3
Thomas Stanley Milligan

Information about Thomas Stanley Milligan's birth differ. Some sources state that he was born in Hardin, Tennessee in May 1810 to William Milligan and Eleanor Michie.

According to the story written by his great-great-granddaughter, Ruth Murray Dannheim, Source: Mason County Historical Book, copyright 1976, p. 193, Thomas was born in Ireland.

The records I found indicate that Thomas' father, William, was probably born in Ireland. and that Thomas Stanley Milligan was born in May 1810 in Hardin, Tennessee. No matter where he was born, Thomas seems to have gotten to Texas as quickly as he could and his life here is what is important.

Thomas Stanley Milligan settled in Titus County Texas in the 1840's. He married, Mahala Maybelle Allen, the 17-year-old daughter of Hugh Joseph Allen in February 1843. There is more about Hugh Joseph Allen and his family in another chapter.

Tom worked at freighting on the Texas Coast. The 1850 census shows the Milligan family living in Travis County. Both Thomas and his wife's birthplaces are listed as Tennessee. At that time, Thomas is listed as a 31-year-old laborer.

The census taker must have written the wrong age. Thomas was born in 1810, he would have been 41 when the 1850 census was taken. Mahala is 24 years old. They have three children ages 8, 6 and 4.

Ruth wrote, "At an early time, Tom was associated with the Fort Clark Community." TSHA | Handbook of Texas (tshaonline.org) has a wonderful article on Fort Clark.

In 1849 Lt. W. H. C. Whiting, was looking for a practicable wagon route between San Antonio and El Paso. He recognized its military potential and recommended the location as a site for a fort. Fort Clark was established June 10, 1852, at Las Moras Springs in Kinney County. The Fort's purpose was to guard the Mexican border, to protect the military road to El Paso, and to defend against Indian depredations arising from either side of the Rio Grande.

According to Bvt. Lt. Col. W. G. Freeman, on August 1, 1853, the quartermaster had only eight wagons available for hauling the materials needed to build the post.

This was an inadequate number since the depot at Corpus Christi was 280 miles distant and wagons required thirty days, under favorable conditions, to make the round trip.

Mail came to the post from San Antonio, "being brought weekly by special express." Perhaps this was Tom's connection with Fort Clark. He was in the freighting business, and everything was supplied by wagons.

In 1855, Tom Milligan settled in Mason County. Here he engaged in ranching and butchering cattle for the soldiers of Fort Mason. He made his headquarters in the locality later known as Hightower's Park, a mile north of Mason.

Some information indicates that Tom purchased this land from his brother-in-law, James Madison (Matt) Allen.

In 1858 Mason County was organized and the first sheriff elected was Tom Milligan. Depredation by Indians was a foremost part of his official work. On Feb. 19, 1860, eighteen months after his election, Tom was killed by Indians.

He was keeping mules for the mail line and had gone to bring in the mules and was surprised by Indians on his return; though he resisted valiantly, he was slain. However, the Indians failed in getting the mules.

Mahala and her six children were in their house when this happened. She could hear the shouts and screams. To calm her children, she read to them all night. One of their descendants, Jane Dunn Sibley, had the book Mahala read from and the spear point that killed Tom.

From the Texas State Gazette in Austin, Texas:

"Thomas S. Milligan was born in Nelson County, Kentucky in 1810 and died about two miles northwest of Fort Mason, February 19, 1860." (This birthplace is incorrect.)

A news item written by G. W. Todd was published in the March 10, 1860, edition of the Texas State Gazette, Austin, Texas. The news item was dated February 20, 1860, and it says in part:

"Last evening, February 19, about seven o'clock our worthy friend and neighbor, Thomas S. Milligan was most brutally murdered by the Indians within 2 miles of Ft. Mason and withing 200 yards of his house. Signed by G. W. Todd"

Thomas S. Milligan and Mahalia (Allen) Milligan, with their six children arrived at Fort Mason, Texas December 5, 1855. At that time the town of Mason was nonexistent.

There were no stores, the settlers bought all their supplies at the fort.

A few families were living on the Comanche and Gamel creeks, and in a radius of two miles of the fort one could find a few log cabins. The fort had been abandoned for almost two years except for a detail of soldiers sent from Fort McKavett.

Tom was buried in Crosby Graveyard. Note: Crosby Graveyard (Cemetery) is also known as Koocksville Cemetery

Ruth Murray Dannheim wrote, "The death of Sheriff Milligan left his widow with seven children, six girls and one boy: the oldest, a daughter of sixteen, and the youngest a baby. Belle Milligan was three years old. No frontier woman faced a heavier task of providing for her family or carried on with more fortitude than did Mahalia Milligan. She was the leader and encourager of her children.

As a young boy James, her son, worked in the fields; holding the plow while one of his sisters led the oxen---they had two yokes of oxen. Some neighbors volunteered help, but most of the tilling of the soil and work about the farm was performed by Mahala and her children. Mahala looked after the land and rode a saddle horse like a man. Not least among the difficulties was the heavy conditions imposed by the Civil War.

Sheriff Milligan left some cattle, and the family continued to increase the herd. The cattle industry became the chief source of revenue: the cattle were grazed on open range.

After selling the original homestead they moved to Honey Creek and later to a place north of Mason. As a means of supplementing her meager income, Mahalia and her daughter made clothing to be sold in the general store.

The seven children of Tom and Mahalia Milligan were: Matilda Ellen (Mrs. John Allen Lindsay), Margaret (deceased as a child), Mary (Mrs. William Henry Caviness and secondly, Mrs. George Bird), James (married Dora Hill and later Josephine Gamel), Belle (Mrs. Tom Murray), Martha (deceased), and Lydia (Mrs. M. Elliott).

This good pioneer mother of seven passed away in the spring of 1890 and was buried in the Crosby Cemetery beside her husband."

Thank you, Ruth, for writing this story about your and Clay's ancestors. I hope you don't mind that I changed a few words and added a thing or two. Deloris Haley Lindsay. Jan. 30, 2021.

There is a historical marker on Fort McKavett Street (US 87) in Mason that tells the story of Thomas S. Milligan. The marker reads as follows:

TWO SHERIFFS OF MASON COUNTY

A native of Kentucky, Thomas S. Milligan (1810-1860) moved to this area in 1855 and operated a change station for the stage line. He was also a rancher and supplied beef to the soldiers at Fort Mason.

Shortly after Mason County was organized in 1858, he became the first elected sheriff. Two years later he was killed by hostile Indians near his home (1.6 mi. NW).

His grandson Allen Thomas Murray (1880-1929) became county sheriff in 1924 and like his grandfather died in the line of duty. He was killed by a bootlegger near this site in 1929. (1980)

Another report about the incident reads:

Thomas Milligan was elected sheriff of Mason County shortly after the county was organized in 1858. He died two years later in an Indian attack on what was then the lawless Texas frontier.

70 years later, his grandson Allen Murray had been elected Sheriff of Mason County. In 1929, he was also killed in the line of duty, by bootleggers, not by Indians.

Sheriff Allen Murray was shot and killed while attempting to arrest two men for possessing containers of whiskey. The gunman was convicted of first-degree murder and sentenced to death on May 22, 1930. He was executed in the electric chair June 19, 1931.

Sheriff Murray was survived by his wife, son, and daughter. His wife was appointed to fulfill his unexpired term as sheriff.

LINDSAY – ALLEN – MILLIGAN FAMILY CONNECTIONS

Many families came from Tennessee to Texas in the 1830'S. Three of those families, the Lindsay's, Allen's, and Thomas Milligan, combined. They are some of Alva Clay Lindsay's ancestors. These families are shown to be living in Titas County, Texas, on the 1850 census.

James Buchanan Lindsay, Clay's 2nd great-grandfather, Thomas Milligan, also a 2nd great-grandfather, and Hugh Joseph Allen, Clay's 3rd great-grandfather, lived in Titus County, Texas, at the same time. They all knew each other. James Buchanan Lindsay's wife, Martha, died in Titus County.

Margaret Allen Coots Smith, Hugh Joseph Allen's oldest daughter, was widowed, for the second time. When Martha Lindsay died, James and Margaret married. Thomas Stanley Milligan married 17-year-old Mahala Maybelle Allen, Hugh Joseph Allen's second daughter.

These families went their separate ways, but between 1855 and 1860, the Lindsay and Milligan families moved to Fort Mason. Margaret Allen Coots Smith Lindsay and Mahala Maybelle Allen Milligan were sisters.

Thomas Stanley Milligan was killed Feb. 19, 1860. He left his widow, Mahala, and seven children. The oldest child, Matilda Ellen, was 16 years old.

The 1860 census shows the James Buchanan Lindsay family living in Mason. James' son, John Allen Lindsay, is married to 16-year-old Matilda Ellen Milligan, the oldest daughter of Thomas Stanley Milligan, who was killed on February 19th.

With that marriage, Matilda Lindsay's aunt Margaret also became her mother-in-law. Margaret's children, John Allen Lindsay's stepbrothers and stepsisters, and half-brothers and half-sisters were Matilda's cousins. And around and around we go. Thankfully, as far as we know, there was no feuding and fighting.

John Allen Lindsay and Matilda Ellen Milligan had twelve children, two sons, and ten daughters. Their oldest son, Alva James (A. J. or "Al") Lindsay, was born April 21, 1863, in Mason, Texas. Alva James Lindsay was Alva Clay Lindsay's grandfather.

No one knows where the name "Alva" originated, but it was passed on for three generations. Alva James named his son John Alva, and he named his son Alva Clay.

Clay's nephew, James Lindsay Long, who spent some time in Scotland, suggested that "Alva" might be a Scottish name. I found that Alva was from the Old Norse Germanic language spoken by ancient Scandinavia peoples; think

Vikings. Those fierce warriors ruled most of Scotland, England, and Europe for over 400 years. Clay's DNA shows 49% from Scotland and 30% from England and Northwestern Europe. Good call, Jim.

4
Sterling Clack Robertson

Sterling Clack Robertson was born Oct. 2, 1785, in Nashville, Davidson County, Tennessee. He served as Major of Tennessee troops in the War of 1812 and 1814 and was honorably discharged. He received a liberal education and was reared in the occupation of planting. He engaged in agriculture in Giles County, Tennessee, but in a few years moved to Nashville.

Mr. Robertson, along with Stephen F. Austin and 10 others, became empresarios of Mexican Texas. An Empresario entered into a contract with the Mexican government to settle a certain number of families in Texas in exchange for sizable land grants.

Enterprising and adventurous, and being possessed of large means, in 1823, he formed a company in Nashville to explore the wild province of Mexican Texas. He penetrated as far as Brazos and formed a permanent camp at the mouth of Little River.

All the party returned to Tennessee, however, except Col. Robertson. He visited the settlements that had been made, and while there, conceived the idea of planting a colony in Texas.

He returned to Tennessee. In 1825 he purchased a contract made by the Mexican government with Robert Leftwich for the settlement of 800 families in Texas.

The enterprise had previously been referred to as the Texas Association, Leftwich's Grant, the Nashville colony, or the upper colony. Please go to The Handbook of Texas website: TSHA Browse Entries (tshaonline.org). His efforts eventually resulted in what was known as Robertson's Colony.

The original contract permitted the introduction of colonists into an area covered by all or part of seventeen present-day Texas counties: Bastrop, Bell, Brazos, Burleson, Burnet, Comanche, Coryell, Falls, Hamilton, Lampasas, Lee, Limestone, McLennan, Milam, Mills, Robertson, and Williamson.

On Oct.15, 1827, the government granted a confirmation in the name of the Nashville Company. This contract extended the colony's boundaries to take in all or part of 13 more present-day counties: Bosque, Brown, Callahan, Eastland, Erath, Hill, Hood, Jack, Johnson, Palo Pinto, Parker, Somervell, and Stephens.

Mexican leaders feared a rebellion of Anglos and annexation to the United States. In 1828, an official inspection tour from San Antonio to Nacogdoches revealed that Anglo-Americans greatly outnumbered native Mexicans in Texas.

Although there was no obvious subversive activity, the Anglos continued to speak only English and conducted legal matters primarily in Anglo tradition. The authorities concluded that Mexico might lose Texas if more Anglo-Americans were allowed to enter. They thought that native Mexicans should be encouraged to settle in the frontier state to "Mexicanize" it.

The government dispatched troops to strategic entrances to Texas in late 1830 to enforce the law and to aid the newly installed customs collectors in levying national import duties. The special exemption from the tariff for Texas pioneer settlers had expired.

It was hoped that the new garrisons would produce native Mexican communities and that the tariff would pay for the troops needed to preserve Texas. However, this inflamed Anglo-Texans, who had come to believe that their exemption from tariffs was permanent.

In 1830, Mexico, alarmed by the influx of Anglo settlers into Texas, sought to erect a line of forts to keep out the intruders. The ancient Aztec name for Mexico City (originally pronounced "Ten-ox-teet-lan") was given this site; it means "prickly pear place."

Fort Tenoxtitlan, constructed in 1830, in what is now northeastern Burleson County, was part of a chain of military garrisons designed to Mexicanize Texas and stanch immigration from the United States according to the Law of April 6, 1830.

The Law was instituted by Lucas Alamán y Escalada, Mexican minister of foreign relations, and was designed to stop the flood of immigration from the United States to Texas. It was reasonable from the Mexican point of view.

Article 11 was intended to prohibit or limit immigration from the United States. Texas colonists were greatly disturbed by news of the law. Austin quickly secured an exemption for his and DeWitt's colonies' restriction when he discovered an ambiguous phrase that seemed to allow immigration to "established" colonies. This he interpreted as those with more than 100 families in residence. The authorities acquiesced.

Application of the law slowed immigration, voided contracts that had been awarded but not carried toward fulfillment and suspended two active enterprises:

the Nashville or Robertson's colony and the Galveston Bay and Texas Land Company.

In the spring of 1830, Sterling Clack Robertson, one of the original stockholders of the Texas Association, acting under a subcontract with them and assisted by his partner, Alexander Thomson, Jr., began to recruit families and brought them to Texas, but the Law of April 6, 1830, prevented them from settling in the Nashville colony.

On June 25, 1830, Lt. Col. José Francisco Ruiz was dispatched from Bexar in command of 100 cavalrymen of the presidia company of Alamo de Parras, with orders from Gen. Manuel de Mier y Terán to establish a fort at the strategic point halfway down the Old San Antonio Road, where the thoroughfare crossed the Brazos River enroute to Nacogdoches. Ruiz reached the Brazos July 13 and established temporary headquarters on the east bank about a half-mile below the Old San Antonio Road.

On October 17, 1830, the garrison moved to a permanent site on a high bluff on the west bank of the Brazos twelve miles above the San Antonio crossing, opposite the spot where the present Brazos-Robertson County line strikes the river. The small spring-fed creek nearby was subsequently known as Dam Creek, probably because its water was diverted into the settlement.

Although Mier y Terán, who envisioned Tenoxtitlán as a future capital of Texas, issued elaborate instructions from Matamoros for the fort's design, the builders probably disregarded most of those instructions. The fortifications themselves were likely of conventional log construction.

Mexico intended this as a bulwark against Anglo-American immigration, but Anglo immigration did not cease. Instead, it thrived on the friendship of the local soldiers and incoming pioneers.

In late October 1830, only six months before the end of their contract, Maj. Sterling C. Robertson of the Texas (or Nashville) Association appeared at Tenoxtitlán requesting permission to select a settlement site for fifty American families accompanying him, provided by the colonization contract that his group had made with the province of Coahuila and Texas.

They arrived three months after the provincial government's official announcement of this contract's invalidation reached the fort. However, Colonel Ruiz, Texas-born himself and sympathetic to the American settlers, evaded orders to apprehend the colonists and turn them over to Nacogdoches' authorities, thus permitting them to scatter into various parts of Texas.

On December 31, 1830, the ayuntamiento of San Felipe de Austin, acknowledging the garrison's importance, established a commission to construct a road from San Felipe to Tenoxtitlán.

Nine families trailed Robertson, and when they reached Nacogdoches, the commandant detained them. Robertson's colonists surreptitiously passed Nacogdoches and reached the Brazos in November.

Amid a flurry of letters to officials, Austin offered the unlucky settlers sanctuary; a step approved officially in September 1831. A long legal tug-of-war ensued between Robertson and Austin. The resulting overlapping claims kept lawyers employed past midcentury.

One of the garrison's most important duties was to assist in the transportation of military funds from Bexar to Nacogdoches. Despite the ban on American settlement, the nearby farming community included an undetermined number of American immigrants. For example, as early as July 1831, Francis Smith operated a thriving general merchandise store at the fort, trading manufactured goods to the Indians for beaver pelts and buffalo robes.

On July 13, 1832, despondent over his grand scheme's failure to settle Mexicans in the Texas wilderness, Mier y Terán committed suicide. The demoralized Colonel Ruiz decided to abandon Tenoxtitlán. He began the evacuation of the garrison and entire Mexican settlement to Bexar Aug. 22, 1832. He withdrew the soldiers, and the fort finally defaulted to the Anglos.

Subsequently, it was a supply center and mustering point for expeditions against the Indians.

Things went back and forth with legal transactions for several months. The former Nashville failed to get a land commissioner appointed, so they did not issue a single land title to actual settlers. However, they did sell permits to nonresident speculators to locate huge grants in that area.

These grants, totaling 1,459,155 acres, later became involved in lawsuits and delayed Central Texas's settling for many years. On May 22, 1834, the governor awarded a new contract to Sterling C. Robertson as empresario.

Afterward, the area was called Robertson's colony. The decree of May 22, 1834, awarding the contract to Robertson, confirmed the boundaries as they had been defined in the Nashville Company's contract of Oct.15, 1827.

It included all or part of the seventeen counties listed in Leftwich's Grant, plus the thirteen shown under the Nashville colony, constituting an area 100 miles wide, beginning at the San Antonio-Nacogdoches Road extending northwest up the Brazos for 200 miles, centering around Waco.

Robertson was to bring the rest of the 800 families into the colony before 29 April, 1838. Each family that dedicated itself solely to farming was to receive one labor (177.1 acres) of land; those who also engaged in ranching were to receive an additional sitio (league, or 4,428.4 acres). Single men were to receive one-fourth league (1,107.1 acres).

For every 100 families introduced, Robertson was to receive five leagues and five labors (or a total of 23,027.5 acres) of premium lands. William H. Steele was appointed land commissioner of the Nashville (or Robertson) colony May 24, 1834, and he appointed John G. W. Pierson as principal surveyor Sept. 17, 1834.

The capital of the colony was laid out at the Falls of the Brazos (near present Marlin, Texas) and named Sarahville de Viesca; "Sarah" for Robertson's mother, Sarah Maclin Robertson, who had lent him money for the project, and "Viesca" for Agustín Viesca, the Mexican official who was presiding over the state legislature when it granted the contract to Robertson.

All the Robertson colony land titles were issued in Viesca. The first was issued Oct. 20, 1834, but all the colonial land offices were closed by Texas's provisional government Nov. 13, 1835, because of the outbreak of the Texas Revolution.

This prevented Robertson from completing the full quota of 800 families. However, according to a ruling handed down by the Supreme Court of Texas, in December 1847, Robertson was given credit for having introduced a total of 600 families.

In 1835, empresario Robertson formed his own Ranger company to deal with Indian depredations at Robertson's Colony. Robertson was a delegate to the convention at Washington-on-the-Brazos.

The Texas Declaration of Independence was produced, literally, overnight. Its urgency was paramount because while it was being prepared, the Alamo in San Antonio was under siege by Santa Anna's army of Mexico.

Immediately upon the assemblage of the Convention of 1836 on March 1, a committee of five of its delegates was appointed to draft the document. The committee, including George C. Childress, Edward Conrad, James Gaines, Bailey Hardeman, and Collin McKinney, prepared the declaration in record time. It was briefly reviewed, then adopted by the delegates of the convention the following day.

It was March 2, 1836, when 59 delegates from Mexico, Scotland, England, Ireland, and 12 U.S. states bravely met in Washington, Texas, to make a formal declaration of independence from Mexico.

Elected as delegates to the Constitutional Convention in 1836, these men determined Texas's future and, ultimately, a substantial portion of the United States. Among them were 12 lawyers, five physicians, four surveyors, three planters, empresarios, and merchants.

Sterling Clack Robertson was one of these men. He signed both the Texas Declaration of Independence and the Constitution of the Republic of Texas. He was also a Senator at the first two sessions of the Congress of the Republic of Texas.

The following characterization of him is from an article, "Gen. Sterling C. Robertson and the Part he Played in Texas History" by Sam Houston Dixon in the Waco (Texas) Times-Herald, 6 Apr 1923: Gen. Sterling C. Robertson has been described as a man of commanding appearance, cultured, refined, and honorable in all his dealings, and highly esteemed as a citizen and official.

William Menefee, who served with him in the convention at Old Washington in 1836 and the congress of the republic, said this of him: "Mr. Robertson was one of the leaders in the convention at Old Washington. He was polished in speech and progressive in thought. He did not aspire to leadership, but his towering intellect, courteous bearing, and pleasing personality gave him that commanding position.

As a senator in the republic's first and second congresses, he measured in intellect and influence with that body's biggest men. In a debate, he was brief and pointed and never tired the senate with long speeches. He was more often applauded than criticized for his stand on measures before the senate. Personally, I admired him very much."

WAR FOR TEXAS INDEPENDENCE

Robertson commanded a company in the army of Texas, commanded by Gen. Sam Houston, which defeated the Mexican army under Gen. Santa Anna at San Jacinto, Texas, and captured its commander.

Robertson was "detailed to guard the encampment near Harrisburg, Ap'l 21st 1836," the day of the engagement at San Jacinto. Robertson and his company were then part of Gen. Houston's army engaged in the campaign that culminated at San Jacinto and won Texas's independence from Mexico.

Robertson's granddaughter's related information that they received from his son, their father, about his activities during the war for Texas independence.

Robertson was present with Gen. Houston at San Jacinto shortly after the battle there when the captured Mexican commander, Santa Anna, was brought before Gen. Houston.

The original of the following order was loaned by Robertson's granddaughter, Mrs. Imogene Robertson Gamel.

The address, "To Sterling Robinson, Esquire," is at the top of the letter; the address, "To Major Sterling C. Robertson, Present," is at the bottom so that when the letter is folded, it appears as the outside address, as was the custom before envelopes came into use.

Robertson was evidently at Gen. Houston's headquarters at Washington, Texas, 5 Mar 1836, when this order was addressed to him.

(Copy of Order)
Head Quarters — Washington 5 March 1836
To Sterling Robinson Esquire

Sir — You will proceed forthwith to the United States and are hereby authorized to raise such number of Troops as may be in your power for the service of Texas for two years or during the present war—in the event of a Company or Regiment being raised the men shall have the power of electing their own officers who will report with their command to the Head Quarters of the Army of Texas without delay.

SAM HOUSTON — Comdr in Chief of the Army.
To Major Sterling C. Robertson — Present.

If he proceeded to the United States and raised troops there, he did so quickly, for he was near Harrisburg, near San Jacinto, a day or two before the battle at San Jacinto.

The original of the following certificate is among the papers of his grandson, Huling P. Robertson:

Certificate

I do hereby certify that Sterling C. Robertson joined the army near Harrisburg, before the Battle of San Jacinto, under my command about the 19th or 20th of April 1836.

(Signed) Robt. McNutt, formerly Major 1st Reg. T. V.
Nashville, Aug 6th, 1838.

GRANTED LAND FOR SERVICE IN TEXAS REVOLUTION

From photostat of record in General Land Office, Austin, Texas-Printed form, manuscript parts shown in italics:

(Endorsed:) File 494 — Milam Co. Donation — Donation Warrant *Sterling C. Robertson.*

STATE OF TEXAS — No. *7* — *640* Acres.

KNOW ALL MEN TO WHOM THESE PRESENTS SHALL COME:

That *Sterling C. Robertson* having — been detailed to guard the encampment near Harrisburg, *April 21st, 1836* — IS ENTITLED TO — SIX HUNDRED AND FORTY Acres of — DONATION LAND, In accordance with an Act of Congress of the Republic of Texas, passed Dec. 21, 1837.

Said *Sterling C. Robertson* — His HEIRS, EXECUTORS, ADMINISTRATORS, OR THEIR ASSIGNS, ARE ENTITLED TO HOLD SAID LAND — But it — CANNOT BE SOLD, ALIENATED, OR MORTGAGED, AND IS EXEMPT FROM EXECUTION DURING THE LIFETIME OP THE PERSON TO WHOM - IT I9 GRANTED.

In Testimony Whereof, I have hereunto set my hand, at Austin — this first day of *May 1846* — *Wm. G. Cook* — ADJUTANT GENERAL.

Approved *Feby 12th 1848* — *C. S. Mann* - Actg, Ad Genl.

INDIAN WARFARE

During the years 1836 and 1837, Sterling C. Robertson, then over 50 years old, served as a captain of the Texas Rangers in Indian Warfare on Texas's distant borders. He was among the first of the Texas Rangers captains.

At that time, he had plenty of business affairs that had to be neglected while he performed this arduous and dangerous duty to defend his country. His patriotism transcended considerations of private fortune—a worthy example, not followed by some "one hundred percent patriots" of later times, and gentlemen who bestowed. "Distinguished service medals" upon each other for "service" arranging for the expenditure of public funds.

Comptroller's Military Service Records No. 7149, Texas State Library:

I certify that Sterling C. Robertson joined the Army of Texas under my command on the tenth day of May 1836. I detached him under orders to raise a company or more of men—he proceeded to Nacogdoches in the discharge of his duties and again reported himself to me about the 25th of July of the same year. I then detached him to go against the Indians. This service was performed by said Robertson upon his own expenses & I considered him entitled to rank & pay as Captn.

(Signed) Thos J Rusk — Late Brig Genl - Coming T. A. - Houston Dec 21st, 1837.

(Endorsed:) 7149 Sterling C Robertson filed 23 Apl 1838. Examined admitted to audit for $300.75. Military services J W Moody Auditor 10 May 1836 Isd 23 Apl 1838 No draft 8541. T Appr April 24th, 1838, Francis R. Lubbock comptroller. Copy Isd.

Order from Gen. Rusk

The order from Gen. Rusk for the service just mentioned is among the papers of Mrs. Johnson.

(Endorsed) General T. J. Rusk — Orders — To Sterling C. Robertson Esq. Present.

Headquarters, Victoria 12th July 1836 to Sterling C. Robertson Esq.

Sir: You are hereby appointed to enroll men for the purpose of protecting the Frontier from Indian depredations. You are expressly prohibited from enrolling any men now in the army or on his way to the army, and you will not enroll any man for less time than Four Months. In all respects, you will subject yourself to such orders as you may receive from Col. Edward Burlison.

THOMAS J. RUSK, Brig Glenn Comdg.

Controller's Military Service Records, No. 5997, Texas State Library:

Recd of S. C. Robertson — Seventy-Eight, 3/4 Lbs. of Powder at One Dollar pr Lb Forty-four Bars of Lead at Twenty-five Cts pr Bar Forty-Eight Flints at Two Dollars, One Hundred Lbs. of Rice at Twenty Cts. pr Lb. Amounting to One Hundred & Eleven Dollars Seventy-five Cts for the Use of the Bttl of Rangers — Nashville — (Signed) Charles Curtis — Asst Qtr Master — Bttl of Rangers — Septm. 5th 1837.

I hereby Certify that S. C. Robinson Left Victory July twelfth, 1836, by order of General T. J. Rusk under my command to return to the frontier in Command of a Company of Rangers for four months which he done and discharged his duty faithfully as Capt in said Core the term of four months and is hereby honorable Discharged from the same this 19 November 1837

(Signed) Edw Burleson — Then Col Comdt Rangers.

Auditors Office — Houston 22 Dec. 1837 — This day came S. C. Robertson and says the annexed instrument is just true and original and the only one that he had offered for liquidation that he owes the Government nothing on his own account or on account of any other person Except Six rangers, at $30 each. — Sworn to before me — (Signed) J. W. Moody, Auditor.

(Endorsed:) $411.75 S C Robinson filed Dec. 21, 1837, Examined same day Admitted to audit for $411.75 Military 12 July 1836 Isd Dec. 21, 1837, No. Draft W.

(Second Endorsement:) 5997 S C Robinson fild Dec. 21, 1837, Examined same day Admitted to audit for $411.75 Military July 12, 1836, Isd Decr 21 1837 No. Draft 7206 W X approved 22nd Dec. 1837 Francis R. Lubbock Controller.

Controller's Military Service Records, No. 6037, Texas State Library:

Columbia July 3d, 1837 — Major Robison — Bot of Hamilton & Henderson — To 4 Kegs Powder at 8.00 $32. — To 2 pare shoes 6 — 1 Round Jacket 3. — 1 doz fishhooks $41.

1837 Columbia Texas — S. C. Roberson Dr — To Hamilton & Henderson — July 3d 4 Kegs powder 64/— 32 00 — 2 pr Shoes & 1 Linen coat 600 — (item not stated) 50 — $38.50 — Recvd payment. — Willis A Faris agent for Hamilton & Henderson — Houston Dec. 22nd. 1837.

Auditors Office — Houston Dec. 1837 — This day came Sterling C Robertson and says the annexed instrument is just true and original and the only one that he had offered for liquidation that he owes the Government nothing on his own account or on account of any other person Sworn to before — J W Moody 1st Auditor.

(Endorsed:) 6037 $38.00 Sterling C Robertson filed 27 Dec. 1837 Examined same day & admitted to audit for—$38.00 the Fishhooks Rejected J W Moody Auditor 3 Jul 1837 Isd 28 Dec 1837 No. of Draft 7248C Approved 26th Jan. 1838 Francis R. Lubbock Comptroller — S C Roberson Act $38.50.

(The bureaucrat who rejected the $38.00 for the Fishhooks, probably never had to find provisions for a force in the field.)

I certify that the distance from Harrisburgh to Nacogdoches is one hundred & eighty miles from Nacogdoches to San Augustine thirty miles & from San Augustine to Victoria about Two hundred- & seventy-miles April 23d, 1838 — (Signed) Thos J Rusk — late Brig Genl — Coming T A.

Auditors Office — Houston 23 Apl 1838 — This day came Sterling C Robertson and says the annexed instrument is just true and original and the only one that he has offered for Liquidation that he owes the Government nothing on his own account or on account of any other persons Sworn to before — (Signed) J W Moody — Auditor.

Texas won its independence from Mexico and became its own country for nine years. It was the Republic of Texas, from 1836 until it joined the United States in 1845.

After the Texas Revolution, the Robertson colony area was broken up to form all or part of the thirty present-day Texas counties listed under Leftwich's Grant and the Nashville Colony.

Tenoxtitlan was again suggested for the capital of Texas during the Republic, but Austin won out. During its brief life, many Texas patriots lived here, including 5 signers of the Texas Declaration of Independence, a martyr of the Alamo siege, and 7 soldiers of San Jacinto's Battle.

According to a letter from Robertson's son, hostile Indians infested his colony's region in 1841, and Robertson, then 56 years old, was still after them. After many Indian raids, the site was abandoned in 1841. By December, only a handful of Americans remained in occupation of the site. A trading post and settlement continued in the vicinity for many years but disappeared after 1860.

In 1936 a granite commemorative marker was erected by the Texas Centennial Commission near the fort's site, fourteen miles northeast of Caldwell off Farm Road 1362. Another was erected in 1970, five miles east of Caldwell on State Highway 21.

WILL OF STERLING C. ROBERTSON

Texas, Milam Co., Clerk of Court, Vol. 8, p. 321. Copied from Abstract of Title to certain lands in Texas, loaned by Mrs. Lela Sterling Robertson.

In his will, Mr. Robertson arranged for $5,000 worth of land to be sold and for that money to be given to his mother, Sarah Robertson Sr.

He also arranged for his two nieces, Mrs. Louisa Flury and Elizabeth Hannum, to receive one-half league of land. He specified that this land would be totally in their control. That neither their current nor future husbands would have control of their land. The land would belong to Louisa and Elizabeth and their heirs forever.

He also gave three of his cousins, James R. Robertson...of the County of Robertson, to H.V. Robertson...and Jonathan F. Robertson...of the County of

Washington, all the Republic aforesaid one thousand acres of land each, to be taken off and out of league No. 6 adjoining the Tenoxtitlan Leagues on the north side of the Brazos River, to have and to hold to them and their heirs forever.

The net remainder and residue of my estate of every description, either personal or real, either in the Republic aforesaid or in any of the United States of the North, I will and bequeath unto my beloved son, Elijah S. C. Robertson to him and the heirs of his body forever, but if my said son shall die without issue, then all of my estate that he has not disposed of to return to the heirs female, of my two deceased sisters Elizabeth Childress and Patsy Hannum, of their bodies begotten and to the children of my brother, Eldridge B. Robertson.

Further, it is my will and desire that part of my estate which falls to the daughters of either of my brothers or sisters last before mentioned shall be and remain for their use alone, not subject by any means or in any manner to the control, entire or in part of their present husbands, or of any person or persons they may or either of them may at any time hereafter marry. (Interestingly, Mr. Robertson made sure that his female relatives and not their husbands would control their land.)

In testimony whereof, I, the said Sterling C. Robertson, have hereunto set my hand and seal, having first read and published this my last will and testament in the presence of the witnesses whose names are hereunto subscribed as such, this tenth day of August, in the year of our Lord, 1840.

HIS DEATH

The Brazos River divides Robertson and Milam Counties. Robertson Co. was formed from Milam Co. and named for him, 1837, before his death.

Sterling Clack Robertson was fifty-seven years old when he died of pneumonia March 4, 1842, at the home of his relative, James Randolph (Randall) Robertson, near Hearne, Robertson Co., Texas. According to family information, he last resided with that relative to whom he bequeathed one thousand acres of land.

Another statement concerning the location of Robertson graves in the cemetery at Nashville was published 27 Oct 1927, in The Rockdale (Texas) Reporter in an article, "Story of Bridge Celebration," by Dr. H. W. Cummings, President, Hearne (Texas) Chamber of Commerce:

"The site selected for this bridge (across the Brazos River) is one of Texas's historical spots. Here was the town of Nashville, one of the early settlements where Sterling C. Robertson, for whom Robertson County was named, first located; and where the graves of the Robertson family can yet be seen. It is said that in selecting a place for the capital of Texas, this place, Nashville, came within one vote of being chosen as the capital city."

Little is known of his wife, Frances King. Sterling's granddaughter, Imogene Robertson, was Alva Clay Lindsay's aunt. She married James Archibald Gamel. (Read more about them in the Gamel chapter.) The Sterling C. Robertson Chapter, Daughters of the Republic of Texas, Waco, Texas, was named for him after his death.

Sterling Clack Robertson had an adventurous life. He was one of many brave men who came to Texas, and he made a difference.

5

Elijah Sterling Clack Robertson

Elijah Sterling Clack Robertson, lawyer, and soldier, son of Frances King and empresario Sterling Clack Robertson, was born in Giles County, Tennessee, Aug. 23, 1820.

He came to Texas in December 1832 and entered school in San Antonio, where he learned to read and speak Spanish. From the fall of 1834 until the fall of 1835, he worked as a Spanish clerk in Robertson's colony's land office.

In 1835-1836 Robertson was a member of a Texas Rangers company engaged in repelling Indian raids. From April 1837 until May 1839, Robertson attended Jackson College in Maury County, Tennessee. On his return to Texas, he became a clerk in the Republic of Texas's post office department. In June 1839, he became chief clerk. On Oct. 9, 1839, he was appointed acting postmaster general, serving until Jan. 8, 1840.

He served as assistant secretary of the Senate during the Sixth Congress (1841-1842). He also served with a company of volunteers that pursued Rafael Vasquez to the Rio Grande. On Aug. 5, 1844, President Sam Houston commissioned Robertson, colonel of the Second Regiment, First Brigade, Militia of the Republic of Texas.

In May 1845, Robertson went to Cincinnati, Texas, taking along in his saddlebags a copy of Blackstone. By clerking in a store during the day and reading law at night, he received his license that fall to practice law in the courts of Texas. He married Eliza Hamer Robertson July 29, 1846. She died March 25, 1852, and on Nov. 8, 1852, he married Mary Elizabeth Dickey.

In 1848 Robertson had been appointed translator of Spanish deeds in the General Land Office in Austin. In 1854 he began construction of his home in Salado, which was still standing in the 1990s. He was elected chief justice of Bell County in 1858 and was commissioned brigadier-general of the Twenty-seventh Brigade, Texas State Troops, April 14, 1860, by Governor Houston.

As a delegate to the Secession Convention in 1861, he signed the secession ordinance. He was appointed aide-de-camp to Gen. Henry E. McCulloch in 1862 and served to the Civil War's close. He was a member of the Constitutional Convention of 1875.

During Reconstruction, he devoted his efforts to building educational enterprises and placing his business interests on a firm basis. Salado College was largely the result of his efforts. Robertson was a member of the Democratic party and the Methodist Church, South. He died at Salado Oct. 8, 1879, and was buried in the family cemetery near his home.

(E. S. C. Robertson's daughter, Imogene Robertson Gamel, married James Archibald Gamel. They were Alva Clay Lindsay's aunt and uncle.)

BIBLIOGRAPHY; William Curry Harllee, KINFOLKS (4 vols., New Orleans: Searcy and Pfaff, 1934-1937. Malcolm D. McLean, comp. and ed., PAPERS CONCERNING ROBERTSON'S COLONY IN TEXAS (19 vols., Arlington: The UTA Press, 1974-93).

Vertical Files, Barker Texas History Center, the University of Texas at Austin. Malcolm D. McLean.

Published in THE NEW HANDBOOK OF TEXAS Austin: The Texas State Historical Association, 1996), Volume 5, pages 615-616.

6
Fort Mason

For over two hundred years, various groups fought over access to or control over the region that is now Texas.

Possession of the region was claimed and disputed by Spain and France's European powers, and the continental countries of Mexico, the United States, the Republic of Texas, and the Confederate States of America.

Ownership of specific lands was claimed and disputed by different ethnic groups, including numerous Native American tribes, Mexican residents, Anglo and African American settlers, and European immigrants.

Access to and control of resources were claimed and disputed by various economic groups, including indigenous hunter/gatherers, farmers, herders, ranchers, colonists, settlers, buffalo hunters, traders, bandits, smugglers, pirates, and revolutionaries.

Military barracks, fortified trading posts, palisades, stockades, lockhouses, strongholds, and fortifications were built to establish, defend, or dispute claims to the area.

In the 17th and 18th centuries, the primary mechanism for colonization was the Spanish mission. Many such missions included defensive structures to protect their operations and communities. Key missions were supported by nearby Spanish army forts, called Presidios.

In the period leading up to the Texas Revolution, Mexico established some new forts in Texas to control or limit Anglo-American immigration into the region. During and shortly following the Revolution, the Texians established several forts to defend Texas towns and cities.

Forts of this period include:

The Alamo – previously Mission de San Antonio de Valero (in San Antonio)

Fort Tenoxtitlán (near Cooks Point) (There is more about this Fort in the Sterling Clack Robertson story.)

Following the annexation of the Republic of Texas by the United States, the US and Mexico did not have a mutual agreement as to the border between Mexico and the new State of Texas. The United States Army established many new forts along the border, and military disputes in this area eventually led to the Mexican American War.

Interference and resistance to the settlement from Indian tribes was a big concern. This was especially true for the Comanche and Apache tribes.

In the 19th century, one of the key organizations for protecting Anglo American settlements was the Texas Rangers. The Rangers operated several Texas posts that were traditionally referred to as forts, though they lacked the kinds of heavy defenses associated with traditional military fortifications.

In the mid 19th century, the US Army was concerned with protecting settlements and towns in eastern, central, and south Texas from Indian interference.

During the Civil War, local Texas militias, law enforcement, and civilians were concerned with protecting the state's entire settled portion from interference from both Indians and Mexican bandits.

In the late 19th century, the US Army was concerned with protecting settlements and towns in west Texas from Indians.

Forts of these periods include:

- Fort Belknap (near Newcastle)
- Bent's Fort, also known as Adobe Walls (near Stinnett)
- Fort Bliss (near El Paso)
- Fort Brown (in Brownsville)
- Fort Chadbourne (Coke County)
- Fort Cibolo (near Shafter)
- Fort Concho (in San Angelo)
- Fort Davis (Jeff Davis County)
- Fort Martin Scott (near Fredericksburg)
- Fort Mason (Mason County}
- Fort McKavett State Historic Site (Menard County)
- Fort Stockton (in Fort Stockton)
- Fort Worth

Several of the most famous generals from both sides of the American Civil War were stationed at Texas forts while serving in the US Army during this period. Robert E. Lee was stationed at the Alamo and Fort Mason. Albert Sidney Johnston, George Henry Thomas, and Earl Van Dorn were also stationed at Fort Mason.

Fort Mason was established July 6, 1851, in present-day Mason County, Texas. It was named in honor of George Thomson Mason, a United States Army second lieutenant killed in the Thornton Affair during the Mexican American War near Brownsville, April 25, 1846.

At various times from 1856 to 1861, this was the home fort for Albert Sidney Johnston, George H. Thomas, Earl Van Dorn, and Robert E. Lee. The Fort was abandoned by the military in the 1870s and restored by a group of local citizens in 1975. Visitors can tour the reproduction officers' quarters at the Fort Mason Museum.

The Fort was designated a Recorded Texas Historic Landmark in 1936, marker number 11275.

Fort Mason, Texas, was established by the United States War Department as a front-line defense against Kiowa, Lipan Apache, and Comanche July 6, 1851. The site on Post Oak Hill near Comanche and Centennial Creeks was chosen by Lieutenant Colonel William J. Hardee and surveyor Richard Austin Howard.

Brevet Major Hamilton W. Merrill, along with companies A and B of the Second Dragoons, established the Fort itself.

The Fort was closed in Jan. 1854, after which horse theft by Native Americans was reported and pursued by the military.

Comanche Chief Katemcy at one point turned over two white captives aged 11 and 12 and again bringing them back when the captives ran away from the Fort to reunite with the Comanches. (For more information about Chief Katemcy and stolen horses, (see the letter written by Hugh Joseph Allen, Sr.).

It was reoccupied in 1856 by Company A, First Dragoons, from March to May. It was occupied by companies B, C, D, G, H, and I of the Second United States Cavalry from Jan. 14, 1856, with Col. Albert Sidney Johnston in command.

Among those in the Second Regiment of Cavalry before the Civil War, George H. Thomas, Innis N. Palmer, George Stoneman, R. W. Johnson, Kenner Garrard, and Philip St. George Cooke became generals for the Union Army.

In contrast, those who became generals for the Confederate States Army included Earl Van Dorn, Nathan George Evans, Charles W. Field, William P. Chambliss, Charles W. Phifer, Fitzhugh Lee, E. Kirby Smith, Robert E. Lee, John Bell Hood, and William J. Hardee.

Originally part of Gillespie County, Mason County is an agricultural community on Comanche Creek southwest of Mason Mountain, on the Edwards Plateau, and part of the Llano Uplift. It was named for the Fort when it was established in 1858. It is in the northwestern portion of the Texas Hill Country.

George W. Todd established a Fort Mason post office March 8, 1858, which became consigned to the civilian settlement June 26, 1858. The protection and commercial possibilities of the fort drew settlers. W. C. Lewis opened a general store that served soldiers and settlers. In 1860, James E. Ranck opened a second store and later became known as "The Father of Mason." He and Ben F. Gooch began leasing 5,000 acres of land to cotton sharecroppers.

Earl Van Dorn was a great-nephew of Andrew Jackson. He served at Fort Mason, Texas, in 1859 and 1860. While at Fort Mason, Van Dorn was promoted to major June 28, 1860. He then was on a leave of absence from the U.S. Army for the rest of 1860 and into 1861.

According to the August 25, 1860, census of Fort Mason, "There is 25 dwelling houses occupied by the officers and soldiers of the Garrison." One hundred and eight people are listed. Most of those were soldiers between 22 and 32 years of age.

One interesting thing about this census was the birthplaces of these occupants of the Garrison. A couple of the officers had their families with them, and three or four of the younger children were born in Texas, but the majority of those living at the Fort came from 15 states and 10 countries.

Alabama, Connecticut, Delaware, District of Columbia, Georgia, Kentucky, Maine, Maryland (listed as Meroland), Massachusetts, Mississippi, New York, Ohio, Pennsylvania, South Carolina, and Virginia.

Denmark, England, France, Germany, Ireland, Nova Scotia, Prussia (listed as PreuBen), Scotland, Switzerland, and Wales.

There were also servants, laundresses, a clerk, and a salter listed as living in the Garrison. These came from the Cherokee Nation, the Creek Nation, Mexico, Ireland, Kentucky, Louisiana, and Tennessee. The settlement of Mason grew up around Fort Mason.

Fort Mason was Robert E. Lee's last command with the United States Army. In a letter dated Jan. 23, 1861, Lee wrote: "I can anticipate no greater calamity for the country than a dissolution of the union. Secession is nothing but revolution."

Fort Mason was evacuated by federal troops March 29, 1861. The Confederate States Army took control of Fort Mason March 29, 1861. In 1862, the CSA held 215 men prisoner, who were transferred to Austin in 1862.

The United States Army reoccupied the Fort Dec. 24, 1866, under General John Porter Hatch's command. During this period, the Fort was renovated with both civilian and military labor. Indian depredations had increased during the Civil War and were worse when the army returned.

The Reconstruction era of the United States left its imprint on the Fort's personnel, often leading to the abandonment of duty and the resulting military discipline. By Jan. 13, 1869, 25 buildings, either unoccupied or in poor shape, remained, with less than 70 soldiers. The order to close the fort was carried out March 23, 1869.

In 1870, the state of Texas organized several companies of frontier forces. Fort Mason was reopened in September of that year as headquarters for Companies A and B, Frontier Forces, under Capt. James M. Hunter, later county judge of Mason County. The Fort was closed for good in 1871. Mason's citizens recycled material from the fort when building their own homes.

Restoration of the Fort began in 1975. Today, the Fort belongs to the Mason County Historical Society. Please visit the site when you come to Mason. Walk out onto the back porch and look north. Look beyond the buildings and see what those long-ago soldiers saw, the beauty of the Texas Hill Country.

Most of Alva Clay Lindsay's ancestors immigrated from Scotland, Ireland, and Germany, and they eventually settled in Mason County, Texas.

7

Mason, Texas

Mason, the county seat of Mason County, Texas, is on Comanche Creek in the county's center. It grew up around Fort Mason, established in 1851, although some settlers were already in the area before that date.

One of the first settlers, William S. Gamel, is thought to have arrived around 1846. Was this a typing error? Should the "S" actually have been a "T"? Was this early settler William Thomas Gamel, Alva Clay Lindsay's great-grandfather?

Perhaps he came to the area and then went back East and brought his family here. Several different dates of the Gamel family's arrival in Texas have been found, but the similarity is too great to ignore.

Peter Birk and Henry Hick were among the first German settlers who moved west from Fredericksburg.

Gamel Spring is where John O. von Meusebach may have signed a treaty with Comanche Chief Ketemoczy in 1847. The area was a favorite Indian campsite, and Gamel Spring was later used as a water source by Fort Mason.

(Other information suggests that this meeting took place near Camp San Saba on the San Saba River, where the Comanche had their winter campground.)

Clay's grandfather, John W. Gamel, used the water from this spring to water his garden. Mr. Gamel gave the spring and the land surrounding it to the City of Mason to be used as a school site. The old rock school building still stands. The water from the spring now fills the city swimming pool.

Early settlers gathered around the Fort, attracted by the opportunities for employment and protection from Indian attacks. Other settlers were soldiers from the Fort whose terms of enlistment had expired.

Shortly after the Fort was occupied, mail service was established from San Antonio to Mason and then on to the west. Supplies were also shipped from San Antonio by mule wagon. A sutler's store and blacksmith shop formed the early town's nucleus when they were moved from the actual Fort on Post Hill to Mason's nearby community.

The Fort Mason post office, one of the county's first, was established three miles from the Fort in March 1858 by George W. Todd. The name was changed to "Mason" in June of that year, and the post office was eventually moved into the town itself. Kathleen Crosby was the postmistress until her marriage to John W. Gamel.

One of Mason's first stores was a picket building erected by W. C. Lewis, who sold ammunition, groceries, and whiskey to soldiers and settlers.

A second store was opened around 1860 by James E. Ranck, known as the "Father of Mason," because of his efforts to develop the town and draw settlers to the area. He and Ben F. Gooch bought 5,000 acres of nearby land to lease to sharecroppers for cotton growing.

In March 1861, the Fort was surrendered to Confederate authorities, but it remained virtually unmanned during the Civil War, except for local militia and rangers. During the war years, settlers suffered severe Indian attacks, and most of the families in the area congregated in or near the Fort for protection. Mason was made the county seat May 20, 1861.

Shortly after the Civil War, a stage route and mail line were established through Mason from San Antonio to El Paso. Comanche Creek received its name because of the dangers that might be encountered there. The stagecoach drivers were warned to be on the lookout for Indian attacks when they slowed to cross it.

A picket house built by S. F. Lace Bridges served as the earliest hotel. Bridges later built the Mason House; a popular stage stop and hotel for several years.

In 1866 the Fort was occupied by federal troops, and there was a resurgence of settlers into the area. The federal government built the first telegraph line in the county through Mason to the western forts; the line was made available to the public until 1868, when the Fort was permanently abandoned.

When the Fort was deserted, both during and after the Civil War, nearby residents appropriated equipment and building materials to use in Mason until eventually, almost all traces of the installation had disappeared.

An election was held confirming Mason as the county seat Aug. 26, 1869. Land within the town was donated for county purposes July 13, 1870, by William and Caroline Lockhart and John W. and Kathleen Crosby Gamel. (John W. Gamel was Alva Clay Lindsay's grandfather.)

During the post-Civil War period, beef was so cheap that cattle were killed for their hides, and the Ranck store became a center of the hide trade. Shortly after, the demand for meat in the eastern and northern markets caused prices to soar, and by the 1870s, Mason was the nucleus of a thriving ranch economy.

William Poffard taught school in W. C. Lewis' home, and Mrs. Lizzie McGuire taught in the Mason House Hotel. James Ranck and John Lemburg built a mill and gin on Comanche Creek sometime before 1870, which burned in 1890.

By 1869 the first stone residences were built in Mason. The Gamel house was built by Alva Clay Lindsay's grandfather, John William Gamel, in 1869. By 1890 nearly all the buildings were of stone.

The first county courthouse and a jail were built in 1869. Court proceedings had previously been held under an old live oak tree near the town well on the town square's northeast corner.

The courthouse and all the county records burned Jan. 21, 1877; a new building was completed by 1878. The jail was replaced in 1882 and again in 1884. One of the oldest church buildings surviving into the twentieth century is the Catholic church, constructed in 1876.

James Kibbee and W. S. Vickery published the first newspaper, the Item or News-Item, beginning in 1877. V. N. Loring took it over in 1886 and renamed it the Mason News. Eventually, it became the Mason County News, which was still being published in 2021.

One news article talked about weather conditions. "A drought in 1887 was so severe that the county had to apply for state aid to assist destitute citizens, but the town's economy suffered no permanent decline."

F. W. Henderson organized the town's first bank; it later became the First National Bank of Mason. Anna Martin became the first woman bank president in Texas when she founded the Commercial Bank in July 1901; this bank was still in operation as of 2021.

In 1900 an entire row of buildings on the north side of the public square burned, including the post office and several businesses.

In December 1902, the first telephone in the county was installed in the county judge's office in the courthouse. Public utilities were slow to develop in Mason. Still, the first electric light plant was in operation by 1898, providing limited services, and the West Texas Utilities Company began providing electricity in 1925.

Mason County has had three courthouses. Two earlier courthouses were destroyed by fire. The most recent was built in 1909-1910 at the cost of $39,786. It was designed by Georgia-born American architect Edward Columbus Hosford, who is noted for the courthouses and other buildings that he designed in Florida,

Georgia. and Texas. Mutual Construction Company of Louisville, Kentucky, built it of Fredericksburg granite and rusticated stone.

The Mason County Courthouse was a fine example of the Classical Revival style. Edward Columbus Hosford designed the Beaux-Arts look of the building with a central dome and clocktower, gabled front porticoes on all four sides, each of which is supported by four two-story Doric columns, and rusticated stonework with contrasting stone lintels.

The Mason County Courthouse in Mason, Texas, was one of the most beautiful courthouses in the Lone Star State. It was added to the National Register of Historic Places in September of 1974. When you drove into Mason, the beautiful courthouse was the first thing you saw. It was right in front of you in the most prominent place. It was the heart of Mason's town square.

On Feb. 4, 2021, about 10 p.m., a depraved arsonist set fire to this beautiful building. One hundred eleven years of Hill Country history went up in flames. The bell tower, clock tower (the mechanism of which predated the building), and third floor, all collapsed through the second floor. Firefighters from Mason and surrounding counties kept the fire contained and prevented damage to other structures, but they could not save the courthouse.

Community members were quoted as saying, "This wanton destruction has broken the community's heart. Everything on the inside is burned and gone. The only thing this town has left are the four walls and columns." Judge Jerry Bearden said, "It was the saddest thing you could possibly imagine. My office in the northwest corner was the last office in that building to catch on fire. I had to sit there and watch my desk and other things burn."

Wendy Hudson, who owns a business on the west side of the square, was quoted as saying, "When I saw the charred and ruined building, I just started crying. It was heartbreaking. This was so unnecessary. It is going to bother me until it is fixed."

The Texas Historical Commission issued the following statement: "Our commission and staff are in shock today as we consider the terrible damage caused to the landmark Mason County Courthouse in last night's fire. We offer our sincere condolences to Judge Jerry Bearden and his constituents across Mason County."

Building inspectors determined that the exterior walls and columns were sound. That was good news. The courthouse does not have to be demolished; it can be rebuilt.

There is an interesting bit of local history about how the 16 two-story Doric columns arrived in Mason. Years ago, Judge Bearden was told, by an elderly Mason resident, that the columns were shipped by rail from Ft. Worth, Texas to Brady, Texas. When they arrived in Brady, each column was placed onto two wagons that had been tied together. Then, they were hauled 30 miles to Mason by several teams of mules.

Since there were no cranes or heavy equipment available, each of the sixteen columns was raised and installed using block and tackle systems and mules and manpower. At that time, the builders completed the construction in two years. It is estimated that it may take five or six years to rebuild.

"We are a poor county, but we are a proud and great county," Judge Bearden said. "We don't have any industry, just ranching, and tourism, so we will take everything we can get from folks who want to help." Individuals interested in donating can contact Judge Bearden's office at county.judge@co.mason.tx.us.

There is also a "Rebuild our Courthouse" PayPal fund and GoFundMe link:

https://www.gofundme.com/f/mason-county-rebuild-our-courthouse

Checks and cash contributions can also be presented directly to the County Treasurer, Mason Bank, Commercial Bank and Bancorp South. Checks payable to "Friends of the Mason County Courthouse" can be mailed to P. O. Box 40, Mason, TX 76856.

Mason, the Hill Country, and Texas lost a beautiful structure and a piece of our collective history.

Texas' oldest standing mansion, the Seaquist House, was built in Mason in 1887. Rev. Thomas A. Broad began constructing a handsome, two-story sandstone house north of Mason's courthouse square on Comanche Creek.

An excellent stone carver and builder, his work featured ornately carved limestone contrasted with the darker sandstone. The Broad family sold their imposing house for $4,000 in either 1889 or 1891 to Edward M. Reynolds, a banker from New York.

Mr. Reynolds hired the German architect Richard Grosse to remodel and enlarge the house. When he completed the home, it was a staggering 22-room masterpiece. Fun fact: Grosse also designed the county jail. (Another beautiful structure).

In 1919, the property was sold to Swedish immigrant Oscar Seaquist, after which the family made several improvements to the house. Oscar Seaquist died in 1933, but the Seaquist family continued to care for the mansion. It received a Texas state historical marker in 1974 and is listed on the National Register of Historic Places.

The sandstone structure continues to stun with its wrap-around porches and incredible interior, including a chapel and a third-floor ballroom. Alva Clay Lindsay was a wonderful dancer, and he danced in the Seaquist ballroom many times.

The Seaquist House Foundation purchased the house in January of 2015 and continues to restore the property. Someone wrote, "Who knew this little piece of history was hiding in the Hill Country"? Be sure to see it when you are in Mason.

In 1923 Mason was the largest town in Texas without a railroad, despite numerous attempts to get one. The story goes that Mr. Reynolds wanted to be able to impress his railroad friends with his wonderful home when they traveled to Mason from the East coast. The railroad was built but it went through Brady.

The increase of automobile use and the development of the Puget Sound-to-the-Gulf Highway minimized the need for a railroad, and by the 1930s, several highways ran through the town. On July 5, 1951, the live oak tree that stood on the town square by the old town well was removed to prevent traffic interference.

The rural county schools were consolidated with the Mason schools in 1946. For most of its history, Mason has been primarily a ranching community. Mason also attracts many hunters, fishermen, campers, tourists, and rock hunters.

Topaz, the Texas State Gem, is found only in Mason County. The Texas blue topaz became the official state gem when Governor Preston Earnest Smith signed House Concurrent Resolution No. 12 March 26, 1969. Texas topaz is found in the Llano uplift in Central Texas, especially west to northwest of Mason.

Topaz was first recognized in Mason County in 1904. The largest gem-quality topaz crystal found in North America, a 1,296-gram pale blue crystal, was found close to Streeter, Texas. It was used as a doorstop for many years. After being displayed in the Smithsonian Institution, this magnificent gem was returned to Mason, where it can be seen in the Mason Square Museum.

In color, size, and clarity, Texas topaz is considered among the best in the United States. Mason County is known for the best quality stones, especially for the beautiful "LoneStar Cut." This cut, designed by two Texans, became the official cut in 1977.

In 2021, the Historic Lindsay Ranch in Mason, Texas, is one place where you can hunt for this elusive treasure. Most of the topaz found on the Lindsay Ranch has been colorless. Go to www.lindsayranch.net for more information.

John William Gamel

8
The Gamel Family — John & Kathleen

No one knows when the Gamel family came to America, and no one knows for sure when they arrived in Texas. Different sources show different dates. I have chosen to use the dates that fit the other facts.

I have included things that were found online as well as family history. I hope you enjoy the Gamel story.

William Thomas Gamel, Alva Clay Lindsay's great-grandfather, was born Jan. 10, 1822, in Columbia, Georgia. He married Catherine Hixie Tucker Jan. 3, 1842, in Monroe, Georgia. They had nine children.

"In 1847, the family came to Texas. They first located in Limestone County, later moving to Llano County, and to Mason, July 4, 1860, when John was 16-years-old."

The date the Gamel's arrived in Texas is uncertain. Some records indicate that other children were also born in Georgia. There is a mention of a William Gamel living in the area in 1847. Was this "our" William, or was it perhaps a relative sent to "scout out" the land?

"William Thomas (Uncle Billy) Gamel was a brave man, a typical frontiersman, and he took a prominent part with those intrepid spirits who withstood the untold hardships to subdue the wilderness and pave the way for the conveniences afforded the present residents of the Lone Star state.

William Gamel and his family were among the first to establish their home here. This ranch was started in the early 'fifties by "Uncle Billy" Gamel, father of John William and Thomas Gamel, and was located on Bluff Creek.

Around 1855, Irish settlers, including William "Uncle Billy" Gamel and the Caveness brothers, began moving to the area. Shortly thereafter, Germans also began to settle in the community.

The greatest source of danger and hardship in those early years were from the Indians and their disastrous raids, and the Gamel family suffered greatly at the hands of the redskins, particularly so in the loss of their horses."

On April 2, 1901, at the age of 79, William Gamel died at his home in Streeter, Texas. He was buried in the Gamel Cemetery. The community of Streeter is between Big and Little Bluff Creeks just north of U.S. Highway 377 and nine miles west of Mason in western Mason County.

John William Gamel, Alva Clay Lindsay's grandfather, was born in Macon, Bibb County, Georgia, Aug. 16, 1844. He was the oldest son of William Thomas and Catherine Hixie Tucker Gamel.

"On July 4, 1860, ten years after they came into the State of Texas, 16-year-old John William Gamel and his family reached Mason County." (They may have gotten to Mason sooner.)

John W. Gamel was in the Confederate service from about the beginning of the war until January 1865, joining first the famous First Texas Cavalry, a part of General Ben McCulloch's command. Mr. Gamel was stationed at Fort Chadbourne under Captain Bill Tobin of San Antonio. Fort Chadbourne, active from 1852-1867, is near the Texas town of Bronte in Coke County.

He was mustered out of that organization at Fredericksburg in 1862 and then joined the Thirty-third Texas Cavalry, under Major Duffy. He was in service at Brownsville, Indianola, and other Texas points, and he took part in one of the expeditions into Indian Territory.

When the Civil War ended, the soldiers came home with next to nothing. Most of their farms and ranches were in ruins. They had no money, but there were longhorn cattle running wild and free for the taking. What happened next is an example of supply and demand.

"The book, "The Long Trail," by Gardner Soule, published in 1976 by McGraw-Hill, tells the real story of early cowboys, longhorns, and the first industry developed in Texas.

This was the chore of capturing, branding, taming, raising, and driving longhorns to market. Legends and myths, plus the exaggerations of many publications are omitted boiling fact down to common sense explanations."

The longhorns originated in Spain. The cattle were not called longhorns but "Spanish cattle" and were smaller in size and had smaller horns.

In 1493, Christopher Columbus brought cattle to America on his second voyage, landing them on the island of Santo Domingo. They probably reached today's Mexico about 20 years later.

Explorers and adventurers brought livestock and large poultry to various shores of North America to supplement their food needs during exploration.

They were driven along in herds and butchered as needed for food. Poor herding allowed many to escape and find themselves left on the prairie to fend for themselves.

Indian attacks, disease, and sickness among the explorers left herding a second priority. In 1685, French explorer La Salle began leaving one cow, bull, mare, and stallion behind after crossing a river to provide meat for the next explorer. Mexican Gen. Alonso de Leon did the same on four excursions across the new lands.

The livestock propagated quickly in the new world. The climate was mild in the south, rains produced millions of acres of good grass for grazing, and there were few predators to keep numbers in check.

These ideal conditions were prevalent for several hundred years, allowing excellent propagation of both cattle and horses. After becoming wild, the cattle lived longer, and their horns became much larger and longer. They became known as longhorns.

The adage, "only the fittest survive," was true. The survivors had the vigor, survival instinct, intelligence, and evolution needed to continue and improve the breed.

Cattle were driven across the Rio Grande into Texas to provide meat for the missions. By the time of the Republic of Texas, wild cattle roamed all over the state.

In the 1850s, Texas longhorns were trailed to markets in New Orleans and California. With their long legs and hard hoofs, Longhorns were ideal trail cattle; they even gained weight on the way to market.

The availability of the wild longhorn, free for the taking, and the poor financial conditions after the Civil War forced the early cattlemen to capture, raise, brand and drive, millions of Texas longhorns to market to survive.

Herds were driven to Indian and military reservations in New Mexico and Arizona, and in 1867 Illinois cattle dealer Joseph G. McCoy arranged to ship cattle from Abilene, Kansas, to the Union Stockyards in Chicago.

Over the next twenty years, contractors drove five to ten million cattle out of Texas, commerce that helped revive the state's economy. John William Gamel was one of these men.

Like the people who forged the state, the longhorn is a product of the land. Or, as Frank Dobie put it, "The Texas longhorn was bred not by man but shaped by nature and man benefited."

Texans benefited the most. The longhorn is credited with lifting the state from the economic ruin wrought by the Civil War and becoming the foundation of a vast cattle empire.

The government wanted meat to supply railroad workers, Indians on reservations, and military posts. The state's only potential assets were its countless longhorns, for which no market was available.

Missouri and Kansas had closed their borders to Texas cattle in the 1850s because of the deadly Texas fever they carried. There was a growing demand for beef in the East, and many men, among them Joseph G. McCoy of Illinois, sought ways of supplying it with Texas cattle.

In the spring of 1867, he persuaded Kansas Pacific officials to lay a siding at the hamlet of Abilene, Kansas, on the edge of the quarantine area. He began building pens and loading facilities and sent word to Texas cowmen that a cattle market was available.

John William Gamel had been a cattleman all his life. Now, cattle equaled much-needed money if you could round them up and get them to Abilene. John joined the many young men ready to saddle up and do just that.

Rounding up longhorns and putting together a herd was hard work, but these former soldiers and young Texas men knew nothing else. They decided to do it, and they did it. An appropriate quote is, "Texans operate best when left alone."

What words describe these men? They were hard-working, forward-thinking, can-do men. They saw possibilities, not impossibilities. They were men of vision. They looked to the future and were not shackled by the past.

They had dreams. They never doubted that they could make their dreams come true. They were energetic men who would not take "no" for an answer. Some were flamboyant, but as the saying goes, "It ain't bragging if you can do it!"

Some were restless and couldn't wait to see what was over the next hill; they got the opportunity to travel. Most made a living and all of them made a difference.

Not all the young men became wealthy or influential, but everyone took pride in their accomplishments and celebrated a job well done at trails end. Most of them signed up for the next drive.

Those youthful trail hands and the longhorns they herded gave a Texas flavor to the entire range cattle industry of the Great Plains. The cattle drives gave us folk heroes everyone called cowboys, but first, these were Texans!

The Chisholm Trail was the major route out of Texas for livestock. From 1867 to 1884, the longhorn cattle driven north along it provided a steady income source that helped the impoverished state recover from the Civil War.

Huge herds of longhorns were gathered and driven north. Sometimes men would merge their herds, and there would be 5,000 to 10,000 animals trailing to Kansas at the same time. Most of the trail drivers were between 14 and 18 years old. The old man, the trail boss of the crew, was perhaps 25 years old.

The longhorn's toughness and endurance made them perfect candidates for the cattle drives out of Texas on the Chisholm Trail. They had long legs, hard hooves and endured hunger and thirst better than other breeds. Longhorns ate grass that other cattle wouldn't. Cattle drives that would have decimated lesser breeds suited the longhorns just fine. Most even gained weight on the drives.

Historian Joe B. Frantz wrote of the longhorns: "They were built for travel because they had strolled their way a thousand miles from Vera Cruz; they grew longhorns because they had to learn to fight off predators in the brush."

John W. Gamel was one of the old-time cattlemen of Central and Western Texas, and he was noted throughout the entire state as one of the best judges of cattle.

On March 25, 1865, John married Kathleen Crosby. Kathleen was born in Ireland in about 1843. With this marriage, Kathleen became a wealthy woman. John measured his holdings by thousands of longhorn cattle. Besides his own land, he leased thousands of acres and sent immense herds up the trail from Mason.

John's home had been principally in the town of Mason since 1865, and at that time, it had one store and four or five small picket houses. When he married Kathleen, they lived in an attractive residence located in the eastern part of the town, near the site of old Fort Mason.

John W. Gamel and his son, either James Arch or John Crosby Gamel

John and Kathleen had three sons, James Archibald b. Feb. 11, 1866, John Crosby b. Feb. 18, 1868, and Walter T. b. June 20, 1870. James and John grew to be adults, but Walter T. died Oct. 1, 1871, when he was only 16 months old.

John W. Gamel and Mr. Lockhart donated the land for the town square. (You will find more information about this in other stories of Fort Mason and the City and County of Mason.)

John's business was buying and selling cattle, and he "went north" with more than one herd. He was recalled by old-timers in Dodge City, Kansas as a "flamboyant, forceful Texan who celebrated at the end of cattle drives by lighting cigars with ten-dollar bills, declaring he had enough money to burn a wet dog."

In 1869, John built his townhouse in Mason on the hill overlooking the courthouse square. It was one of the first rock homes in the city. He owned the Mill Creek Ranch, which he built into a holding of over 50,000 acres. He lived part of the time at the ranch but saw the need for a townhouse near schools for the children.

John, Kathleen Crosby Gamel, and their two young sons, James Archibald (Arch) and John Crosby (Johnny), moved to the rock house, just a few blocks east of the current town square, when the construction was completed. (There is more information about the house in another story.)

The compound consisted of a rock house, a wooden bathhouse, a rock potato house, a wooden carriage house, a rock stable and barn, a bunkhouse, and a log smokehouse. Mr. Gamel could sit on his fifty-foot-long west front porch and see his large garden.

A three-foot rock wall was built on the west, north, and east sides of the property. The original west wall still stands in 2021. In later years, the other rock walls were moved back by the highway department and lowered in height.

Mason was not always a quiet, peaceful community. The following is a brief account of what was known as the Mason County War (Hoo Doo War). Why was it called the Hoo Doo War? The members of the vigilance committee covered their faces with masks so that they wouldn't be recognized. So, the question, "Who do it?"

This deadly episode began as a feud over cattle rustling but grew into a conflict between the community's Anglo and German elements. In Feb. 1875, the violence began when a mob took five suspected cattle thieves from jail and killed three.

(Lucia Holmes wrote about this in her diary. She ran across the road to stay with Mrs. Gamel because she was frightened by what was happening and her husband was out of town. She wrote that they could see and hear what was happening from the Gamel's porch.)

Shortly thereafter, another suspected rustler was killed by twelve men with blackened faces, prompting his friend Scott Cooley, a former Texas Ranger, to seek revenge. Cooley and his men, including Johnny Ringo (later at OK Corral), killed at least a dozen men, whereupon Maj. John B. Jones and twenty or thirty Texas Rangers were sent to quiet the difficulties.

One of the Texas Rangers who came to Mason, Texas with Major Jones was Ira Long. In 1967 the Texas State Historical Survey Committee erected Marker Number 5268 to Captain Ira Long. It is in Decatur, Wise County, Texas.

The inscription reads, "Dedicated and courageous. Born in Indiana; reared in Missouri. Wounded twice in Confederate service during the Civil War.

On reorganization of Texas Rangers, 1874, was commissioned first lieutenant; promoted 1875 to captain, Company A. official escort of Major John B. Jones, Commander of Ranger Force. Did outstanding duty against Indians and outlaws, and in quieting such feuds as Mason County War. Served six years."

John William Gamel likely met Major Jones and his official escort, Captain Ira Long. He probably hosted them in his home. Neither Ira Long nor John Gamel knew that 63 years later, their grandchildren, Clabe Scott Long and Effie Mary Lindsay, would marry and that their great-grandsons, John Clabe Long and James Lindsay Long, would be significant contributors to this book. It is a small, small world.

Jones searched for Cooley and his followers without success before discovering that some of his rangers were former comrades-in-arms of Cooley. After Jones discharged them, Cooley fled into Blanco County and died a short time later.

A few people were eventually arrested, but most of the cases were dismissed. After many months of violence, a strained peace returned to Mason County in the fall of 1876. On Jan. 21, 1877, the Mason County Courthouse burned. The fire destroyed all the early county records, including those about the Mason County (Hoo Doo) War. This fire ensured that many of the details of the Mason County War would remain unknown.

These books are available from the Mason County Historical Commission:

The Lucia Holmes Diary 1875-1876, The Hoo Doo War Years, $10.00

Contains transcriptions of Holmes' eyewitness account of the Mason County Hoo Doo War.

Holmes was a seamstress for men and women in Mason. She notes the travels of her attorney husband, Hal Holmes, visitors to their home, clients, weather, and feelings about the Hoo Doo War. 1985, now in its 6th edition with an index, 127 pp., softbound.

Life of Thomas W. Gamel, $15.00

1930s recollections of Tom Gamel about the early events of Mason County from the 1850s to the 1880s. Many contemporary authors refer to this book, which has been out of print for many years. Mason County Historical Society is pleased to reissue this with annotations from Dave Johnson. Revised in 2003, 59 pp., softbound.

("*The Life and Times of Thomas Gamel,*" is a first-hand account of happenings at that time. Thomas Gamel was John William Gamel's brother.)

Mason County 1877 News-Items stated, "The grass was probably never better in Mason and surrounding counties than it is at present. The eyes of the cattle, sheep and horses are literally standing out with fatness."

John William Gamel was one of the influential men of his time. He made his fortune in the cattle business. He was away from Mason much of the time. He and other cattle buyers went all over the state buying and selling and putting together the herds going up the trail to Kansas.

Another news item in the same paper said, "Mr. John W. Gamel is expected home soon with four thousand cattle which he bought in Victoria and Kendall counties. He proposes to winter them in his James River, Mason County pasture, in which he already has several thousand head of beautiful home-raised cattle."

THE DRIVE

From the Dodge City Times Dodge City, Kansas May 26, 1877:

100,000 Cattle Passed Griffin on the First. Bound for Dodge; Three Herds Arrived To-day

Messrs. Hutchinson, Bassett, and Campbell came up the trail this week. They went down to direct the leading herds to Dodge City over the best route. From these gentlemen we learn that forty herds are this side of the Washita and will be at Dodge City between the 1st and 10th of June.

The ranges in the vicinity of the Dodge City trail are superb. Water in abundance is found at short intervals and the grass has never been finer since the 'oldest inhabitant' can remember. The stock will arrive here in splendid condition.

Doc Burnett arrived to-day with a herd belonging to Burnett & Mayberry; also, Charles Slaughter and brother's herd and John C. Gamel's herd.

From Judge Beverley and other sources, we learn that 100,000 cattle had passed Fort Griffin up to the 1st inst., with more coming. All the above drive is headed for Dodge City.

The following herds bound for Dodge City have passed Fort Worth before May 12th: Geo. Miller 1817; Dillard R. Fant 5100; Dillworth & Littlefield 14250; W. G. Butler 1760; Brocker Bros. 2770; Wheat 2260; McCarty 2506; Holstein & McCoy 2400; M. Kenedy 2000; Hood & Holmsley 5500; Ellison & Dewees 7100; Bennett & West 1650; Caruthers 2250; S. Hay

1700; Dillard R. Fant 1100; Dillworth & Littlefield 4500. All the above herds are mixed cattle except those of George Miller.

Many of the approaching herds are close together, having been detained by high water, and will arrive in large numbers when they do come.

FORT GRIFFIN

From Legends of America, legendsofamerica.com:

Fort Griffin was established in 1867. Built on the rolling hills between the West Fork of the Trinity River and Clear Fork of the Brazos River, the area was a dangerous place as settlers made their way into Texas, conflicting with the Plains Indians who had long called the area their exclusive hunting grounds.

By the time it was finally complete, the fort would accommodate up to six companies of soldiers and included an administration building, a hospital, officers' quarters in eleven buildings, numerous barracks, a guardhouse, a bakery, a powder magazine, five storehouses, forage houses, four stables, a laundry, and a workshop.

Almost immediately after the fort was completed, a new settlement began at the bottom of the hill that was first called "The Bottom," "The Flat," or "Hidetown," before it took on the name of the fort. In addition to the honest pioneers who settled the area for legitimate reasons of ranching, agriculture, and commerce, in flooded several ruffians and outlaws.

The settlement was bustling with buffalo hunters, businessmen, cowboys, outlaws, gamblers, gunfighters, and "painted ladies," quickly gaining a reputation for lawlessness.

Some of these people would become well-known in the annals of history, including Doc Holliday and Wyatt Earp, who first met at Shaunissy's Saloon in Fort Griffin. Also, there were Big Nose Kate; famous lady gambler, Lottie Deno; lawman, Pat Garrett, and gunfighter, John Wesley Hardin.

Fort Griffin continued to serve as a major supply source for buffalo hunters from 1874 through 1877, and a stop off for the many cowboys herding cattle up the Western Trail to the Dodge City, Kansas railheads.

Businesses of all kinds sprouted up to meet the needs of the growing population which including numerous stores, saloons, and restaurants. A newspaper called the Fort Griffin Echo was published from 1879 to 1882, and the town even sported an academy for several years.

At its height, Fort Griffin had a permanent population of about 1,000 and an estimated transient population of nearly twice that. After 14 years of guarding the area population, the US flag at the fort was lowered for the last time May 31, 1881.

Fort Griffin, fifteen miles north of Albany on U.S. Highway 283 was one of the wildest places in all the Old West.

John Gamel bought and sold cattle. Wealthy buyers from the East rolled into Mason riding in Concord Coaches. Here they were met by John, who drove them out to his many ranches.

Usually, they stayed at the Mason House, the most prominent hotel in town. The Mason House joined the stage stop, making it still more popular. At times, though, John proudly brought these cattle buyers to his own beautiful home.

In the beginning, John spent many hours with the herds but now, when his business was completed, he turned the chuck wagon and horse remudas over to the men he hired and took the stage back to Mason.

John was out of town when his wife, Kathleen Crosby Gamel, died Jan. 1, 1880.

Kathleen was more than a wife and mother. She took care of the family business as well as her home and children. Before she married in 1865, Kathleen was the first postmistress of Fort Mason, and she was active in the community. The Crosby family also owned land and cattle, and Kathleen had a good head for business. When John was away, she took care of the family and their money.

John would make hand-shake deals with other cattlemen. They would come to Mason, and Kathleen would finalize the transactions. She took money from those who had purchased cattle from John and paid them for the cattle he bought.

These cattle deals involved substantial amounts of money, and there were no banks in Mason in those early years. The closest banks were more than 100 miles away in San Antonio and Austin.

The Koocksville Store, about two miles west of Mason, was the largest store in the area at that time and it was frequented by cowboys, drovers, and cattlemen. The store owners handled a lot of money. They put their extra cash on a packhorse and turned the horse loose in the pasture. When they needed money, they would get the horse.

John had no interest in the money, except when he needed to buy something, so he would give it to Kate and say, "Do something with it." Kathleen had a special place where she kept the money. It was a secret place, a place known only to her.

One day, Kathleen needed something from the potato house. This was a rock cellar-like structure about 100 yards west of the main house. Rock steps led down into the potato house. The walls extended about four feet above and below the ground, and there was a vaulted roof. This structure still stands in 2021.

John was out of town, but he was due to return shortly. Kathleen told one of the boys to get some potatoes from the potato house. Being young boys ages 12 and 14, they had other things to do. After a few minutes, Kathleen went to get the potatoes herself.

No one knows what happened next. The story passed down in the family was that when she opened the door go in, a man, who had been hiding in the potato house, ran out.

Did he accidentally strike her as he bolted out of the potato house and up the stairs? Did she fall and hit her head on the rocks? Was she so startled that she had a heart attack? Was she pregnant at the time? Did she lose the baby? No one knows exactly what happened, but 37-year-old Kathleen died a short time later.

John was returning to Mason from a business trip when this happened. In the few hours before her death, John pieced together a bit of the story. Kathleen died, leaving a stunned husband and two young sons, but she took the secret of the gold's location to her grave.

After the shock wore off, John began to look for their money. He knew she had hidden it, but where? John and others searched and searched, but no one found the Gamel Gold.

Years later, when the highway was being widened, John's daughter, Jesse Gamel Lindsay, made sure that she was on hand just in case something "turned up." Nothing did.

John was a 37-year-old widower with two teenage sons; James Archibald was 15 years old and John Crosby, 13, when he married his second wife, 19-year-old Alice Kettner, Sept. 15, 1881. Alice, the daughter of Franz (Francis) and Catarina Keller Kettner, was only a few years older than John's sons. In fact, John could have been her father.

John was a wealthy man. He was so wealthy that when he re-married, he built each of his sons a rock house across the street from where he and Alice would live, and he gave each of them $75,000.00.

That is the equivalent of giving them each more than $1.9 million in 2021. The houses are still standing. One is the current Mason County News office, and the other is across the street from the Gamel Guesthouse.

Many things have been written about John W. Gamel. "The first of the big ranchmen of the early days in Mason County was John W. Gamel. With his brother, George Jefferson Gamel, he operated some large outfits in the days of the open range."

"John W. Gamel was early inured to the hardships of pioneer life. He began working with cattle at an early age, and he continued as a cattleman throughout all of his active life, only retiring from the vocation within the past few years."

His sons learned from their father. They also became well-known cattlemen.

As Paul Harvey famously said, "Now, for the rest of the story."

The following information is from "The Gamel Treasure" by James Archibald Gamel's great-grandson, Ambrose Archibald (Arch) McNamara, Copyright 1995, and from "Kinfolks" by William Curry Harllee. Deloris Haley Lindsay, Aug. 15, 1999, and Jan. 6, 2021.

"Unusual incidents seemed to follow the Gamel family. John Gamel's son, James Arch Gamel, and his brother, John Crosby, attended St. Mary's in San Antonio during the period 1875-1878."

Private tutors educated James and John, and they attended St. Mary's College, San Antonio, Texas. They entered Georgetown University, Washington, D.C. Sept. 8, 1881, and the University of Missouri, Columbia, MO, in 1882.

There is no evidence that either of the brothers earned degrees from these institutions, although the experience probably gave them a degree of polish unusual for cattlemen of that era.

While at Missouri, James Arch joined a small fraternity named Zeta Phi, which later affiliated with the distinguished national fraternity Beta Theta Pi. He was given the privilege of becoming a Beta, which he accepted--he was number 111 on the chapter rolls.

In 1885, James and Johnny bought a 13,000-acre ranch near Mason with its herd of 1,500 cattle for $30,000. Although they had their father's backing, they paid this sum off quickly without calling on their father's resources. They continued to add to their holdings and sold out to their father after three years.

In 1885, John Archibald Gamel, then 19-years-old, his disabilities as a minor having been legally removed, became the administrator of the estates of his father, John, and his uncle, Christopher Crosby.

They continued to add to their holdings and sold out to their father after three years and headed for the Indian Nation where they had large holdings and leased land from the Indians, "while the grass grows and the water flows." A nice poetic touch. Some land in Mason was traded to Christopher Crosby for land that he controlled in the Indian Nation.

(Historical and biographical Record of the Cattle Industry and the Cattlemen of Texas, Antiquarian Press, Ltd., New York, 1959, Vol. II, no page).

What happened to James Archibald Gamel, Sr., Imogene Robertson Gamel, and their family?

James Archibald Gamel, Sr. and Imogene Robertson married Oct. 1, 1888, in Tom Green County at the home of her brother. Imogene Robertson was the daughter of the late Colonel and Mrs. E. S. C. Robertson. The Robertson's were large landowners in what was then called Salado Springs.

By coincidence, this happened to be one of the places where the Gamel's had stopped on their western travels before they settled in Mason County. (See the stories of Sterling Clack Robertson and his son, Elijah Sterling Clack Robertson.)

James Archibald Gamel, Sr. and Imogene Robertson Gamel had three children. Their individual stories follow.

The following comments are copied from "The Gamel Treasure," written by Ambrose Archibald (Arch) McNamara, Copyright 1995. Arch was Imogene Gamel McNamara's son. He was the great-grandson of James Archibald, Sr., and Imogene Robertson Gamel.

"The Gamel's (James Archibald Gamel, Sr. and Imogene Robertson Gamel) had everything. They were young, rich, good looking, and had three children, but the livestock market was about to collapse. To add to their problems, the United States government opened the Indian territories to white settlement.

James Arch took his family to Mexico, where the government of Don Porfirio Diaz welcomed foreign investors. Gamel opened a chain of soft drink bottling companies (Coca Cola) and prospered in Mexico, but that country was about to explode in a civil war.

With the revolution's coming, the anti-American feeling in that country made it too dangerous to remain there, and they returned to the United States. James Arch Gamel had made his fortune too quickly and at too young an age. He went through one business failure after another."

This is a listing of some of the places the Gamel family lived in Mexico and some of the business they engaged in while living there. The information on a passport application made in 1920 states that J. A. Gamel had lived in Mexico from 1901 - 1907.

- They moved to Monterey, Mexico, and owned a match factory and engaged in mining in the state of Nuevo Leon.
- Saltillo, Coahuila, Mexico; engaged in mining and owned bottling works. James and his brother John Crosby Gamel received a contract to build a Brewery for $20,000 dollars. That equates to $580,000 in 2021 currency.
- Queretaro continued mining and bottling business. James' brother, John Crosby Gamel, died in Queretaro, Mexico in 1906.
- Saltillo, Celeya, Auga Caliente and Morelia bottling business.
- Morelia and then again to Saltillo, bottling business.
- "With the revolution's coming, the anti-American feeling in that country made it too dangerous to remain there, and they returned to the United States."
- El Paso, Texas, engaged in mining.
- Waco, Texas, engaged in real estate business and operated a ranch near Aquila, Hill County, Texas.
- Waco, Texas, lived on a 1,000-acre ranch that Imogene inherited from her father. Resided there three years.
- Waco, Texas real estate business.
- Houston, Texas; oil business.
- Shreveport, LA; oil business.
- Palma, Oriente, Cuba, then to Havana, engaged in sugar business. (James stated that he needed to go to Jamaica to accompany his daughter, Marion.)

- El Paso, Texas, President, Southern Chemical Co.
- Los Angeles, California, where he died July 12, 1933.

"James Arch Gamel had made his fortune too quickly and at too young an age. He went through one business failure after another."

The following is a copy of a death notice found in the family bible:

RELATIVES HERE LEARN OF DEATH OF ARCH GAMEL. (This references the death of James Archibald Gamel, Sr.)

"Local relatives have recently received news of the death of James Arch Gamel, which occurred July 12 in Los Angeles, Calif. Mr. Gamel was born in Mason, being a son of the late John Gamel of this place. He was born, February 11, 1866, being 67 years, 5 months, and one day of age at the time of his death.

His widow, one daughter, and one grandchild, all of California, survive. His stepmother, Mrs. John Gamel (Alice Kettner), and one half-sister, Mrs. John Lindsay (Jesse Gamel Lindsay), live here. Mrs. W. C. Lauderdale (Nellie Mary Gamel) of San Antonio is a half-sister, and Herbert Gamel (Herbert Zork) of Harper is a half-brother."

James' widow, Imogene Robertson Gamel, lived a full life. She was well-known because of her father and grandfather and because she was married to James Archibald Gamel. Imogene traveled to many places.

She and James lived in Shreveport, LA, when she filled out her passport application Jan. 3, 1919. She stated that she was going to Cuba to visit her two daughters, one of whom was ill. She stated that she had lived in Saltillo, Mexico, from 1901 to 1907.

Imogene was a suffragette. She was co-vice president of the Waco, Texas chapter. She was one of the ladies who traveled to Dallas "to extend a welcome to Mrs. Cunningham, State President, to visit Waco and deliver an address to women suffragists here."

The 1940 census lists Imogene Gamel, her daughter, Imogene McNamara, and grandson, Archie McNamara, living at 309 South Hobart Boulevard, Los Angeles, CA.

Family information shows that Imogene Robertson Gamel probably died in 1945 in Saltillo, Coahuila de Zaragoza, Mexico. Find A Grave does not list a death date, place, or burial location. The Gamel family lived in Saltillo for several years.

Saltillo is famous for producing the traditional multi-colored Mexican blanket, the sarape, and floor tile. Nachos are said to have originated in Piedras Negras.

INDIAN TERRITORY - OKLAHOMA TERRITORY - STATEHOOD

The Oklahoma land rush began April 22, 1889. At precisely high noon, thousands of would-be settlers make a mad dash into the newly opened Oklahoma Territory to claim cheap land.

The nearly two million acres of land opened to white settlement was in Indian Territory, a large area that once encompassed modern-day Oklahoma.

Initially considered unsuitable for white colonization, Indian Territory was thought to be an ideal place to relocate Native Americans who had been removed from their traditional lands to make way for white settlement. The relocations began in 1817, and by the 1880s, Indian Territory was a new home to a variety of tribes, including the Chickasaw, Choctaw, Cherokee, Creek, Cheyenne, Comanche, and Apache.

By the 1890s, improved agricultural and ranching techniques led some white Americans to realize that the Indian Territory land could be valuable. They pressured the U.S. government to allow white settlement in the region. In 1889, President Benjamin Harrison agreed, making the first of a long series of authorizations that eventually removed most of the former Indian Territory from Indian control.

To begin white settlement in the area, Harrison chose to open a 1.9-million-acre section of Indian Territory that the government had never assigned to any specific tribe. However, subsequent openings of designated sections to specific tribes were achieved primarily through the Dawes Severalty Act (1887), which allowed whites to settle large swaths of land that had previously been designated to specific Indian tribes.

On March 3, 1889, Harrison announced the government would open the 1.9-million-acre tract of Indian Territory for settlement precisely at noon April 22. Anyone could join the race for the land, but no one was supposed to jump the gun.

With only seven weeks to prepare, land-hungry Americans quickly began to gather around the borders of the irregular rectangle of territory. Referred to as "Boomers," by the appointed day, more than 50,000 hopefuls lived in tent cities on all four sides of the territory.

The events that day at Fort Reno on the western border were typical. At 11:50 a.m., soldiers called for everyone to form a line. When the hands of the clock reached noon, the cannon of the fort boomed, and the soldiers signaled the settlers to start.

With the crack of hundreds of whips, thousands of Boomers streamed into the territory in wagons, on horseback, and on foot. All told, from 50,000 to 60,000 settlers entered the territory that day. By nightfall, they had staked thousands of claims either on town lots or quarter section farm plots. Towns like Norman, Oklahoma City, Kingfisher, and Guthrie sprang into being almost overnight.

An extraordinary display of both the pioneer spirit and the American lust for land, the first Oklahoma land rush was also plagued by greed and fraud. Cases involving "Sooners" – people who had entered the territory before the legal date and time – overloaded courts for years to come.

The government attempted to operate subsequent runs with more controls, eventually adopting a lottery system to designate claims. By 1905, white Americans owned most of the land in the Indian Territory. Two years later, Nov. 16, 1907, Oklahoma became the 46th. state.

9

James Archibald (Arch) Gamel, Sr.
& Imogene Robertson Gamel's Children

James Archibald (Archie) Gamel, Jr. was born Sept. 6, 1889, in Mason. TX. Archie first married Frances Ray Riveroll. She was born July 4, 1894, in Mexico City, Mexico.

Their names are listed on a passport application dated July 10, 1917. His reason for traveling to Tampico, Mexico, was "Construction of pipeline for Mexican-Gulf Oil Co."

The 1913 City Directory of Waco, Texas lists Miss Frances R. Riveroll and Robert Riveroll, a student at Today's Business College. They are both boarding at 1009 Columbus. Indications are that James and Frances had one daughter, Sara Maria Gamel.

James married Manuela Gougnet June 9, 1923, in Mercedes, Provencera de Corrientes Argentina.

Archie died June 10, 1927, in San Paulo, Brazil. Manuela and Arch had no children.

"REPORT OF DEATH OF AN AMERICAN CITIZEN, AMERICAN CONSULAR SERVICE San Paulo, Brazil July 1, 1927.

James Arce Gamel died in Hospital Santa Catharina, San Paulo, Brazil. The Cause of death: Delirium tremens, also said to have had been consumptive.

He was buried in "Araca" Cemetery. Local law stated when his remains could be disinterred: Can be removed after three years and perhaps earlier by special permission. As to the disposition of his effects: effects? He had none, except a few clothes which were handed to his wife, Mrs. Gamel. His wife, Manuela Gougnet Gamel, was with him.

Her address was Caixa Postal 3300, San Paulo. Manuela was said to be in indigent circumstances and was returned to her home in Argentina by the Argentine Counsel at San Paulo. The letter was signed by C. R. Cameron, American Counsel for the Department of State.

Marion Dickey Gamel (named for her grandmother Mary Elizabeth Dickey), was born Sept. 1, 1892, in Waco, TX.

The 1916 Waco, Texas, City Directory lists Marion as a stenographer for Southern Union Life Insurance Company. The three siblings are living at 2100 Ethel Avenue. Her brother, Archie Jr., is working in the real estate business.

A passport application was filed Sept. 11, 1918, by Marion. She stated that she was living in Houston and would be leaving from Key West, Florida, to travel to Cuba as soon as she received her passport. She planned to return to the United States within six months.

Marion was probably going to visit her newlywed sister, Imogene "Brownie," and her brother-in-law, Ambrose Archibald McNamara, working in Cuba in the sugar and molasses industry. Marion's nephew, Arch McNamara, wrote that Marion earned a law degree in Los Angeles in the 1920s, an unusual achievement for a young woman at that time.

The New Orleans passenger list of the SS CHALMETTE lists the following "American Citizens Sailing from Havana Cuba Sept. 3, 1923, arriving New Orleans Sept. 5, 1923".

- Gamel, Imogene age 50 born in Salado, TX. Destination Los Angeles.
- McNamara, Imogene "Brownie" age 25, born in Chickasaw, Indian Territory. Destination Los Angeles.
- Gamel, Marion age 22, was born in Waco, TX. Destination Los Angeles.
- McNamara, Ambrose A. (Archibald), age 2, born in Central Palma, Cuba Aug. 29, 1920, of American Parents, destination Los Angeles.

Marion Dickey Gamel died in Oriente, Matanzas, Cuba, Jan. 6, 1925, at 32. She was probably living with her sister's family and working with her brother-in-law, Ambrose Michael McNamara, who managed a sugar and molasses business in Cuba.

Imogene "Brownie" Gamel was born May 23, 1894, in the Chickasaw Nation, Indian Territory, many years before Oklahoma became a state.

She married Ambrose Michael McNamara Aug. 14, 1918, in Harris County, Texas. Ambrose, born July 20, 1885, in Limerick, Ireland, loved traveling and adventure. His lifestyle fitted perfectly with that of the Gamel family.

Many passenger lists show his arrival in the United States by ship and by plane. The first lists his arrival in New York May 20, 1907, from Queensland, Ireland, on board the SS ETRURIA. Ambrose, a 22-year-old student, listed his last permanent address as Sramelebred (Ireland) and Galveston (Texas). Rev. P. R. McNamara, his brother, was living in Cathedral Leavenworth, Kansas.

The 1910 census shows him living in Colorado County, Texas. He is working as a bookkeeper at a sugar mill. He and the Barbe family are listed as boarders in Louise Morris and her two children's home. Mr. Barbe also works at the sugar mill.

Sept. 22, 1912, 26-year-old Ambrose sailed on the SS CAMPANIA from Queenstown, Ireland, to New York. His last address is listed as Houston, Texas. He states that he had become a naturalized citizen of the United States "six years ago at Galveston."

By the time he married in 1918, Ambrose had worked with the molasses and sugar industries in Cuba and Jamaica. His son, Ambrose Archibald (Arch) McNamara, was born in Centra Palma, Cuba, Aug. 29, 1920.

The following is a list of some of his travel documents.

- 1920: Arriving from Kingston, Jamaica, Assistant Manager at a sugar company in Palma, Cuba.
- 1921: Vice President of the Dunbar Molasses Company.
- 1921: Sailing from Queensland, Ireland to New York on the SS SYTHIA. Ambrose, an Assistant Manager, lists his previous address as Six Mile Bridge. His father is Patrick McNamara from County, Clare, Ireland.
- 1924: His home in Hatillo, Cuba. He is working in the Molasses and Sugar Industry.
- 1925: The records from the SS NORTHLAND show that the McNamara family sailed from Havana, Cuba, Jan. 9, 1925, and arrived in Key West, Florida, on the same date. Ambrose was 37 years old; Imogene was 29, and their son, Archie, was four years and six months old.
- 1929: Manager
- 1929: August 32, Ambrose is the Vice President of Dunbar Molasses Co. He is staying at the Alban on 82nd. & Central Park West in New York. He is 47 years old, 6' 1/4" tall, weighs 180 pounds, and his hair and eyes are gray.
- 1936: Executive

- 1937: Broker
- 1938: Executive - Ambrose is living at 11 W. 42nd. New York, City. He speaks English and Spanish.

Ambrose McNamara was never in one place very long. He traveled to Ireland many times and to England, Kingston, Jamaica, the Dominican Republic, and Cuba. In America, he lived in or visited Key West and Miami, Florida, New York, Houston and Galveston, Texas, and Los Angeles, California.

In 1934, Imogene and Archie lived in El Paso, Texas, and Los Angeles, California. The Los Angeles City Directory of 1934 shows them living at 604 S. Andrews Place. Imogene is listed as a teacher. A California voter registration record states that she taught Dramatic Arts.

The 1940 census shows that Ambrose is married and living in New York. The other occupant of the home is his servant, Agapeto G. Garcia. On the line that asked about his education, Mr. McNamara listed: College 5th or subsequent year. In 1940, his wife and son, Imogene, and Archie, were living in Los Angeles.

Imogene "Brownie" Gamel McNamara died Aug. 7, 1971, in Temple, Texas, at the age of 77, and was buried in Salado, Texas.

Ambrose Michael McNamara died in Suffolk County, NY, in 1980 at the age of 95. He was buried in the Cemetery of the Holy Rood in Westbury, Nassau County, NY.

Their son, Ambrose Archibald (Arch) McNamara, died March 30, 2000, in Temple, Texas. He is buried there.

These exciting people, James Archibald Gamel, Jr., Marion Dickey Gamel, and Imogene Gamel McNamara, were Alva Clay Lindsay's maternal first cousins.

10
John Crosby Gamel & Katherine Hewins

John Crosby Gamel and his older brother, James Archibald Gamel, traveled together, went to school together, worked together, and owned property and cattle together. They both went to live in the Indian Territory in the 1890's.

John Crosby Gamel left the Indian Territory and went north to Kansas. Why Kansas? Was he going to meet old friends? Was he traveling on business? Was he trying to make a cattle deal, or was he looking for a wife?

In Cedar Vale, Kansas, John became acquainted, or reacquainted, with Mr. Edwin Mortimer Hewins. Mr. Hewins had had some recent reversals of fortune, but he was still a well-known and well-respected cattleman in Kansas.

Of Scottish heritage, Mr. Hewins was born in Lorain County, Ohio, March 22, 1839. When he was 18 years old, he went to the Territory of Kansas. He settled in Wabaunsee County, took up a claim, although he was a minor, and improved it as well as he could.

When Pike's Peak fever broke out in 1859, Edwin was one of the first immigrants to that region. He engaged in prospecting in Colorado and New Mexico for about one year before returning to Kansas in the fall of 1860.

Governor Crawford commissioned him to be Captain of a military company for the State's defense against the Indians.

He served in the Union Army during the Civil War. Skirmish, Coon Creek near Lamar: KANSAS--2d and 6th Cavalry. Union loss, 2 killed, 22 wounded, 6 missing. Edwin was one of the wounded.

After the war, Edwin married Julia Elle Ross. Julia was the daughter of Sylvester Flint Ross and Synthia Rice. The Ross family was well known in Kansas. They were very vocal in their opposition to slavery. Edmund Gibson Ross published a newspaper in Topeka, and he was elected to the US Senate in 1868.

Senator Ross is famous or infamous for casting his vote against convicting President Andrew Johnson of "high crimes and misdemeanors." This allowed Johnson to stay in office by the margin of one vote.

The vote June 6, 1868, set off a national uproar. Overnight, Ross became America's most hated man. Millions cursed him. A hometown newspaper blasted him. Ross endured death threats and subsequently lost his Senate seat at the next election.

Over the course of a century, Ross and his vote became an American legend—so much so that John F. Kennedy featured him in Profiles in Courage. President Grover Cleveland appointed Mr. Ross to be the Governor of New Mexico Territory in 1885.

Julia's father, Sylvester Flint Ross, a Justice of the Peace for Wabaunsee County, Kansas, at that time, officiated at her wedding. Julia, a cultivated and highly accomplished lady, was 17, and Edwin was 27 when they married May 22, 1866.

Edwin and Julia had four children, Minnie, Katie (Katheryn), Charles, and Ellie. Katheryn was born Feb. 20, 1871, in Topeka, Kansas. The Hewins family was well known and prosperous.

"From his boyhood, he has been a lover of a good horse, and he took great interest in all kinds of livestock. A taste he has cultivated and gratified since unto manhood until he has become one of the foremost stock-raisers and dealers in the state of Kansas.

Mr. Hewin's farm was one of the largest in that part of the state and specially arranged for handling stock, having all the modern conveniences, scales, corrals, and everything necessary for that business.

Besides his stock-raising and drover's business, Mr. Hewins was a member of the well-known livestock commission firm of Shough, Hewins & Titus, Kansas City."

Lives and fortunes can change overnight. This happened to Mr. Hewins and many other cattlemen during the winter of 1885-1886. For more information, read: the "Blizzards - The Big Die Up" chapter.

The winter of 1885 and 1886 was particularly severe. A series of cold spells and heavy snowfalls culminated in the first week of January when a huge snowstorm accompanied by high winds hit the central plains.

Drifts of six feet or more were common, and the temperature dropped to 30 degrees below zero in some places. Many prairie homes had been quickly and cheaply built, leaving settlers ill-prepared to protect themselves from such cold. The snow and wind were so fierce that people became lost a few yards from their homes.

It has been estimated that 100 Kansans froze to death during the storm. Neither were the settlers prepared to protect their livestock. Cattle turned their tails to the wind and 'drifted' for miles across the open range until they dropped from hunger or exhaustion.

Losses were high, up to 75 percent in some areas, and consequently, some large western Kansas cattle companies were bankrupted.

Ed Hewins was a remarkably successful rancher until this devastating blizzard hit in December 1885, continuing into early 1886. Most of his and his partner Titus's 15,000 cattle died, leaving only "sixty-two head." He had to sell his ranch, and his fortunes took a major downturn.

He was a member of the Kansas state house of representatives 95th District, 1877-79; member of Kansas state senate 21st District, 1885-87; and a delegate to the Democratic National Convention from Kansas, 1888.

This blizzard had a devastating effect on other parts of the country, including the Texas Panhandle. Read: "Blizzards - The Big Die Up."

Thousands of cattle had died. There was now a market for more and James A. and John C. Gamel had cattle. We do not know why John left the Indian Territory and traveled north to Cedar Vale, Kansas, but it was a life-changing trip. He met the young lady who would become his wife.

John felt right at home with Mr. Hewins. The Gamel and Hewins family were in the same business, and they spoke the same language, cattle.

John was 25 years old, handsome, wealthy, well educated, and from a well-known Texas family. John and 17-year-old Catherine (Katherine) were married in Cedar Vale, Chautauqua Co., Kansas, Feb. 12, 1893.

John's wife's name was spelled numerous ways. Catherine is on the wedding certificate. One of the early censuses lists her as Kathy. The notice from Mexico about her husband's death lists her as "Catarina." Katherine was used in several places. We will use Katherine but note that these are the same person.

The young couple left Kansas and went back to the Indian Territory. They lived there when their son, Clayton Hewins Gamel, was born in 1894. Their daughter, Byna Dorothea, was also born in the Indian Territory in 1897. The John Gamel family then moved to Colorado, where their youngest son, Hewins Archie Gamel, was born in 1899.

In the early 1890s, Ed Hewins "got some backing and started ranching on Salt Creek, in Indian Territory." How far was this from John and Katherine's ranch? No one knows.

After a few years, he opened a store in Woodward, also in Indian Territory, and started a cattle ranch just northwest of Woodward. "Not long after, he closed out and went to Douglas, Wyoming." We do not know the year Mr. Hewins and his wife, Julia, went to Wyoming. His son, Charles, went with them or followed them there.

Wyoming was admitted as the forty-fourth state of the Union July 10, 1890. There was a conflict between large cattle ranchers and small homesteaders in northern Wyoming in the spring of 1892. This has been referred to as "the most notorious event in the history of Wyoming" for its influence in reshaping the cattle industry and political landscape of Wyoming.

"Ed's son, Charlie, stocked a ranch at the foot of a mile-high peak, at the north base of the Medicine Bow Range."

Competition between newly arrived farmers and the established ranchers led to a cattleman's war, making it "the hottest outlaw spot the Northwest has ever witnessed." Douglas, Wyoming, was drawing the kind of gangs and corruption that should be avoided, but Ed Hewins joined in. His health deteriorated.

He was buried "on the slope of" the peak "overlooking the ranch he was operating."

(Summary condensed from "Sam Jent Recalls Rancher, Ed Hewins," "Cedar Vale Messenger," July 12, 1962, which appears on pages 33-39 of From Whence We Came: A Little History of Hewins, Kansas.)

It is not known when they arrived or how long they were in Wyoming before 59-year-old Edwin Hewins died Nov. 28, 1898, in Douglas, Converse County, Wyoming. Perhaps his family moved his body as records indicate that he is buried in the Pioneer Cemetery.

At some point, John, Katherine, and their family also moved to Wyoming. The 1900 census shows John, Katherine, their three children, and Katherine's mother, Julia, a widow, living in Upper Labonte, Converse County, Wyoming.

How long did the Gamel family stay in Wyoming? No one knows.

After his father's death, Charles Hewins moved back to Woodward, OK. The 1900 census lists Charles and his family and his sister, Ella Nay, and her family living there. It is likely that John and his family also moved back to Oklahoma.

John Crosby and his family were in Mason June 18, 1905. From Mason, they traveled to Corpus Christi. They were in San Antonio Aug. 15, 1905, when John wrote this letter to his father. The letter was written on letterhead from the Brown Beer Brewing Co.:

Brown Beer Brewing Co.
1317 West Commerce Street

New Phone No. 877
San Antonio, Texas, Aug 15, 1905

Mr. J. W. Gamel

Dear Father

Your letter received some time ago but did not answer it sooner as there is very little to write about. It is certainly hot here, and if these people get Yellow Fever, they will be out of luck.

I will leave here for Queretaro about the first and believe I will be able to make a 10 strike in this beer and it is a good proposition either in this country or Mexico. There are 4 of these boys here and they are all making money but Harry, and it is a good deal his own fault that he is not doing the same.

Suppose Nellie has arrived at Mason by this time. *(This is a probable reference to Nellie Mary Gamel, John's half-sister.)* We just got back from Corpus Christi & had a good time. The kids are all well. See Jess Presnall *(The man for whom his half-sister Jesse was named)* every few days and a great many of your old friends, who want to know how you are & ask to be remembered to you.

San Antonio is a very dead city at present it seems to have outgrown itself. Harry is trying to sell his business & go back to Loyal Valley. Well, I hope you are feeling as good as when I was up there. Remember me to all the folks.

Kitty & kids send love

Your Son

J. C. Gamel

The first notice below was published Dec. 1905. This information shows part of what the Gamel brothers were doing in Central Mexico:

John Crosby Gamel: "Cold Storage and Ice Trade Journal," Volume XIV, No. 6, December 1905 ("News of Companies and Plants"), page 105 ("Queretaro"):

QUERETARO. -- Concessions have been obtained by J. Arch Gamel and John C. Gamel for the establishment of a brewery and ice plant to cost $20,000.

A January 11, 1906, supplement to the "Engineering News," page 15, indicates John C. Gamel will soon get the contract for a large brewery's construction in Queretaro, Queretaro, Mexico.

Page 24 of "The National Provisioner," December 31, 1905, reports:

Queretaro, Mexico. Concessions have been obtained for the establishment of a brewery and ice plant here to cost $20,000, by J. Arch and John C. Gamel of the Queretaro Bottling Works.

John and his brother appear to have been shuttling between Texas and Mexico for their projects. It seems that they were exploring a construction opportunity in Mexico to add an ice plant and brewery to the Queretaro Bottling Works," which they may have already owned and/or operated.

The $20,000 that they were going to invest equates to $580,000 today. These young men had money to spend.

Did Katherine and their children go to Mexico with John? Did they travel back to Oklahoma, or did John move his family to the Texas Panhandle before he went to Mexico?

The railroad's arrival contributed to a booming cattle business in the Texas Panhandle. Katherine's mother, brother-in-law, John (Jack) Forbes Hall, and her sister Ella Hewins Nay Hall were all living there so this seems to be a logical place for her to go while John was in Mexico.

There are a lot of unanswered questions. We know that John went to Central Mexico, either alone or with his brother James or other family members. We also know that he died there. No death or burial records have been found except the following notice:

Died in central Mexico. Juan Gamel y Crosby Mexico, Querétaro, Civil Registration, 1864-2005. Name: Juan Gamel y Crosby Event Type: Death Registration Event Date: 4 Sep 1906 Event Place: Querétaro, Querétaro, México

Event Place (Original): Querétaro, Querétaro, México Gender: Male, Age: 48 Birth Year (Estimated): 1858 (should be 1868) Death Place: Querétaro, México

Father's Name: Juan Gamel Mother's Name: N Crosby Spouse's Name: Catarina Henins Spouse's Gender: Female Registration Number:1334

We do not know who furnished this information. According to James (Jim) Lindsay Long, family history reported that John Crosby Gamel's death was related to the political unrest between supporters of Porfirio Diaz and Pancho Villa. Perhaps some thought that John, an Americano, was supporting the wrong side.

John Gamel was not alone in his business ventures in Mexico. One of his cousins from Mason, John Christie "J. C." Crosby, was also involved.

The story from Kathleen Crosby St. Clair's daughter, Christie St. Clair, is that Uncle John escaped Mexico disguised as a priest. Things changed, and he returned to Mexico. In 1914, he married Esther Otamendi in Salvatierra, Chiapas, Mexico. John was 47. Esther was 22 years old. A few years later, Esther owned the Internationally Famous Ma Crosby's Café and Hotel in Ciudad Acuna, Mexico, across the border from Del Rio, Texas.

Three years after John Crosby Gamel's death, the 1910 census lists Katherine Hewins Gamel and her family living in Canyon, Texas. In addition to having family living in the area, there were also a lot of people that had a common interest, cattle.

Katherine's story continues in another chapter.

11
Katherine Hewins Gamel – After John

Three years after John Crosby Gamel's death, the 1910 census lists Katherine Hewins Gamel and her family living in Canyon, Texas. In addition to having family in the area, her mother, Julia, and her sister, Ella, there were also a lot of people that had a common interest, cattle.

"On Feb. 2nd, 1909, Mr. Lee John Hutson married Mrs. Katherine Gamel, a widow with three children. She was the daughter of ex-Senator Edwin M. Hewins of Kansas."

HUTSON, LEE JOHN (1850–1911). Lee John Hutson, a Panhandle rancher, was born Nov. 9, 1850, in Herefordshire, England.

Little is known of his parentage or early life. After immigrating to the United States, he was involved for several years with the Armour Packing Company and lived in Kansas City, where he represented an English loan company.

Having managed a ranch in Kansas, he was employed in Feb. 1889 by the Cedar Valley Land and Cattle Company as foreman of the T-Anchor Ranch, headquartered in Randall County, Texas. (See T-Anchor Ranch History.)

His primary task was to close out the company holdings due to the losses that the T-Anchor had suffered from the drought and blizzards in 1885–86.

However, after arriving at the ranch Feb. 16, Hutson urged the syndicate not to sell out. He argued that more profits could be made by buying and selling steers, improving the herds with blooded stock, and drilling wells in pastures where water was not easily accessible.

Mr. Hutson seemed always anxious to make friends. In a letter written May 18, 1889, to C. D. Fisher about his appointment as manager of the T-Anchor Ranch he wrote: "I think my reference will satisfy the Directors. I am aware of the unsuccessful state of all English Cattle Companies and assure you that under my management the strictest economy with efficiency will be enforced.

"I do not wish to brag on myself, but I am ambitious and wish to make a success of the Company that will have full confidence in me and believe I can provide an estimate of the value of the cattle after the count is made."

In a letter dated June 4, 1889, about four months after his arrival he said, "I have made acquaintance with all my neighbors and can safely say I have made friends of them all."

Since he desired to keep the ranch intact, he initially opposed Randall County's organization and the selection of a county seat, Canyon City, so near the headquarters. He saw it would mean the breaking up of the T-Anchor Ranch.

At first, as the country was opened for filing on the land, he would fire any of his cowmen who filed on land. When he saw he would be unable to stop the flow of settlers he helped his cow-hands file on land and began buying land himself.

As soon as he saw the breaking up of the Ranch was inevitable, he changed his course and aided in every way in the building of the town of Canyon. He soon became a leading booster of the county.

On Sept. 2, 1890, he wrote: "Settlers are coming in fast and within a year most of the school land will be filed on. They are a good class, not fencing much of their land but appear to be speculating on a Big Boom next Spring."

He bought his land mostly along the creeks for $3.50 per acre, and on Dec. 30, 1890, wrote that he had control of nearly all the water on both creeks. Hutson formed a partnership with Emmett Powers and leased several blocks of land on which he ran cattle under the Crescent G brand. He sold out this interest to Vinson Roe in 1900 but continued as foreman of the T-Anchor until 1902.

"A drive to Fort Reno, Okla., contributed one of the most widely known tales of the T-Anchor drive. Some of the boys wrote home that they were going into Indian Territory. One boy received the following letter, which the cowboys got and read in his absence:

Dear Bud:

   I don't want you to go where those old Indians are. They might scalp you, and if they did, I would surely die. Be careful, Bud, and don't let them hurt you, because you are the roasting-ears of my heart and the cornbread of my existence.

"It is sad as you watch the T-Anchor being gradually crowded out of existence, sad as you watch John Hutson struggle against his inevitable defeat, for it had been the policy of the T-Anchor to lease, not to buy their land and the settlers had filed on the land right under the herd.

"But you glory in the man as he turns immediately to the new order and begins the development of his fine herd of Herefords. With the open range it was impossible to build up the herds by introduction of graded stock. Now, using the very fence he had fought, John Hutson concentrated on his own properties and built up his exceptionally large herd of Registered Herefords."

Adept as a dealer in high-bred cattle, he won numerous blue ribbons and other prizes at stock shows in Fort Worth, Denver, Chicago, and Kansas City.

"One of Mr. Hutson's greatest contributions to Randall County and the Panhandle was his preservation of the live timber in the Palo Duro Park. When the ranches began breaking up and the settlers came, he kept two of his cowhands stationed in the Park and would not let the settlers cut any of the live timber.

"He would give them all the dead timber they wanted but none were allowed to cut the live timber in the Park. So scarce was wood on the plains some of the early settlers might have denuded the Park. This action of his has preserved the wooded beauty of the Park for the thousands of people who now visit yearly.

"Mr. Isaiah Jenkins was one of his cowmen he had stationed at the Park for this purpose and when the young people of Wayside came to the Park for a picnic, they invited Mr. Jenkins to join them. It was on this occasion that Mary McGeehee and Isaiah Jenkins first met, and this was the beginning of their courtship."

John Hutson played a prominent part in the first Press Convention held in Amarillo in 1894, two years after J. R. Gaut, pioneer Canyon and Amarillo newspaper publisher, established the Canyon City Searchlight.

There were three papers in Amarillo, but they were always fighting and could not get together even to entertain visitors. One day during the Press Conference J. R. Gaut met John Hutson. Hutson asked Gaut how the meeting was going and Gaut told him the trouble they were having.

Hutson invited the pressmen to Canyon for a barbecue. He and his men butchered and barbecued a fat steer and the last day of the Press Conference was held in Canyon. When the delegates got home their newspaper accounts of the Convention did not mention Amarillo but confined their accounts to the wonderful hospitality of the Canyon people and particularly John Hutson.

As a civic leader, Hutson dedicated himself to Canyon's growth. At one time, he was said to have owned at least half of the property in town. Mrs. Ed Harrell tells an interesting tale of Mr. Hutson:

"In 1891 Mr. L. G. Conner had built a hotel in Canyon which he had named The Victoria Hotel in honor of his wife, Victoria Conner. The Hotel was completed July 4th, 1891.

"In the fall of 1896, Mr. Hutson was expecting friends to visit him and wanted to entertain them at the Hotel. He wanted to serve drinks and the Conners would not allow him to serve drinks in the Hotel; so, Mr. Hutson asked them what they would take for the Hotel and when they named their price, he bought it, entertained his friends, serving liquor, and continued running the Hotel until it burned in 1908."

Mrs. Harrell says he ran a first-class Hotel. Heb Smith was the cook and in January of 1897 Mr. Hutson gave a party at the Hotel to which he invited everyone in the county and Mrs. Harrell says she thinks everyone came. He served supper to everyone and had everything that was available at that time to eat. After the supper he gave a dance at the Court House. He had hired a fiddler, a guitar player, and a banjo player.

Mrs. Harrell tells another tale about Ed Trigg which illustrates the type of Hotel Mr. Hutson ran. Mr. Trigg rode up to the Hotel on his horse and went in to eat. Mr. Hutson would not let him in the dining room without his coat on. Since Mr. Trigg did not have a coat with him, he had to go somewhere else to eat. Mr. Trigg often told this tale and laughed heartily at it.

Mr. Hutson was a friendly man. All who knew him speak of his friendliness, his generosity. He was a well-educated man, a man of refined tastes, always well groomed, erect on stature. Mamie Conner Bradford, daughter of Mr. and Mrs. L. G. Conner and Mrs. C. J. L. Lowndes, as well as many others, say he was an accomplished pianist. Mamie says he used to come to their home and play the piano for hours at a time.

Mr. Tom Dowlen, who worked for him longer than any other man, says he knew the cattle business. He knew how to select, how to breed, and how to develop his stock into better cattle. He never exploited the land, the cattle, or the people.

Mrs. Harrell remembers Mr. Hutson as a very dignified man, an interesting man whom all enjoyed knowing. She says he contributed much to the development of this country. This seems to be the opinion of all who knew him.

Thereafter he concentrated on his own properties and built up an exceptionally large herd of registered Herefords. Adept as a dealer in high-bred cattle, he won numerous blue ribbons and other prizes at stock shows in Fort Worth, Denver, Chicago, and Kansas City.

In April 1907, he was one of thirteen ranchers who met at the old Amarillo Hotel to form the Panhandle Hereford Breeders Association; in 1910, he was elected vice president.

By 1909 Hutson was the owner of two large ranches in Randall County, one on Palo Duro Creek northwest of Canyon and the other on Tierra Blanca Creek south of Umbarger. He also owned a ranch in Arkansas and land on the future townsite of Texico, New Mexico, some of which he sold for $30,000.

As a civic leader, Hutson dedicated himself to Canyon's growth. At one time, he was said to have owned at least half of the property in town, including the Victoria Hotel, which he bought from Lincoln G. Conner in 1896. In 1898 he used his influence to get the Pecos and Northern Texas Railway routed through Canyon.

Hutson helped organize the First National Bank and served as its vice president and on the board of directors. He also donated land to build an Episcopal church, gave money for establishing West Texas State Normal College (now West Texas A&M University), and helped establish the German Catholic community at Umbarger.

Jan. 14, 1911, Mr. Hutson suffered a fatal heart attack while conducting business at the Amarillo Hotel. Mr. Hutson drove by Tom Dowlen's place on his way to the Hotel to see some horses Tom had at pasture for him and when he left told Tom, "If I don't come back, I want you to have those horses." He died that night. He was 61 years old. Both Mrs. Hutson Day (Katherine) and Mr. Dowlen said that they had never known him to be sick a day in his life. He was buried in Llano Cemetery, Amarillo.

"John Hutson believed in this country. A new economic era had come, and Hutson was able to adjust himself to the new way. His death was a loss to his many friends, the cattle industry and the County of Randall."

Mrs. Katherine Hutson Day writes: "I still have fond memories of my life with John. He was one of the finest gentlemen I have ever known and was well known all the way from Texas to New York, with many friends in Chicago, Denver and Kansas."

The Dobbs Corporation, Inc. in Canyon, Texas was founded by Clay Lindsay's sister and brother-in-law, Doris, and L. R. Dobbs more than fifty years ago. It is still family owned and is operated by Clay's niece, Debbie Dobbs Green, and her children, Tiffany, and Lance Green. Debbie reports that the Hutson family is still well known and active in the Canyon community in 2021.

Seven years later, there was another death in Katherine's family. Her oldest son, Clayton Hewins Gamel, died May 17, 1918, in Liverpool, England, while serving in WW I.

A notification in the Washington D. C. newspaper and an official document states that his body was returned and buried Sept. 14, 1920, in Arlington, Arlington County, Virginia, United States of America.

Clayton Hewins Gamel's name is on the memorial erected on the Canyon Court House lawn to those who gave their lives for the defense of their country.

Katherine's daughter, Byna Dorthea Gamel, married Mr. William Nicholas Wood in Amarillo, Texas, in 1919. They were the parents of two daughters, and they lived in Ohio, Maryland, and Washington, D. C.

Byna and William were living in Washington, D. C. when she died May 22, 1942. She was 45 years old. Byna Gamel Wood was buried May 25, 1942, where her brother Clayton was buried, in Arlington, Arlington County, Virginia, United States of America.

Was Byna in the military? Did she work for a special government agency? How did she qualify to be buried in Arlington? Her uncle had been a U.S. Senator so that may have been the reason. Again, no one knows.

Katherine, now twice widowed, inherited all of John's property. She continued managing the estate for a few years. But eventually sold most of the property. In the 1920 census, she is living in California.

The 1920 census shows that Hewins Archie Gamel, John and Katherine's youngest son, lives in Potter County, Texas. Hewins is a boarder, working as a cowboy, on the ranch owned by J. T. and Ella H. Hall. He is living with his aunt and uncle.

Katherine moved to California. Her daughter, Byna, was married and living back East and her son was living with and working for her younger sister, Ella and her brother-in-law, John (Jack) Forbes Hall, on their ranch a few miles west of Amarillo.

It is interesting that people in Texas came from so many other places. This census shows that J. F. Hall, age 55, was born in Scotland. His wife, Ella H., age

25, was born in Kansas, and their border and ranch hand, 20-year-old Hewins Gamel, was born in Colorado.

After working as a cowboy in Texas, Hewins also moved to California. He married Lazette Wiseman in 1926, and their son, John Clayton Gamel, was born July 18, 1927, in San Diego.

The San Diego City Directories show that in 1927, Hewins Gamel was a clerk at the U.S. Grant Auto Equipment Company. In 1931 and 1932, he is a salesman for the same company.

This company and many of the buildings in San Diego are named for U.S. Grant, Jr. "He was a son of the famous Civil War General and the President of the United States, but his contributions to his adopted 'hometown' San Diego, CA. were outstanding."

Hewins A. Gamel is listed on a ship's record of the JARED INGERSOLL.

The SS Jared Ingersoll was a Liberty ship built in the United States during World War II. The Jared Ingersoll was laid down 24 June 1942 by the Bethlehem-Fairfield Shipyard, Baltimore, Maryland. She was launched 15 Aug. 1942. She was allocated to American West African Line, Inc., 25 Aug. 1942.

The report shows that Hewins A. Gamel signed on in Norfolk Sept. 16, 1942. The ship arrived in port April 12, 1943, and was expected to sail May 2, 1943, but nine seamen had deserted. Hewins A. Gamel is listed as one of the nine seamen who deserted the ship.

The report is stamped "SECRET" Ellis Island, N. Y. Harbor Record Division. There is no more information.

Hewins Archie Gamel returned to California and married Elanora Maria Louisa Cerrato. He died Nov. 30, 1982, in Torrance, Los Angeles County, CA.

After moving to California, Katherine Hewins Crosby Hutson married Mr. John Lee Steele April 13, 1927, and after his death, she married Mr. James Arthur Day June 11, 1943. Katherine was married four times and outlived all four husbands. She died June 29, 1958, in Long Beach, LA. County, California.

These people traveled everywhere! From coast to coast and border to border, in America and in other parts of the world, they never stayed in one place for a prolonged period.

This concludes the story of John William Gamel and Kathleen Crosby Gamel's two sons, John Archibald, and John Crosby Gamel, and their extended families. I hope you have enjoyed getting to know them.

12
Blizzards – The Big Die Up

Ablazing hot summer in 1886 had parched the Great Plains so that when the snow began falling in early November livestock were already stressed and in no condition to face a harsh winter. Then Jan. 9th, 1887, a severe blizzard hit burying parts of the plains under more than 16 inches of snow. Icy winds blew in out of Canada dropping the temperature to fifty degrees below zero.

Because of the drought, farmers had been unable to store enough hay for their cattle and millions of livestock that weren't killed by the brutal winter died of starvation. Some ninety percent of the open range cattle were rotting where they perished.

As far as the eye could see the carcasses clogged up rivers and tainted drinking water. Many ranchers went belly up while others pulled up stakes and moved back east. The loss was also felt by Europeans who had invested heavily in America's cattle business.

Ranchers and farmers had been dealing with brutal winters since 1881 and after the 1886-1887 winter hope was raised that the plains were about due for milder weather, but August began cooling early and September was prematurely chilly. By late November folks found they were in for another severe winter. This one would prove deadlier than the previous year.

In late December, a string of blizzards hit. The snow and gale-force winds killed sixty people in Kansas. A storm swept down from Alberta blowing across the plains of eastern Montana. The howling artic wind raced along at 45 miles an hour. The temperature dropped to forty below.

Children were caught between school and home. A farmer was lost between his barn and house. His wife perished when she went looking for him. In hours, the storm swept over 780 miles. After three days the winds died down and the death toll was more than three hundred. During the following spring, bodies were found in melting snow drifts and isolated refuges.

Charlie Russell came to Montana in 1880 at the age of sixteen where he hired out on a sheep ranch. He later went to work for a former trapper Jake Hoover, who owned a ranch in central Montana's Judith Basin.

Over the next few years, he worked as a night herder on several cow outfits in the area spending his free time becoming an artist. During the brutal winter of 1886-1887 he was working on the O-H ranch in the Judith when the owner wrote to the foreman asking how the cows had weathered the severe winter.

Instead of using words to tell the story the foreman used one of "Kid" Russell's watercolors titled "Waiting for a Chinook." A chinook was a Blackfoot Indian word meaning "snow-eater," a warm dry wind that blows down the east side of the Rocky Mountains at intervals and can cause a rapid rise in the temperatures melting the snow and exposing the grass.

The watercolor depicted a gaunt steer under a gray winter sky being stalked by wolves. Someone added the line, "The Last of the 5,000."

The rancher showed the grim illustration to friends and business acquaintances. It was eventually displayed in the window of a shop in Helena and before long Charlie began to find steady work as an artist and in a few years, he would be earning, in his words, "dead man's wages."

The disastrous blizzards of 1886-1887 and 1887-1888 brought far-reaching changes to ranching and farming in the West. It marked the end of open range ranching where cattle roamed far and wide.

Ranchers reduced the size of their herds, began farming operations to grow food to feed their herds and began fencing the ranges. It marked the end of an era. The days of the open range cowboys and the wild and untamed West were gone for good.

Information about this tragic event was obtained from numerous sources including:

Texas State Historical Association Handbook of Texas. "The Big Die-Up" by H. Allen Anderson.

Smithsonianmag.com January 5, 2015, by Laura Clark.

History.com/news/great-plains-blizzard-1886-kansas-big-die-up

Truewestmagazine.com/the-great-cattle-die-up

Americancowboy.com/lifestyle/big-dieup by Ron Soodalter

13
Quarter Circle Heart Ranch

The Quarter Circle Heart Ranch was established when Lewis H. Carhart, the original Clarendon colony's founder, invested part of his fortune in cattle.

Since his colonization scheme occupied most of his time, Carhart initially ran only a few hundred head. However, the success of other large cattle companies prompted him, in 1883, to extend his operations.

His brother-in-law, Alfred P. Sully, of the New York investment firm of Austin and Corbett, visited Clarendon to arrange for a syndicate and then returned east to begin foreign negotiations. At the same time, Carhart worked to increase the herd and improve the ranch properties.

The ranch had been under J. C. Murdock's temporary management, but Carhart sought out an experienced cowman with its enlargement. He found him in Al S. McKinney, an Irishman who came highly recommended after working for the Spade Ranch.

Early in 1884, a debenture company was founded in England, and Carhart sailed there to sell company stock to prospective buyers. Organization of the Clarendon Land Investment and Agency Company followed.

After returning to assume the managerial responsibilities, Carhart registered his Quarter Circle Heart brand and added to his original holdings (343 sections: 219,520 acres) those of Frank Houston and S. V. Barton on McClellan Creek.

Foreman Al McKinney took charge of the increased herds. Archie Williams, an elderly English veterinarian, was chosen to manage the new horse ranch that Carhart had established on the former Houston property.

A dugout on Carroll Creek served as the first company headquarters; nearby was a two-room bunkhouse constructed of rock and sod. When McKinney married, he moved the ranch office to his new house's front room on an adjoining section.

Also, the ranch contained three division line camps. At its peak, the Quarter Circle Heart range covered 250,000 acres of land, in the center of which lay Clarendon's town. Its longhorn cattle numbered from 15,000 to 35,000 head.

Neighboring ranches included the JA, the RO, the Half Circle K, and the Diamond F. As the only settlement in their midst, Clarendon became the supply center and social hub. Noted cowboys who worked for the "Hearts" included Jesse S. Wynne, Frank Groves, Tom Martindale, Al Gentry, and Henry W. Taylor.

The Quarter Circle Heart prosperity was short-lived, especially after 1887, when Clarendon moved its townsite five miles south to the Fort Worth and Denver City Railway tracks. The drought and blizzard of 1886–87, the "Big Die-Up," had taken their toll.

Increasing dissatisfaction among the company's British stockholders, many of whom had never received a dividend from their investments, prompted the executives to send the company secretary, Count Cecil Kearney, to the Panhandle for an on-the-spot investigation.

Carhart and McKinney, upon learning that Kearney would arrive on a specific day, both resigned without notice and left Clarendon. Kearney's inspection tour revealed conditions worse than he had suspected. On the range where 35,000 head of cattle had grazed, he could find only a fraction of that number.

Signs of gross mismanagement in all enterprise areas led to a complete reorganization, with Henry Taylor as range boss and Charles O'Donel, Kearney's nephew, as manager. Over the next few years, the Quarter Circle Heart range was divided into farms, school land, and settlements. By 1895 the brand had been discontinued.

14
JA Ranch

The JA Ranch is the oldest privately-owned cattle operation in the Panhandle. It began in the summer and fall of 1876, when Charles Goodnight drove 1,600 longhorn cattle from Pueblo, Colorado, to the Palo Duro Canyon. He established his "Home Ranch" near the Prairie Dog Town Fork of the Red River in southwestern Armstrong County.

After getting his men and cattle settled in for the winter, Goodnight returned to Colorado and arranged to bring his wife, Mary Ann (Molly) Goodnight, to the new homestead. In Denver, he met John G. Adair, an English aristocrat interested in going into the cattle business himself.

As a result of their meeting, Adair agreed to furnish the capital Goodnight needed to build up the ranch. In May 1877, the Goodnights and Adair, along with four cowboys, arrived at the Home Ranch with 100 Durham bulls and four wagons loaded with provisions.

On June 18, before the Adair's left for Ireland, the partners drew up a five-year contract under which two-thirds of the property and profits were to go to Adair and one-third to Goodnight. There were to be as many as 1,500 cattle and 2,500 acres of land. Goodnight borrowed his third of the investment from Adair at 10 percent interest. He was to receive an annual salary of $2,500.

At Goodnight's suggestion, the ranch was named Adair's initials. The letters of the JA brand at first were separated; three years later, the present connected design was adopted.

After the money was made available, Goodnight bought the first 12,000 acres from Jot Gunter and William B. Munson, Sr., who agreed that he could pick the land wherever he pleased. Over the next two years, he continued buying choice pieces of property crazy-quilt fashion in and around a seventy-five-mile stretch of Palo Duro Canyon, carefully selecting areas with good grazing land and water until the ranch was solidified.

In 1878 he drove the first JA trail herd, led by his famous bell ox Old Blue, north to Dodge City, Kansas, then the nearest railhead. In 1879, desiring a more central location for the ranch headquarters, Goodnight moved it to a choice site at the foot of the Caprock, twenty-five miles east of the old Home Ranch.

There he built a new four-room house of cedar logs and supervised the construction of several other buildings, including a bunkhouse, a bookkeeper's house, a wagon boss's house, a blacksmith shop, a wagon yard, and an ingenious milk and meat cooler. Later, the two-story, nineteen-room, main house was added. The old Home Ranch house was used as a line camp until it burned down on Christmas Eve, 1904.

As manager of the JA, Goodnight allowed no gambling, whiskey, or fighting and would not take anyone who had been fired elsewhere for drunkenness or theft. Even so, he usually was able to hire the men he needed.

Cape (Caleb B.) Willingham, Wint Bairfield, Jim (James T.) Christian, Frank Mitchell, J. W. Kent, George Doshier, Mitch Bell, and the brothers Judd, Jeff, and Lige Campbell were among the outstanding JA employees during its early years.

Goodnight's brothers-in-law, Walter and Leigh R. Dyer also worked off and on for the JA, particularly during trail drives and roundups. Almost from the start, Goodnight had sought to improve the JA cattle's quality by bringing in blooded stock.

In 1882 he built what is thought to have been the Panhandle's first barbed wire drift fence across a canyon bed above the Home Ranch to separate the purebred cattle, on which he used a JJ brand, from the main JA herd. He also kept a buffalo herd, which he sought to cross with cattle to produce the "cattalo."

By the time their contract expired in 1882, Goodnight and Adair had bought 93,000 acres and were looking for more. Also, Goodnight had purchased the Quitaque (Lazy F) range in Briscoe County for Cornelia Adair, and the Palo Duro post office had been established at the JA headquarters.

To Tom Adair's satisfaction, the enterprise had realized more than $512,000 in profits; thus, the partners opted to extend the contract for another five-year period. In 1883 Goodnight fenced the Quitaque properties and added the Tule Ranch in Swisher County, which he fenced in 1884–85, to the JA properties.

He also made other purchases from Gunter and Munson, the railroads, and the state that increased the ranch's size to 1,325,000 acres in parts of Randall, Armstrong, Donley, Hall, Briscoe, and Swisher counties.

After John Adair's death in 1885, following his third visit to the JA, his widow continued the partnership with Goodnight. By 1887, however, the building of the Fort Worth and Denver City Railway, falling beef prices, the influx of settlers, and attempts by politicians to curb large-scale ranching, the colonel was ready to sell out and limit his ranching activities; thus, their partnership was terminated on the expiration of the contract.

Nevertheless, Goodnight, who acquired the Quitaque Ranch in the property division, continued to act as manager until 1888, when he was succeeded by John E. Farrington, who served in that position for three years. James W. (Jack) Ritchie, Mrs. Adair's son by her first marriage, served briefly as foreman of the ranch's steer division in Tule Canyon before returning to New York City to handle the purchase of JA horses for the New York police department.

Arthur Tisdale managed the JA in 1891 and was succeeded the following year by Richard Walsh, an Irish immigrant who had been with the ranch since 1885. Under his leadership, improvements continued to be made through crossbreeding with blooded Hereford and Angus stock in the JA herd, which had increased to 101,023 head by 1889. Walsh soon built up one of the finest-quality herds of cattle in the nation.

As the railroads brought in more settlers, the JA began leasing and selling much of its excess pasture. When several nesters located on school lands within the JA boundaries, Walsh shrewdly purchased their claims or traded land outside the range for their holdings within, thus consolidating the JA properties.

In 1891 a school was opened for the children of ranch employees and neighboring settlers in the Palo Duro community near the ranch headquarters. Over the years, the ranch was gradually reduced in size as longtime employees like George Doshier, Wint Bairfield, Mitch Bell, and Jim Christian began their operations on former JA lands.

In 1917 Edward D. Harrell purchased the acreage where the old Home Ranch was located, and the Mulberry Ranch, named for the creek that drains it, was formed out of the JA's Mulberry Division.

After Walsh resigned as a manager in 1910, John S. Summerfield served for a year in that capacity and then was succeeded by James W. Wadsworth, Jr., a nephew of Cornelia Adair. Wadsworth held that position until 1915 when he was elected to the United States Senate from his home state of New York.

At that time, Timothy D. Hobart of Pampa was named to succeed him; he and Henry C. Coke, a Dallas attorney, were named executors of Cornelia Adair's estate after her death in December 1921. In her will, she left the bulk of the JA properties to her son, Jack Ritchie, and his heirs.

Clinton Henry came as the ranch bookkeeper in 1924 and assisted Hobart in the management.

In 1935, after Hobart and Coke died, Montgomery H. W. (Monte) Ritchie took over as manager. J. W. Kent retired in 1940, after having worked for a record number of years (since 1883) for the JA. Not until 1948 was the Adair estate, with its accompanying debts and inheritances, entirely settled.

By 1945 the JA's operations were confined to 335,000 acres in Armstrong, Briscoe, Donley, and Hall counties. Subsequently, a tract of 130,000 acres was divided into eight leaseholds to decrease labor and costs further.

Watered by the Prairie Dog Town Fork and its tributaries plus several hundred natural lakes, dirt tanks, and fifty-eight wells, the ranch had twelve winter branch camps and five farms that raised feed for the livestock.

Palo Duro Canyon's winter range afforded maximum protection, and the summer range was singularly free from land waste. Nearly two-thirds of the extant JA properties were rolling pastureland; even the land north and west of the headquarters was relatively flat.

As of 1990, the ranch was substantially fenced and cross-fenced and noted for its purebred Herefords and Angus bulls. Quarter horses were raised primarily for ranch use, and a small buffalo herd was maintained. Some commercial hunting of buffalo and deer was allowed. Tillable land continued to be leased. The Ritchie family also owned ranchland at Larkspur, Colorado, near Colorado Springs.

In 1988 the JA headquarters comprised several ranch outbuildings, including a supply store and garage, and was dominated by the "Big House," whose grounds were well manicured. A herd of longhorns, courtesy of the JA, roamed in Palo Duro Canyon State Scenic Park.

In 1960 the house was designated a national historic landmark. Two of the JA's historic buildings were given by Monte Ritchie to the Ranching Heritage Center at Lubbock. The old milk house in 1971 and an oat bin in 1988.

15
T-Anchor Ranch

The following is a brief history of the T-Anchor Ranch and the Cedar Valley Land and Cattle Company.

The T-Anchor Ranch originated in the fall of 1877, when Leigh R. Dyer, a brother-in-law of Charles Goodnight, drove his herd of about 400 cattle to Spring Draw in Randall County near the junction of Palo Duro and Tierra Blanca creeks.

He and his brother Walter cut cedar logs in the canyons, hauled them by the old Timber Creek Indian trail, and constructed a two-room log cabin for their headquarters. The Dyers' only claim to land was that of priority, and they sold that claim to the surveying firm of Gunter, Munson, and Summerfield in 1878.

Operating from their home office at Sherman in Grayson County, Jot Gunter, William B. Munson, Sr., and John S. Summerfield obtained title to the acreage by locating land certificates and by surveying on a partnership basis for land companies. Using money borrowed in Illinois to supplement their own funds, they were among the state's outstanding purchasers of land certificates.

They began their ranching activities in 1880 by bringing in mostly poor-grade cattle from Louisiana, Arkansas, and East Texas and herding them together in Kaufman County. These cattle, which numbered more than 3,600 head and bore the partners' GMS brand, were then sent west under Jud Campbell, who occupied the log cabin on Spring Draw.

W. H. (Harry) Ingerton and Vince Terry were among the cowboys who accompanied Campbell and who stayed to help build line camps and corrals and round up strays during the winter of 1880–81. The severe winter weather killed some of the cattle but, in the spring of 1881, Campbell trailed another GMS herd from Grayson County and fenced in about 240,000 acres to prevent them from drifting too far; this was said to be the first extensive fencing operation in the Panhandle area.

That fall Jule Gunter, Jot's nephew, bought Summerfield's interest, and the firm became Gunter, Munson, and Gunter. In addition to the GMS, the firm started using a Crescent G brand. However, when Jule Gunter brought a herd branded T-

Anchor from his Burneyville Ranch in the Indian Territory, the company dropped the other two brands and formally adopted the T-Anchor.

According to Jim Wright, foreman of Gunter's Grayson County holdings, Joe Harris had originated the brand on the head of Ellum Creek in Montague County near Saint Jo.

Early in the summer of 1882, Jim Wright, and Vas Stickley drove another 3,500 cattle from Grayson County to the T-Anchor. This herd was allowed to drift south with the other stock to the summer pasture in Tule Canyon.

On August 24th., the T-Anchor men began combing the canyons and rounding up the cattle to drive them back to the home ranch. Though Gunter had planned to divide the herd into two groups, a chance decision resulted in the largest single cattle drive in history.

Sixteen cowboys with a remuda of 125 horses herded 10,652 cattle to Big Lake and took half a day to run them through the fence line gate while Vas Stickley and Jule Gunter counted them. That night the cattle were bedded down over an area so large that it took over an hour for a horse to circle them at a fast trot.

In the fall, the T-Anchor men made their first drive north to the railhead at Dodge City, Kansas. On the trail, there were two divisions, each with a chuck wagon and 1,050 cattle. At about the same time, in October 1882, Munson and the Gunter's began leasing more grazing lands on Dixon Creek, east of the home ranch, and putting up more fences.

Jule Gunter continued to act as manager, with Jot as trader and buyer until 1883, when they sold out to Munson. Blooded stock was introduced to the T-Anchor in the spring of that year when Vas Stickley brought in its first herd of Hereford cattle from Dodge City. Munson continued to be the sole owner of the ranch until 1885, when he sold about 275,000 acres in Randall and Deaf Smith counties to the Cedar Valley Land and Cattle Company of England for $800,000.

Included in the transaction were 25,000 cattle and 325 horses. The new owners retained the T-Anchor brand, leased additional lands, and were the first to hire outside help (from the JA Ranch) to tally the cattle. Sam Dyer, Jim Moore, Hank Siders, and Lee John Hutson served successively as foremen. In 1895 the forfeiture of the syndicate's leases marked the end of the T-Anchor as such.

Nevertheless, the Cedar Valley Company operated the remaining lands until 1902, when the ranch was broken into blocks and sold to farmers and smaller ranchers. Later, the state purchased the old headquarters and the surrounding 200 acres to use as an experimental farm for West Texas State College.

The T-Anchor brand was discontinued in the Panhandle, but between 1906 and 1910, J. G. Hardie, a grandson of Jot Gunter, used the brand on his cattle in Duval County. Subsequently he ran it in Maverick and Zavala counties and in Coahuila, Mexico.

For several years, an annual reunion of former T-Anchor employees, known officially as "The Old Time Cowpunchers' Roundup of Each Other on the T-Anchor Range," was held at the old log headquarters near U.S. Highway 87 north of downtown Canyon. In 1975, however, the building, the oldest surviving Anglo structure in the Panhandle, was moved to a site near the Panhandle-Plains Historical Museum and fully restored.

16
John (Jack) Forbes Hall

John (Jack) Forbes Hall was born Jan. 8, 1864, in Farnell Parish (now Angus), Montrose, Scotland. He landed in New York aboard the FURNESSIA, March 10, 1883.

John was a cattleman. He left New York and took a job with the Western Land and Cattle Company. He was in Kinsley, Kansas, Nov. 1, 1884, when he declared his intention to become a U.S. citizen. (There is more about Kinsley, Kanas in the "Blizzards – The Big Die Up" chapter. It is likely that Mr. Hall became acquainted with the Hewins family while he was in Kansas.)

Four years later, he was in the Texas Panhandle. He began punching cattle for the Quarter Circle Heart ranch near Clarendon. He was engaged in the mercantile business in Clarendon for several years and returned to the cattle business when he became the JA Ranch assistant manager. (More details about Quarter Circle Heart and JA Ranches are found in other chapters.)

"The prominent Plainsman came to Amarillo shortly before the turn of the century. He was engaged here in cattle and commission work. He also served three terms as a Potter County commissioner."

The 1940 census shows that Mr. Hall is a rancher, that he owns a cattle ranch, and that he worked 52 weeks in 1939. That is a rancher's life, work!

The following information was taken from the Amarillo Daily News, Amarillo, Texas:

John (Jack) Forbes Hall, pioneer, cowboy, rancher, and businessman, died of a heart attack Saturday, Aug. 10, 1940, in an Amarillo, Texas, hospital. He was 76 years old. He was buried in the Llano cemetery.

As a member of the board of commissioners, he arranged for the purchase of land for the Northwest Texas Hospital. He is survived by his wife, the former Ella Hewins Nay of Amarillo. They were married in 1904.

He retired from active business life several years ago and sold all but 160 acres of his ranch northwest of Amarillo.

John (Jack) Forbes Hall and Ella Hewins Nay Hall were John Crosby Gamel's brother-in-law and sister-in-law. Ella Hewins was the younger sister of Katherine Hewins Gamel, John Crosby Gamel's wife.

17
A Trail Driver's Story

Trail drivers were cowboys who moved cattle, typically in herds of about 2,500, from a home range to a distant market or another range. The typical outfit consisted of a boss, who might or might not be the owner of the herd; ten to fifteen hands, each of whom had a string of from five to ten horses; a horse wrangler, who drove and herded the horses; and a cook.

The men drove and grazed the cattle most of the day, herding them by relays at night. Most considered ten or twelve miles a good day's drive, as the cattle had to thrive along the route. Wages for a trail driver were about $40 a month.

The trail drivers' code presupposed that no matter what the hazards, hardships, or physical torture, a man would stay with his herd as loyally as a captain stays with his ship at sea.

I DROVE A HERD OVER THE TRAIL TO CALIFORNIA

By W. E. Cureton of Meridian, Texas

I was born in the Ozark Mountains of Arkansas, in 1848, came to Texas with my father, Captain Jack Cureton, in the winter of 1854–55; settled on or near the Brazos River below old Fort Belknap in what is now Palo Pinto County, and began raising cattle. The county was organized in 1857. (Mason County was organized in 1858.)

In 1867 we (my father and John C. Cureton) drove a herd of grown steers from Jim Ned, a tributary of the Colorado of Texas, now in Coleman County, up the Concho at a time when the Coffees and Tankersley's were the only inhabitants there. That year the government began the building of Fort Concho, which is now a part of the thrifty little city of San Angelo.

The Indians killed a Dutchman and scalped and partly skinned him a little ahead of us, and Captain Snively, with a gold hunting outfit, had quite a skirmish along the Concho with them.

From the head waters on the Concho, we made a ninety-six-mile drive to Horsehead Crossing on the Pecos River without giving the cattle a good watering. Our trail was the old military stage route used by the government before the Civil War. The Indians had killed a man and wounded a woman ahead of us at the old adobe walls at Horsehead Crossing on the Pecos and captured a herd of cattle belonging to John Gamel and Isaac W. Cox of Mason, Texas.

A few miles above Horsehead Crossing the Indians stole eleven head of our horses one night; only having two horses to the man; we felt the loss of half our mounts very severely. A little further up the river the Indians wounded Uncle Oliver Loving, the father of J. C. and George B. of the noted Loving family of the upper Brazos country and the founder of the great Texas Cattle Raisers' Association.

The old man died at Fort Sumner of his wounds. They also killed Billy Corley, one of Lynch & Cooper's men, from Shackleford County, the same drive.

We left the Pecos near where now stands the town of Roswell, and traveled up the Hondo out by Fort Stanton over the divide to San Augustine Springs, near the Rio Grande, and wintered the cattle and sold them in the spring of 1868 to Hinds & Hooker, who were the United States contractors to feed the soldiers and Indians, as they were pretending to subdue and keep the Indians on reservations, but in reality were equipping them so they could depredate more efficiently on the drovers and emigrants.

In the summer of 1869, I sold a bunch of grown steers in Palo Pinto County, Texas, to Dr. D. B. Warren of Missouri, and we trailed them to Baxter Springs, Kansas. We swam Red River at the old Preston Ferry. We camped near the river the night before and tried to cross early in the morning. The river was very full of muddy water, and the cattle refused to take the water.

After all hands had about exhausted themselves Dr. Warren, who was his own boss, said to me: "William, what will we do about it "I answered him that we had better back out and graze the cattle until the sun got up so they could see the other bank, and they would want water and go across. You should know that you can't swim cattle across as big a stream as this going east in the morning or going west late of an evening with the sun in their faces." About one P.M. we put them back on the trail and by the time the drags got near the river the leaders were climbing the east bank. The doctor looked at me and said, "Well, I'll be damned — every man to his profession."

In the spring of 1870, my father took his family along, and turned over more than eleven hundred cattle to us boys, John C., and J. W., to drive to California. We went out over the old Concho Trail to the Rio Pecos, up the river to the Hondo, out by the Gallina Mountains, crossing the Rio Grande at Old Albuquerque.

We went over to and down the Little Colorado of the West; through New Mexico into Arizona, by where Flagstaff is now; on the Santa Fe` Railroad, parallel to the Grand Canyon on the south side of the Colorado; crossed the Colorado at Hardyville above the Needles; crossed over the California desert; climbed over the Sierra Nevada's and wintered the cattle between San Bernardino and Los Angeles in California, a fifteen-hundred-mile drive.

(Note the way he says, "Crossed the desert, climbed over the Sierra Nevada's" …no description of the hardships they endured."

In the spring of 1871 we drove the cattle back across the Sierras, north up the east side of the mountains to the head of Owens River, where we fattened them on the luxurious California meadows; then drove them to Reno, Nevada, five hundred miles from our wintering grounds, and sold them, and Miller & Lux, the millionaire butchers of San Francisco, shipped them to their slaughtering plant in San Francisco, California—and, by the way, the firm still controls the California market there.

We paid ten dollars for grown steers in Texas; got thirty dollars after driving them two thousand miles and consuming two years on the trip. After all, I honor the old longhorn; he was able to furnish his own transportation to all the markets before the advent of railroads.

I made many other trips but think these will give a fair idea of the hardships of the pioneers.

I have been interested in cattle raising for sixty years, ranching in Texas, New Mexico, Arizona, and California during that time, but always claimed Texas as home; was a schoolboy with the late Colonel C. C. Slaughter of Dallas and George T. Reynolds of Fort Worth more than sixty years ago.

18
The Gamel House

The Gamel house, one of the first rock homes in Mason, was built in 1869. John W. Gamel, his wife, Kathleen Crosby Gamel, and their two sons, James Archibald (Archie) and John Crosby (Johnny), lived there until her death on January 1, 1880. (There is more information about her death in the Gamel chapter.)

The Gamel house, except for the kitchen and dining room, was built of rock and consisted of seven rooms. There are two fireplaces, and the walls are two feet thick. Ceilings in the front rooms were twelve feet high, and ninety-inch windows came within eight inches of the floor. The roof was of cypress shingles, and the woodwork, doors, and floors were also of cypress.

Cypress shutters that opened and closed decorated the windows as well as tempering the heat and cold. The rock walls were left rough; however, the gallery's wall was plastered and marked off with mortar to resemble cut stones in the 1880s.

John married Alice Kettner in 1881, and there were some changes made to the house. The plastered inside walls were wall-papered. The wooden bathhouse was moved to the south side of the house, and a rock tank house was built by the well when a windmill was installed.

In the early 1900s, a screened porch was added to the southeast portion of the house, and the bathhouse was connected to the porch. In the 1920s, the wooden floor on the gallery was replaced by a cement floor, and the wooden posts were replaced by square pillars mounted on cement bases.

In the 1930s, the house was stuccoed and painted white. P. C. Rode built the cement steps from the street to the house. Alice Kettner Gamel lived in this house until her death May 27, 1942.

In 1978, Jesse's daughter, Effie, returned to Mason to live and restore the old Gamel house which had been heavily vandalized in the few years it was vacant

Effie conferred with the Texas Historical Society in Austin and began a general restoration. The house was found to be structurally sound despite the vandalism.

Two bathrooms, one at each end of a former long hall, were added. Closet and storage spaces were built on each side of the remaining hall. A new living room was built where the old, screened porch had been, and the old bathhouse moved to an outside yard to be used as a garden and tool shed. Mrs. Effie Lindsay Long White finds that the project goes on and on and on

During the 1980's restoration, the workmen were astounded at the size and excellent condition of the cypress logs used for bracing the floors. Almost all the cypress floors survived. Only one floor and one interior wall needed extensive repair.

At that time, the Gamel house was the oldest house in Mason's township that was still owned and occupied by a member of the original family. After Effie Lindsay Long White's death June 1, 1989, the house was sold.

Gene and Patsy Zesch are the current owners in 2021. Patsy reported that they recently hired an architect to inspect the house and that he was amazed that it was in such excellent condition. He was also impressed with the hand-dug well and the rock tank house.

John William and Alice Kettner Gamel had four children, Effie, Nell Gamel Lauderdale, Herbert Zork, and Jesse Gamel Lindsay, who was the only surviving child when this article was written.

However, both Jesse Lindsay and her daughter, Effie Lindsay Long White, are deceased. Jesse Gamel Lindsay died March 23, 1987. Her daughter, Effie, died June 1, 1989.

John W. Gamel paid for quality, and he got it. The people who built the Gamel house in 1869 did an excellent job. This house holds many beautiful memories for the Lindsay family.

Clay Lindsay loved his grandmother, Alice. According to him, she was the best woman in the world. There are photos of Clay when he was 10 years old, lying on the front steps of her house. When he gathered eggs on the ranch and took them to her, she bought everyone, even though most of them were rotten.

The Lindsay family of seven went to Alice's house every Sunday for dinner. Clay also went to his grandma's house for lunch when he no longer attended the country school. His new school was just up the hill, and, of course, grandma had his favorite food waiting for him.

There are also sad photos. Standing in front of the Gamel house in May of 1942, wearing his Merchant Marine uniform, 20-year-old Clay holds his two young nephews, John and Jim Long. Clay was home, on leave, to attend the funeral of his beloved grandmother.

Franz (Francis) Kettner

19
Franz (Francis) Kettner

Clay's great-grandfather, Franz (Francis) Kettner, was born Oct. 23, 1826, in Oberkirch, Baden-Württemberg, Germany. His parents were Dr. Franz Lambert Kettner and Maria Clara Strickfaden.

Records from the Galveston County. Gen. Soc. Ship Passenger Lists show that Franz Kettner departed from Antwerp on the Ship LOUIS. He was from Baden. His destination was Texas.

Franz was 22 years old when he landed in Galveston, Texas Nov. 20, 1848. This young man was a stranger in a strange land but there were many Germans in Texas when he arrived, and more were on their way. He was not totally alone. He was involved in many endeavors, and he wrote his parents telling them of his new life in this new land. A few of his letters were published by the Southwestern Historical Quarterly, Volume 69, July 1965 - April 1966. This little booklet was entitled, "Letters of a German Pioneer in Texas."

The first letter was written Aug. 12, 1853, from Castell, Texas. Castell, the oldest town in Llano County, is about 30 miles east of Mason. It was settled in 1847 by a group of German settlers led from Fredericksburg by Count Emil von Kriewitz to a site selected by John O. von Meusebach to comply with the terms of the Fisher-Miller land grant, which the organization had acquired. The town was named for Count Carl Frederick Castell-Castell. Many of those living in the community in 2021 are descendants of the original German settlers. In 1964, Castell was designated a Recorded Texas Historic Landmark. The marker is number 9440. The first letter is dated August 12, 1853. He tells his parents a little about his experiences in the Texas Hill Country:

"Our store is doing well. My main occupation is in the store but for relaxation, I go fishing. Our river, the Llano, is so full of fish that you could not imagine it. Many times, I have caught thirty or forty pounds of fish in two hours, so many that we cannot stand to look at, much less eat, any more fish for a week.

Hunting is also excellent. And I am quite content if I can ride out every eight or ten days to shoot a buck.

Concerning my health, I am still well and happy, and people insist that I never grow older and still look like a man of twenty-three or twenty-four years.

They envy especially my good humor, which I did not lose even when we ran out of food on the way back from the Rio Grande. We had to go hungry and thirsty for almost two days, and the temperatures were between 95-and 100-degrees F.

My body is somewhat hardened, and I maintain that the more stresses and strains a person has to endure, the stronger and more energetic he becomes. But now we are able to take better care of ourselves. If I may say so, I liked traveling better than sitting in the store and selling."

The next letter was written almost two years later. His old Texas Ranger outfit was mustered temporarily into service of the United States Army to act as military escort for wagons moving to El Paso. He received a small pension for that service through the rest of his life. Upon being discharged, he returned to Castell, but the Indian troubles obliged him to resettle near Fredericksburg.

Fredericksburg – April 23, 1855

Dear Parents,

"Since your last letter, which I received in December of last year, I have had no news from you. I am rushing this letter to tell you about my military service, since I have been discharged. Our whole military expedition consisted only of escorting wagon transporters for the regular army.

We had six companies and escorted about 400 six-span mule-wagons to a fort that lies a little below El Paso, about 600 miles from San Antonio. (This was Fort Bliss, founded in 1848) It took us, going and coming, about three months.

Other than the fact that many died, due to the bad weather, nothing of interest happened. (The height of understatement.) It was a wild, rocky land, deficient of water, and we sometimes had to travel for two days before reaching water again. I myself bore the hardships very will and did not get sick a single time."

Think about what he said and what they did. Calculate the numbers of people and livestock that made that journey. It was an enormous task. Would you like to make that trip?

To learn more about the amazing life of this daring young man and to learn about the hardships and dangers of frontier life faced by Franz in the Texas Hill Country, read "Die Kettner Briefe," aka "The Kettner Letters." This book was published by Charles Kettner, PhD and Ilsa Wurster. It can be purchased from Amazon and other book sellers.

"The book consists of 39 letters exchanged between Franz Kettner and his family in Germany from 1850 to 1875. The letters, printed in German with their English translations, read like a good adventure novel with each letter providing a much-anticipated new chapter. The story is enhanced by photographs, both old and new, and other supporting documents."

Francis married Katharina Keller Sept. 3, 1857, in Fredericksburg, Texas. They had five children. Clay's grandmother, Alice, their third child, was born June 24, 1862.

Franz was an early farmer and stockman in Comal, Gillespie, and Mason Counties. He participated in several campaigns with the Texas Rangers and later, during the Civil War, was a member of the Minute Men. He ran a store and post office in Castell. He hauled freight from the Texas coast to Fort Mason.

He was a sheriff in both Gillespie and Mason Counties. He held the prestigious position of Cattle and Hide Inspector during the era of large cattle drives from Mason County.

Address delivered upon the Funeral of Francis Kettner Sept. 9, 1907, by R. Runge:

Dear Friends:

Again, we have marched to the city of the dead to deposit in its sacred precincts the remains of one of the best. At his request I address to you a few words, giving a short sketch of some of the principal events of his life, not to pronounce a eulogy upon him; for such is told much more eloquently by a long and noble life than words can express it.

He was a man with whom "to do good" was religion. A man who by virtue of his many sterling qualities and noble character, from the early settlement of this country, has held a fond place in the hearts of the people. Coming hither when Mason County was a wilderness, infested by hostile Indians, when the few white settlers each were acquainted with the other, all soon learned to know, respect, and love him.

Francis Kettner was a man of indomitable courage, scrupulously honest and conscientious, pronounced in his views, indulgent toward others, unbounded in hospitality.

In the perilous, early days, when none but the best would do, he was frequently called upon by the citizenship of his county to fill the office of a sheriff and other responsible positions. And the efficient and energetic manner in which he discharged the hazardous and difficult duties of those positions, under adverse circumstances, ever was a credit to himself and of untold benefit to his constituents.

Nor is his good name and fame confined to the bounds of Mason County, nor to this state, nor, indeed to this continent. Our beloved dead was born (nearly 81 years ago) in the Grand Duche of Baden, Germany, on October 12, 1826, a date which coincides with the natal day of the ruler of his native state, the venerable Grand Duke of Baden.

Our departed friend received a careful education in the celebrated institutions of learning of his fatherland. But before his education was finished, he in 1848, joined the revolutionary party, which had for its object the throwing off of the yoke of petty and greater tyrants and the unification of what is now the German Empire.

This territory was then divided in about 34 separate and theoretically-- independent sovereignties; the inhabitants of the smaller ones having to submit not only to the arbitrary will of their own rulers, but as well to the tyranny of the more powerful of these countries, while none of them was strong enough, single handed, to defend against any of the great powers of Europe.

Some of these revolutionists had far advanced ideas, dreaming of a "Republic of Germany," while united Germany, strong enough to defend herself against any of her neighbors, with a ruler whose powers were to be limited by a constitution, was all that the more conservative and thoughtful demanded or hoped for—a hope that was realized as the result of the Franco-German War 23 years later. "Union and Liberty" was the slogan of the revolutionists of '48 with which they went to battle under Franz Sigel, later a celebrated general of the U.S. Army.

And our departed friend in this fight for the oppressed people against potentates and tyrants, risked his all. The revolutionary movement was crushed by forces of the strongly disciplined armies of the princes, and our friend, to escape persecution, together with many of the nation's best, was compelled to part from his native land and sought a new home in the new state of Texas, in 1848.

He at once went to work with a will, but not acquainted with the conditions and workings of this country, it was years before he acquired a competency. In the first year of residence in Texas he tried farming in a bend of the Guadalupe in Comal County, which on account of its particular form is called "Demijohn Bend."

The next year we find him in Captain Connor's company of Texas Rangers in the Rio Grande country, protecting the state against invasions of hostile Indians and Mexicans. This company was later mustered into the service of the United States from which the departed during the last few years of his life has drawn a small pension for his service in the campaigns of that company.

Of the 80 and some young men that composed his company 57 years ago—so far as known, only 2 survive our departed friend, namely, Gustav Schmeltzer of San Antonio, and Charles C. Schreiner of Kerrville.

This period was full of adventure and dangers, and our friend would most interestingly talk of them. I regret that the limited time will not permit me to relate some of them.

Robert Brodemann of New Braunfels, Mr. Kriewitz of Castell, and Captain Dosch of San Antonio, whom many of you know, were with Kettner in this service. They all preceded him in death.

Upon the completion of this service, Mr. Kettner lived for a short time with this friend Kriewitz at Castell, thereupon he moved to Gillespie County, where he was elected sheriff, making one of the best sheriffs that county ever had.

Still making Gillespie County his home he engaged in farming and freighting. Freighting was then done by means of large ox teams, and a single trip to the coast or to one of the military posts far off on the frontier, would often require months.

While such journeys over the long and lonesome routes were not bare of charm to those who in loneliness loved to commune with nature and to some romantically inclined youths, it was full of hardship and perils incident to the early frontier life. Our friend having by this time seen considerable of the frontier life was of great service to his comrades who were new or "green" on the frontier.

On Sept. 3, 1857, he was married to Katherine Keller at Fredericksburg. Two years later he moved with his young wife and child to Mason County, settling on the south bank of the Llano River, on the place now owned by Adolph Keller at what is now known as the Foley Crossing.

Here he and his family suffered untold privations and dangers. During the Civil War, the conditions were exceedingly bad. For years afterwards, the Indians were very bad, and this place seemed to be on their "trail" or route they were accustomed to travel when going on their depredations in the white settlements.

It finally became so bad that to longer attempt to stay on that place would have been little short of suicide.

In 1875, while Mr. Kettner was at work in the field a bunch of Indians swept down upon the ranch attempting to drive off the saddle horses grazing within 75 yards of the house. The oldest, Louis, then a lad of 13, boldly attacked them, firing upon them with his six-shooter, while Mrs. Kettner took a Spencer Carbine to her husband in the field. When Mr. Kettner arrived on the scene, gun in hand, the Indians called the fight off, fleeing with all speed to the mountains, Mr. Kettner firing on them as they fled.

This occurred while there was a company of rangers stationed within 2 miles of the ranch. Soon after even this supposed protection was withdrawn, when the family moved to what was then known as the McSwane place, six miles below the town on Comanche Creek, where they lived until 6 years, when they moved to our town where Mr. & Mrs. Kettner have since resided.

During this residence in Mason, the departed held many important positions. He was sheriff in early days, later he was revenue officer, in the early 70's he held the then highly important office of cattle inspector and in that capacity probably did more than any other man to see that everyone got his dues.

Later he was elected county commissioner and re-elected many times—so long as he could be persuaded to accept the office—and to his ability and faithful performance of the duties of that office, it is largely due that Mason County was rescued from a state of bankruptcy and placed on a cash basis.

There were born to Mr. and Mrs. Kettner 5 children: the sons, Louis, Will and Charles, and the daughters, Ida, and Alice, now Mrs. August Keller, and Mrs. John Gamel, all of whom survive him and now stand at his grave; 15 grandchildren also survive him.

The departed lived to see 2 happy events, which are of rare occurrence in the short span of time allotted to man. The one was the birth of a great grandchild; the other was the 50th Anniversary of his wedding day - The Golden Wedding.

It is sad to know that the latter of these 2 events was destined to be the beginning of the end. For while the day opened brightly and beautifully, shortly before noon, while the table was spread, and the happy children and grandchildren in anticipation of a most joyous time gathered around the parental board, the beloved groom, the father, and grandfather suffered a paralytic stroke to which he succumbed, yielding up his life 8 days later, at 4 o'clock yesterday one week to the hour after we laid to rest the remains of his kinsman and lifetime friend, Major James Hunter.

While the departed, in his long life by industry, and economy accumulated a handsome fortune, his aim in life never was the acquisition of riches. He was one of the old school of idealist, now nearly extinct, who saw his happiness in the elevation of mankind, whose deeds were directed by his principle, "To do unto others as he would have them do unto him."

Most of you have known him the greater part of your lives-speaking for myself, I for the first time grasped his hand over half a century ago. You all remember good and noble deeds of his. No one can point to any wrong that he ever committed.

You men and women of a younger generation who knew him in life, whenever you meet with an occasion where you do not know whether to do a certain thing is right or not, ask yourselves this question: "What would he have done under like circumstances?" Do what you know he would have done, and a clear conscience will be your reward.

While we submit his remains to the grave, surrounded by those of many friends, who have gone before, let his life be our beacon-light.

John William Gamel

Alice Kettner Gamel

20
John William Gamel & Alice Kettner's Family

Alice Kettner was born June 24, 1862, in Mason, Texas to Franz (Francis) and Catharina Keller Kettner. On Sept. 15, 1881, 19-year-old Alice married John William Gamel, a 37-year-old widower with two teenage sons. Even though his first wife Kathleen had died without telling anyone where she had hidden their gold, John was still a wealthy man.

He was so wealthy that he gave each of his sons, James Archibald, and John Crosby Gamel, $75,000 dollars and a rock house after his marriage to Alice. That was equivalent to $1.9 million dollars in 2021 currency. John continued to buy and sell cattle and operate his large ranches.

The Gamel family grew. They had three children in seven years. Their first child was Effie Mary Gamel b. Nov. 12, 1883, Mason TX; d. July 15, 1913, Mason TX.

Things changed and many Mason ranchers went broke in the next few years. Their big cattle spreads were being hampered by fencing. There as a searing drought in 1885 and then the horrendous blizzards of 1885-1886.

Alice's second child was Nellie Mary Gamel b. Aug. 27, 1886, Mason TX; d. Oct. 13, 1960, Austin TX; m. W. C. Lauderdale, San Antonio, TX.

Their son, Herbert Zork Gamel was b. April 30, 1888, Mason TX; d. April 03, 1934, Harper, TX.

The Great Panic of 1893 dropped cattle prices to $6.00 a pair for cow and calf and John Gamel went broke. He began hunting in earnest for the gold that Kathleen had hidden 13 years before.

Stella Gipson Polk, Fred Gipson's sister, wrote about this in a magazine article, "The Gamel Gold," Where did the Rancher's Wife Hide Their Money?"

"When John was away from home, others also hunted, with the result that the well-kept lawn was spotted with their diggings. It was never found. Like an elusive dream, vague and sad, the Gamel gold had vanished."

Alice and John's last child was Alva Clay Lindsay's mother, Jesse Presnall Gamel, b. Oct. 23, 1897, Mason TX; d. March 23, 1987, Mason TX.

Jesse never liked her name because she was named for a man, one of her father's closest friends, a well-known cattleman from San Antonio, TX. Jesse Presnall. Jesse changed the spelling of her name to Jessie because it was more feminine.

The John Gamel family was well-known and well-respected, but tragedy awaited. July 15, 1913 was a hot day. John and Alice's oldest daughter, Effie, decided to go to the Llano River with her fiancé, her younger sister, and friends.

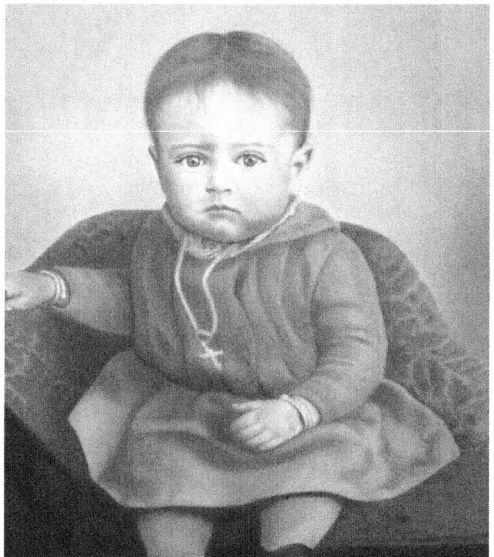

Jesse Presnall Gamel, youngest child of John W. & Alice Kettner Gamel

These newspaper clippings were kept in the Gamel family bible. Jesse Gamel, Effie's younger sister, watched helplessly from the bank of the river, as her sister drowned. After a few years, Jesse would go to the river, but she would never go into the water, and she never learned to swim.

Notes for EFFIE MARY GAMEL: Effie Gamel and Charles P. Burkes were drowned in the Llano River. The following accounts tell the tragic story:

CHARLES P. BURKES VAINLY GIVES LIFE FOR SWEETHEART

Mason, Tex. July 15. Responding to a call for help from his sweetheart, going into deep water to rescue her and reaching her side only to become helpless, too, Charles P. Burkes, former sergeant at arms of the Texas House of Representatives and since Deputy United States Marshal, with headquarters at Waco, was drowned with the young woman this morning in the Llano River, eight miles south of here.

Mr. Burkes' fiancée was Miss Effie Gamel, daughter of John Gamel, a prominent ranchman of this county, and she had been a Deputy County Clerk. The body of Miss Gamel was recovered within a few minutes. Burk's body had not been recovered late this afternoon.

The victims were members of a pleasure party composed of Mr. and Mrs. H. C. Burst (should be Durst) and Miss Jesse Gamel, besides themselves. All were in bathing when Miss Gamel got beyond her depth and gave alarm. Burkes did not hesitate in going to her assistance and both sank before the eyes of the other members of the party.

Six touring cars carrying a number of persons left here immediately on receipt of the news and many now are engaged in attempting to find the missing body.

Mr. Burkes was well known throughout the State and was a son of D. C. Burkes, Sheriff of Bell County for six years, and who made the race for State Comptroller four years ago. Charles Burkes was a member of the Ben Hur Temple of the Mystic Shrine. He resided in Belton, Texas until recently, when he moved to Waco. He was 30 years of age.

Mrs. Burkes Prostrated.

Belton, Tex., July 15 -- Belton and the entire community was shocked when the news of the drowning of Charles P. Burkes of Belton and Miss Effie Gamel of Mason, in the Llano River, near Mason, reached here. Mrs. D. C. Burkes, mother of Mr. Burkes, is in a serious condition and requires medical assistance. D. C. Burkes and Hosea Robinson left here in an auto for the scene of the accident. The body will be brought here for burial.

Austin, Texas. Messages broke the news here of the drowning of Charles P. Burkes and Miss Effie Gamel this morning in the Llano River near Mason. The double tragedy has cast a gloom over the Capitol, Mr. Burkes having many close friends among the heads and employees of the departments.

Burkes Was Away on Vacation.

Captain John H. Rogers, United States Marshal for the Western District of Texas, was notified early last night of the death of his deputy by The Express. He was deeply shocked by the news and could make no comment except to laud Mr. Burkes for his many excellent qualities as a man and an officer. When Captain Rogers was sworn in April 4 last Mr. Burkes also assumed office and was assigned to station in Waco.

Several days ago, he applied for leave of absence to be in effect from July 10 to 18. He said he wished a brief vacation and it was readily granted him. Captain Rogers will leave today to attend the funeral.

A TRIBUTE TO MISS EFFIE GAMEL

Belton News. Tis hard to give up our loved ones are they called away in youth or in old age, but when the summons comes just as they are entering upon the rich, full measure of manhood or womanhood the loss seems doubly great. Not only are we deprived of the companionship that has been comfort and pleasure to us, but it seems to us that the world has been robbed of so much that that life would have given.

Such is the feeling that links with the thought of the death of Miss Effie Gamel of Mason, who for several years made this city her home, and who during her residence here won the confidence and

Effie Mary Gamel, daughter of John W. and Alice Kettner Gamel

esteem of all with whom she was associated.

Capable, efficient, prompt in the discharge of every duty devolving upon her, her services were indeed valuable to those with whom she was associated in business life.

Quiet and unassuming in social life, she was yet a friend, faithful and true to those with whom she was brought in contact. Those who knew her best loved and trusted her most.

She stood quietly and firmly for the highest principles of life. Miss Effie was a young lady of attractive personality as well as of high culture. She held the love and esteem of those who knew her both by her fine intellect and gentle womanliness.

In her true love and regard for him who had chosen her to be his life companion was the sweetness and gentleness of her nature shown.

'T would seem that God loved truly these faithful lovers and called them to that home above that their love might be made perfect, free from earthly cares and sorrows.

Friends here sorrow over the loss of the companionship of Miss Gamel and Charley P. Burkes but we know that there is a reunion in the great hereafter in which there shall be no parting when all shall be reunited.

A Friend

BURKES' FUNERAL FRIDAY

Former Sergeant of Arms of Thirty-third Legislature Will Be Buried at Belton.

Belton, Tex., July 16. The body of Charles P. Burkes, drowned in the Llano River yesterday, will reach here tomorrow night. The funeral will take place Friday morning at 10 o'clock.

C. P. Burkes was born in Llano, January 1882, and lived in Bell County most of his life. He served the county in the capacity of Deputy Sheriff for a number of years, also as Justice of the Peace of Precinct No. 1.

He resigned the position of sergeant at arms of the lower house of the Legislature last March to accept a position as Deputy United States Marshall.

Burkes was to have been married to the young lady who drowned with him, in a few weeks. He was a Knight of Pythias, a Shriner, and an Elk.

THOUSANDS AT FUNERAL

Friends From All Over State Show Regard for Charles P. Burkes.
Special Telegram to The Express.

Belton, Tex., July 18. The funeral of Charles P. Burkes, who was drowned in the Llano, held here today, was attended by over 2,000 persons.

The services were conducted by Rev. M. Story and Rev. A. F. Cunningham, and Father P. A. Heckman also spoke briefly on the life and character of the deceased. A large number of prominent persons from different parts of the Sate attended.

The active pall bearers were John W. Hornsby of Houston, Dayton Moses of Burnet, Sam Sparks of Austin, John McKay of Temple, H. B. Savage of Belton, Bob Barker of San Antonio, Albert Mace of Lampasas, and J. L. Beringer of Belton.

Captain J. L. Rogers, United States marshal, tendered to D. C. Burkes the deputyship made vacant by the death of his son, Charles Burkes. Mr. Burkes declined to accept.

Mr. Burkes' body reached this city on the midnight Santa Fe train last night, accompanied by a number of his personal friends from Llano, Mason and Lampasas. The body was taken to the home of his parents, Mr. and Mrs. D. C. Burkes, on North Pearl Street, to await the funeral.

Long before the hour set for the service great crowds were thronging from every direction to the residence, and after the services were concluded one of the largest processions ever seen in this city followed the body to the North Belton Cemetery, where interment was made.

The floral offerings were numerous, and the grave was a complete mound of flowers. Some forty or fifty people from Killeen were present, also several from Mason, Llano, Lampasas, Austin, San Antonio, Temple, Waco, Houston and Dallas and other places.

Among those from a distance were, W. L. Escaville, Burnet; Captain J. L. Rogers, San Antonio; Dayton Moses, Burnet; Judge John Hornsby, Houston; Albert Mace, Lampasas; Sam Sparks, Austin; Otto Schmidt, Mason; Sheriff P. C. Baird, Mason; Bob Barker, San Antonio; Pat Dougherty, Anson, Elmer and Jack Smith, Llano.

Hon. Chester Terrell of San Antonio would have been present, but owing to a misunderstanding in the funeral arrangements, he was unable to get here in time

The Commissioners' and other courts of this city adjourned for the funeral.

CARD OF THANKS

To all those who shared our sorrow and contributed all that human kindness could suggest to help and comfort, we return most heartfelt thanks, and although such devoted friendship cannot remove the sad memories that linger around our vacant chair, it brings into view the brightest side of humanity and throws the pure light of an unselfish friendship into a darkened home.

May the time be far away when the friends who gathered will need similar attention, but should that time come, we pray that they may receive the same full measure of generous aid and tender sympathy they brought to us when our hearts were crushed with a weight of sorrow.

Mr. and Mrs. J. W. Gamel and Family

This poem was found in the Gamel family bible:

The time is drawing near
that I must faint and die.
My body to the dust return
and there in silence lie.

Through heat and cold
I have often went and wandered in despair
to call dear sinners to repentance
and seek their savior dear.

My little children near my heart
nature seems to bind,
how it greaves my soul to part

and leave you all behind.

Oh Lord a father to them all
and keep them from all harm,
Until they learn to worship thee
and dwell upon thy charm.

My loving wife my bosom friend
the object of my love.
The time that I have spent with you has been sweet
my dear and harmless dove.

Often times you looked for me,
and often you seen me come,
but now I must part from you
and never more return.

I can never come to you,
let this not greave your heart
for soon you will come to me
where we will never part.

"By Grandpa Gamel"

John William Gamel was 73 years old when he died March 21, 1917. John was a remarkable man. He was flamboyant. He worked hard and played hard, but he always played fair. He was well known and well respected both for his knowledge of cattle and for his dealing with all men.

He was not a man to be ignored nor forgotten. In 2021, more than a century after his death, his name is still known in Mason, Texas.

In his hometown, the home he built in 1869 still stands. Gamel Creek flows through town when it rains. The courthouse and the town square occupy land that John Gamel and Mr. Lockhart gave to the city. The water that fills the city swimming pool comes from the well that watered his garden. Some of his descendants, his grandson, Alva Clay Lindsay's family, still live in Mason.

OBITUARY

August 16, 1844 – March 23, 1917

MR. JOHN WILLIAM GAMEL IS DEAD

Mr. John W. Gamel, aged 72 years died on Wednesday morning of this week at his home in Mason. Mr. Gamel had a stroke of paralysis early Wednesday morning and at 9 o'clock he died.

Mr. Gamel was born in Georgia Aug. 16, 1844, and came to Texas with his parents at the age of ten years. When they first came to Texas, they located in Llano County, where they resided for several years and in the year 1860, they moved to Mason County.

He was married twice, his first wife being Miss Katherine Crosby. To this marriage there were born three children: Archie, Johnnie and Walter, the latter died while a baby and Johnnie, the eldest of these died a few years ago in Mexico. (John Crosby (Johnnie) was their second son.) Archie is still living and makes his home in Houston, Texas.

His first wife died in the latter part of the seventies (January 1, 1880) and in the year 1881 he was married to Miss Alice Kettner, who with 3 children survive him. To this marriage were born 4 children, the eldest, Miss Effie preceded him in death only a few years. The living children of this marriage are Mrs. W. C. Lauderdale, of Galveston, Mr. Herbert Gamel of Yates, and Mrs. John Lindsay of this place.

He is also survived by two sisters and two brothers: Mesdames Jim Milligan and M. F. Carter of Mason and Messrs.' Alf and Tom Gamel, of Streeter. The deceased had been a member of the Catholic Church from early childhood.

Mr. Gamel was very widely known having been one of the biggest cattlemen in Texas in his early days and it is said that he controlled great ranching interests throughout the two states of Texas and Oklahoma. He was known everywhere he went and especially is this true among the old settlers.

Had it not been for his generosity and liberal disposition he could have easily been one of the richest and most wealthy citizens of Texas. He often remarked that he had had lots of money in his time and while he spent a great deal, he had not failed to enjoy it and would never regret having spent it for it had not only made he and his family happy but in numerous instances it had made many poor hearts happy.

It can truthfully be said that a more liberal and generous man never lived than was John W. Gamel. The funeral services will be held at the family residence this afternoon at half past four o'clock and interment will be made in the Crosby cemetery.

John and Alice Kettner Gamel were married 36 years. After John's death Alice remained in their home. She died May 27, 1942, at the age of 79. John and Alice were both buried in Mason, Texas.

Matilda Ellen Milligan, Clay's great-grandmother

21
John Allen Lindsay & Matilda Ellen Milligan

The Lindsay Ranch in Mason, Texas, the current residence of Deloris Haley Lindsay, has been home to five generations of Lindsay's and their families.

- James Buchanan and his second wife Margaret Allen Coots Smith Lindsay
- John Allen and Matilda Ellen Milligan Lindsay
- Alva James (A. J.) and his second wife Alice Coalson Lindsay
- John Alva and Jesse Gamel Lindsay
- Jack Gamel and his second wife Doris Anderson Lindsay
- Alva Clay and Deloris Haley Lindsay

John Allen Lindsay was born July 22, 1836, in Jackson County, Alabama to James Buchanan and Martha Lindsay. Matilda Ellen Milligan was born Sept. 10, 1842, in Titus County Texas to Thomas Stanley Milligan and Mahala Maybelle Allen. John and Matilda Ellen married in Mason, Texas, in 1860.

During their marriage, they had 12 children, two sons, and ten daughters. One daughter, Eddie May, died when she was only 17 months old. Their other children lived to be adults, married, and had families of their own.

- Priscilla m. James Jackson (J. J.) Jones
- Alva James m. Mary Ellen Turner
- Louise Margaret m. Charles E. Turner
- Annie Wardlow m. John Thomas Jones
- Olathe Elizabeth m. Charles McDonald Coalson
- John Hamilton m. Alpha Eletha Edith Polk
- Martha Ellen m. William Frank Edmiston
- Eddie May d. June 23, 1877, at 17 months of age
- Cordelia (Della) m. Gratten Christie Crosby
- Emma m. Thomas Franklin Nix
- Ivy m. John Moody Smart
- Katherine (Kate) m. James T. Brown

John Allen died Oct. 1, 1891, at 55 years of age. He is buried in the family cemetery on the Lindsay Ranch. Matilda lived for 41 years after John Allen died.

When she was older, she traveled between her children's homes and stayed a few weeks at a time with each of them. Matilda came home to the Lindsay Ranch often. Clay was twelve years old when she died. He remembered her very well. There is a family photo of Matilda sitting in the ranch's back yard, hand-feeding her pet deer.

At the time of her death, Dec. 22, 1934, Matilda was 92 years old. At that time, she lived with her daughter and son-in-law, Cordelia (Della) and Gratten Christie Crosby, at their ranch in Schleicher County, between Ft. McKavett and Eldorado, Texas. She is buried in Mason.

Cordelia (Della) Lindsay Crosby's granddaughter, Lillian Kathleen Crosby St. Clair, inherited the ranch when her parents, John Christie, and Lillian May Hannie Crosby, died.

Kathleen operated the large cattle and sheep ranch until her death June 5, 2012. Kathleen's daughter, Christie St. Clair, is the owner of the Crosby Ranch in 2021.

The Crosby Ranch was a wonder-filled place. It holds fond memories for family and friends who were welcomed there.

Alva James (A. J. or Al) Lindsay, Clay's grandfather

22
Alva James Lindsay,
Mary Turner,
& Alice Coalson

Alva James Lindsay was born April 21, 1863, in Mason, Texas, to John Allen and Matilda Ellen Milligan Lindsay. On June 28, 1883, he married Mary Ellen Turner. A. J. was 20, and Mary was 17 years old.

This young couple lived in Mason for a year or two, then they left their family and friends and moved to Leakey, Texas. Moving is never easy and, in the mid-1880s it was even more difficult. Their journey of more than 100 miles required a lot of planning and preparation.

The Lindsay family was well established and successful in Mason. Why did this young man want to leave? Perhaps the fact that his family was well established and successful was the very reason that he had to go. Alva James knew about ranching and raising cattle, and he was young, ambitious, and confident. He knew that he could accomplish important things, and he was anxious to do it. He wanted to make his own way, and he saw no opportunity for him to make it big in Mason.

Cattlemen from all over the state came to Mason. Perhaps it was Captain Charles Schreiner or Mr. Alexander Auld who said, "You've never seen such pretty country as there is around Leakey. There is so much water and grass that you can see the cattle getting fatter overnight. All anyone needs to do is file on a piece of land and bring in a few head of cattle. In a few years, he could make a fortune."

Words like these would appeal to a young man ready to strike out on his own. It is more than likely that Alva James loaded his packhorse, saddled up, and rode south to check out what he had heard, to see if it was true. That part of the Hill Country was more rugged than it was back home, but there was water and grass, and he liked what he saw. He saw his future, and it was full of promise and endless possibilities.

The spark of an idea turned into a flame. Al was young and confident, and he knew where he wanted to go. In that new place, he could make a good living and a good life for his family. He was eager to make it happen. It was not hard to convince Mary that Leaky was the perfect place for them. A. J. must have had backing from his family because they needed many supplies and a wagon and horses. Making lists of things they needed and checking those things off the list as they were loaded was exciting. This move was going to happen!

They needed food for their journey. A. J.'s mother, Matilda, would have taken care of that. She probably prepared fried chicken, hard-boiled eggs, loaves of bread, a ham or two from the smokehouse, a sack of jerky, jars of peaches, preserves, and pickles from the cellar. Last of all, she would have added cookies, a fruit pie, or a cake.

There may have been a house waiting for them in Leakey but, they had to take all their clothing, bedding, and household supplies. When they finished loading the wagon, the young couple was ready to leave for their new home.

The departure would have filled Al's brothers and sisters with excitement. The little ones jumping up and down, the older ones smiling and waving, but there were probably a few tears also. Their big brother was leaving, and they did not know when they would see him again.

John and Matilda had mixed feelings as their oldest son, and his family drove out of sight. They were happy for Al and Mary and little Evva, but they also knew the possible hardships that awaited them. They traveled south through a rugged country filled with hills and valleys and rivers and were excited about what awaited them in their new home.

Leakey was close to the Frio River in the southeastern part of what would become Real County. John Leakey, for whom the town was later named, his wife Nancy, and five others settled near the site, at springs that were later known as Leakey Springs, in 1856.

Shingles and lumber were produced from the abundant cypress trees lining area streams. The lumber was processed at water-powered sawmills along the Frio. (Perhaps this is where builders acquired the cypress lumber used in constructing John William Gamel's house in Mason.) Lumbering, freighting, cotton, and corn were initially important to the local economy. These activities were eventually superseded by ranching and raising Angora goats.

It is not known when A. J. and Mary arrived in Leakey, nor where they lived. They may have purchased land, leased land, or filed on a homestead. Their daughter, Evva Marie, was born July 13, 1884. Her birthplace is listed as Mason, but this may be incorrect. Their son, John Alva Lindsay, Alva Clay Lindsay's father, was born March 13, 1887, in Leakey. Things went well for this young family until May 12, 1890, when the unthinkable happened. Mary Ellen Turner Lindsay died. She was only 24 years old.

No death certificate or paperwork of any kind has been found to indicate the cause of her death. Was she involved in a horrible accident? Did she die in childbirth? Did she die of a sudden illness? No one knows. A. J. buried his young wife in Leakey. Mary's grave, the oldest grave in the cemetery, is surrounded by a beautiful, old, wrought-iron fence.

Leakey, Texas was no longer a special place. Leaving his hopes and dreams and young wife behind, Alva James Lindsay loaded what he needed on a packhorse, saddled up, and returned to Mason with his young children, seven-year-old Evva Marie and four-year-old John Alva.

Mary Ellen Turner had always been a mystery. The family story was that her mother, John Alva's grandmother, was Mary Rainwater, a full-blood Cherokee from Arkansas, but there was no documentation or other information.

In 1925, John Alva was notified that he had inherited some land from his grandmother, Mary Ellen Rainwater. The land was part of the Cherokee Reservation in Arkansas. John traveled to Union, Arkansas, looked at the land, and reportedly said, "I don't want it. You can keep it."

A few years ago, I ordered a DNA kit for my husband, Alva Clay Lindsay. Everyone was anxious to see if there was any sign of "Indian blood," but it was not listed. However, the results did show a connection to two men named Rainwater. I dug a little deeper and found a common ancestor. John Sanford Rainwater is listed as Clay's 2nd-great-grandfather.

John Sanford Rainwater married Lucinda Shehan. Their daughter, Mary Ellen Rainwater, was born Aug. 22, 1847, in Cumberland, Russell County, Kentucky. Mary Ellen Rainwater married George Washington Turner May 20, 1861, in Webster, Missouri. Their first child, Mary Ellen Turner, was born Sept. 7, 1865, in Arkansas.

Mary Ellen Rainwater had three more children with George Washington Turner. She then married Joseph W. Mills, and they had one son. Mary Ellen died May 9, 1925, at the age of 77, in Crawford County, Arkansas. She was buried in Union Town, Arkansas, in the Macedonia Cemetery.

Finally, we have proof of the Rainwater connection. However, there are a few more questions that may never be answered. How did Mary Ellen Turner get to Texas? Did she have relatives here? Was her father, George Washington Turner, related to the William R. Turner family that lived in Camp San Saba, Texas? It seems likely that young Mary Ellen had relatives or friends in the Mason area, that she came to visit them, and while here, she met and fell in love with Alva James Lindsay, and as they say, the rest is history.

Alva James Lindsay and his two young children moved back to Mason, but the bad times were not over. A. J.'s father, John Allen Lindsay, died Oct. 1, 1891. He was only 55 years old. Now the responsibility of caring for his children, his mother, and his younger sisters was on Al's shoulders. His youngest sisters, Ivy and Kate, were close to his children in age.

ALVA JAMES LINDSAY- ALICE COALSON

In 1894, the 31-year-old widower married 22-year-old Alice L. Coalson. The Lindsay and Coalson families already had a connection as Alice's brother, Charles McDonald Coalson, was married to Al's sister, Olathe Elizabeth. Al and Alice had four children. They were living on the Lindsay Ranch in 1900.

- Ruby b. 1895 m. Ervin Ellebracht

- Hattie Bell b. 1898 d. 1899
- Walter William (Pete) b. 1900 m. Loma Katherine Turman
- Sadie M. b. 1900 m. Bert Raab Tucker

They were living on the Lindsay Ranch in 1900. When I was researching land deeds and documents needed to apply for the Texas Department of Agriculture Family Land Heritage Certificate, I found that Alva James Lindsay purchased nearly every parcel of land that came up for sale in Mason County.

At one time, most of the land between Mason and the Lindsay Ranch was owned by Lindsay's. As his sisters and children married, they were given land. 320 acres south of the Ranch were deeded to his older sister, Pricilla and her husband, James Jackson (J. J.) Jones. The land just north of our current location was given to Walter William (Pete) Lindsay. Ruby and Ervin Ellebracht were given land on the east side of the highway and on and on. It was interesting to see that there were times when the price A. J. paid in legal and processing fees exceeded the price of the land he purchased.

Over time, these family-owned pieces of land were sold to others. In the 1970s, Jack Gamel Lindsay sold 640 acres out of the middle of the current Ranch. Two portions, totaling approximately 1,000 acres, remain of all the land that A. J. and his ancestors purchased.

When his son, John Alva, married Jesse Gamel, A. J. moved closer to Mason to what would become known as the John O'Donnell place, so that John and Jesse could live on the Ranch. He was living there when he died of apoplexy and high blood pressure Nov. 2, 1926. He was 63 years old. He was buried in Mason, Texas. Four-year-old Alva Clay Lindsay remembered all the cars at the house when he and his family arrived for the funeral. He also remembered seeing his grandfather in his casket.

Alva James Lindsay left Mason to make his fortune when he was a young man. Sudden life-changing events brought him back to Mason after only a few years. He was where he needed to be when his father died.

Despite all that happened, or perhaps because of it, A. J. Lindsay made the most of every opportunity. He did what needed to be done, and he did it well.

23
John Alva & Jesse Gamel Lindsay

John Alva Lindsay, the son of Alva James (A. J. or Al) Lindsay and Mary Ellen Turner, was born March 13, 1887, in Leakey, Texas. John was four years old when his mother died May 12, 1890. 1891 was a tragic year for the Lindsay family. A. J.'s aunt, Elizabeth Lindsay Burns Adams, died Sept. 1, 1891, and his father, John Allen Lindsay, died Oct. 1, 1891. Elizabeth and her brother, John, were living in Mason, Texas.

At the time of their deaths, Mary was 24, Elizabeth was 56, and John Allen was 55. There was an outbreak of Asiatic flu in Europe in 1889-1891 that spread to America. Many people from all over the world traveled to Texas. Did this flu reach the Hill Country and cause these deaths? It is possible.

After Mary's death, Alva James left Leakey and took his two young children, Evva Marie and John Alva, back to Mason, Texas.

John Alva Lindsay was a "favored son" he wanted for nothing. He was given the best of everything. He owned the best horses, the best saddles, the best tack, and the first automobile in Mason County. In

Jesse Gamel Lindsay with son Jack Gamel Lindsay at Galveston, Texas.

addition to that, he was handsome and well-liked by the ladies.

Jesse Presnall Gamel, the youngest child of John William and Alice Kettner Gamel, was born Oct. 23, 1897. Jesse was a beautiful young lady. She was "daddy's little girl," and she was also used to having the best that money could buy.

They were both from large, well-to-do families. Jesse's father, John William Gamel, was well-known throughout Texas and beyond. The Lindsay family had lived in Mason since the town was founded. If there was ever a "royal couple" in Mason, it was Jesse Gamel and John Alva Lindsay.

Jesse Gamel Lindsay with children Jack Gamel and eEffie Mary Lindsay.

They married, in Mason, Sept. 12, 1914. Jesse was 17 and John was 27. Friends commented that John and Jesse Lindsay were the most handsome couple and the best dancers in Mason.

John and Jesse had five children in 10 years.

Jack Gamel Lindsay was born Jan. 13, 1916, in Mason. Jack married Jean Johnson Jan. 20, 1944, in Dodge City, Kansas. Jack and Jean were the parents of six children:

- Sherry Joy Lindsay b. Nov. 06, 1944.
- Carolyn Grace Lindsay b. Jan. 04, 1946.
- Alica Gamel Lindsay b. March 23, 1947.
- John Clay Lindsay, b. Aug. 27, 1950.
- Thomas William Lindsay b. Sept. 20, 1952.
- Jay Sam Lindsay b. Nov. 03, 1953.

Jack died June 19, 1989. He is buried in the Crosby Cemetery, Mason, Texas.

Effie Mary Lindsay was born Dec. 10, 1918, in Mason, TX. Effie and Clabe Scott Long married on Jan. 02, 1938, in Brownwood, Texas. They had three children:

- John Clabe Long b. Oct. 22, 1938.
- James Lindsay Long b. Aug. 25, 1940.
- Janet Lee (Dolly) Long b. April 16, 1953.

Effie was living in Mason when she died June 01, 1989.

Courthouse records indicate that a child was born to John and Jesse Lindsay in January 1921. No one in the family had any knowledge of this child. It is assumed that the child was stillborn.

Alva Clay Lindsay was born Aug. 15, 1922, in Mason, Texas. He married Myrtis Deloris Haley Smith Oct. 30, 1971, in Leakey, Texas. Alva Clay and Deloris Lindsay had two children:

- Alica Kay Lindsay b. Jan. 07, 1975.
- Clay Haley Lindsay b. Nov. 06, 1976.

Clay was where he wanted to be, on the Lindsay Ranch, a stone-throw from where he was born, when he died June 14, 2020.

Doris Dea Lindsay was born June 04, 1924, in Mason, Texas. Doris married Louie Raymond Dobbs Aug. 27, 1946. They adopted one daughter, Deborah Dea Dobbs b. Jan. 25, 1958.

Doris was living in Canyon, Texas, when she died Nov. 02, 2005.

Peggy June Lindsay was born May 31, 1926, in Mason, Texas. Peggy married Ernest Davis April 29, 1950. They were the parents of two children:

- Lindsay Davis b. March 29, 1951.
- Michael E. Davis b. Feb. 16, 1954.

Peggy was living on South Padre Island, Texas, when she died Dec. 02, 2002.

John Alva Lindsay was a rancher and an old-time cowboy. He could ride before he could walk, and he could rope anything. His grand-daughter, Sherry Lindsay, recalls John roping a goat and getting all four legs with one throw.

That was a great throw, or it might have been an accident. My friend, Milton Bailey, told me about one of his experiences. "I roped a horse once by catching his two front feet. The other guys said, "I didn't know you could do that!" I replied, "Well, I just wanted to show you boys how it was done." Then, he confessed, "I was aiming for his head."

The Lindsay's owned horses, cattle, sheep, goats, hogs, and chickens, and the animals had to be fed and watered and cared for daily. As John rode around the ranch, he checked the stock tanks (Texan for what Yankees call ponds).

He needed to make sure that there was water for the animals and also that nothing was mired down in the mud. He rode the fence line to make sure there were no broken wires, and that no deer or coyote was stuck in the fence.

John slaughtered the meat for the family, and the smokehouse was used to help preserve it. Jesse had a large garden and fruit trees. Ranch life was not an easy life, but John and Jesse provided for their family.

Of course, life was not all work. The family would go to Alice Gamel's house for dinner every Sunday. That was one of the highlights of Clay's week because, as he said many times, his grandmother, "Was the best woman in the world."

I do not know what car they had in the 1930s but, many times, the car would not start when they were ready to go to town. John Lindsay was a good horseman, he knew livestock, but he was not a mechanic.

John would try to start the car by "popping the clutch." He always parked on the hill by their house. He would start the car rolling down the hill and then abruptly release ('pop') the clutch. When it worked, the engine would turn over and start.

Often, it did not work the first time. John would walk up the hill, harness a team of horses, hook a chain to the bumper and pull the car back up the hill to try it again. After two or three tries, there was probably a lot of steam coming out of the car that was not coming from the radiator.

The family would go to Hightower's on Saturday night. There was music, a dance floor, a skating rink, and food. The kids would skate and play while the grownups danced. These were family outings, and everyone joined in. John and Jesse were said to be the best dancers in the county.

There was a dance club in Mason. Clay was 14 years old when he was dancing in the third-floor ballroom of Mason's Seaquist Mansion. He never forgot that he was supposed to ask ALL the ladies to dance.

The family occasionally drove to San Antonio to visit Jesse's sister, Nell Lauderdale. Clay said that even though his dad owned the first automobile in Mason County, "He never did learn to drive!" They always got lost and they would drive around San Antonio for half a day trying to find Aunt Nell's house.

The Lindsay family played games. They grew up playing dominos, Pitch, Bridge, and other card games. All the men still play Pitch at every family get-together. Sometimes the women join in to show them how the game should be played. As competitive as they were and are, I don't know how anyone survived.

Jesse enjoyed playing Bridge. A group of friends played every week. One lady who came each week was Pearl. Pearl was always there, and she always lost. Someone asked her, "Pearl, why do you keep playing when you always lose?" She replied," Where else can I go and have this much fun for $5.00?"

There were notices posted in the San Antonio News about Bridge parties at Jesse's mother's home in Mason. Effie Lindsay Long made her living playing, teaching, and authoring books about Bridge. She co-authored books with Charles Goren.

She traveled on Norwegian Cruise Lines and others as a Bridge Instructor. She said, "All the Lindsay's played cards, but I'm the only one who made a living doing it." The members of the local Bridge Club were delighted when Effie moved back to Mason.

The "Buzzin' Cousins" was the name given to the bi-monthly get-together of the Kettner relatives. Because there were so many young children, Peggy renamed it the "Buzzin' Cousins and the Crying Dozen."

The families took turns hosting the gathering. Everyone brought a covered dish for the noon meal. After lunch, the ladies visited, shared recipes, and caught up on the latest family news. The men spent the afternoon visiting, pitching washers or horseshoes, or playing cards and dominoes.

I first met Clay's extended family at one of these gatherings. We drove up to his mother's house the afternoon of Oct. 31, 1971, the day after we married. The party was in full swing. We were there about five minutes before Clay was playing dominoes, and he probably won.

At any family gathering, someone would say, "Let's make some fudge." That was Peggy's specialty. Jack's daughter, Caroline, said, "Lots of good fudge was made in the kitchen with Jesse, Peggy, Doris, Sherry, and me, taking turns stirring and waiting for that wonderful vanilla to hit the chocolate. My mouth is watering. I can close my eyes and bring it all back. Such a delicious memory of my summers at the Lindsay Ranch."

At Christmas time, they made Divinity and Pecan Pralines. When we went to the Creek's swimming hole or to the Llano River and the Bat Cave for the evening,

I made hamburgers, and Peggy would bring potato salad and chocolate cake. Oher favorites were Tacos and Tamale Pie. Good food, good times, good memories.

Peggy Lindsay Davis' Tamale Pie

1 pound ground round
1 large onion
1 large green pepper
3 teaspoons chili powder
2 teaspoons garlic salt
1 large can of tomatoes
1 medium can ripe olives, drained
Salt and pepper to taste

Brown onion and green pepper in a dab of shortening. Add meat and cook till done. Add seasonings, tomatoes, and olives. Set aside.

Now, boil two cups of salted water and add 1 cup cornmeal. Stir well, remove from heat.

Add 1 cup cornmeal (another) to 1 cup cold water and mix well. Add to the first cornmeal and mix again.

Add half of the combined cornmeal mixture to the meat and stuff.

Pour into a greased 13x9" pan. Spread the rest of the cornmeal on top. Bake 1 hour at 350 degrees. When ready to serve, sprinkle Parmesan Cheese on top.

The Lindsay men were handsome, and the women were beautiful. Peggy did some modeling in San Antonio. Best of all, their children and grandchildren were and are honest, hardworking, good people.

You now know a little about John and Jesse and their children, but there is more to their story. Daddy John and Nana Jesse, as their grandchildren called them, were complicated people. Want to know more? Read the next chapter.

Nana Jesse and Daddy John

24
Daddy John & Nana Jesse

John Alva Lindsay and Jesse Gamel Lindsay were married Sept. 12, 1914. Jesse was 17, John was 27.

John Clabe Long, a conversation with Jesse: "Grandmother, why did you marry Daddy John?" Answer: "He was the best-looking man in Mason County."

Their marriage ended in an acrimonious divorce in the early 1950s.

John Clabe Long, another conversation with Jesse: "Grandmother, why did you divorce him?" Answer: "He would have lost the rest of the ranch with his gambling and drinking if I had not saved my half by divorcing him."

When Clay married, everyone in his family was shocked. He was a 49-year-old bachelor, and, in their minds, his life was settled. Then a 35-year-old, blonde divorcee came along. Everyone was sure that he was being taken advantage of by a woman who was only interested in his money.

Clay and his partner, W. T. Scott, owned the White Top Package Store, located between Crosbyton and Post, Texas, 260 miles from Mason. Clay worked Wednesday through Tuesday, one week on and one week off.

Clay and his dad were very close. Until his health deteriorated, John lived with Clay and traveled with him each week. John was living in an assisted living facility in Mason when Clay and I married.

We would leave the store each Tuesday at midnight and drive to Mason. The first stop would be Anna Lee's, where John lived. John would say, "Where have you been? You haven't been here in a long time?" Clay would answer, "Dad, I just got here from the store; you are my first stop."

Usually, John wanted to go to "his" Ranch, even though he had not owned it in years. Clay would just smile. It didn't matter who the current owner was; to John, it was always "his" Ranch. Into the truck and out to the Ranch we would go.

Of course, I was the official gate opener; there were four and sometimes five gates. I can hear John saying, "Clay, this is the roughest road I've ever been on! Why don't you fix this road?"

After driving two- and one-half miles on that rough road, we would arrive at Clay's house on the Mason Mountain part of the Ranch. After a short visit, a glass of tea, some peanut butter and crackers, and sometimes a game of dominos, John was ready to go back to town.

We made the trip in reverse and got John settled into Anna Lee's. Clay bought his dad anything he needed, gave him money, and never complained about making the trips.

When Clay and I married, Jesse lived in the big house. The first time I saw it, I was very impressed with the white pillars and dormer windows. I thought, "It looks like Tara, the 'Gone with the Wind' house."

Jesse was an elegant lady. She would never go to town without make-up and without being dressed for the occasion. One shop owner said, "When Jesse Lindsay comes into the store, a little 'class' comes in with her."

Jesse and I were not enemies, but we were never friends. I didn't feel that I came up to her standards, whatever they were. When I asked Clay, "Why doesn't she like me? She doesn't even know me." He replied, "She doesn't like me; you're with me, so she doesn't like you either."

Clay and I decided that it didn't matter what his family, my family, or anyone else thought about us. If we were happy with each other, that was enough. And we were happy with each other for 49 years.

John and Jesse were complex people. There is a 38-year span between their grandchildren, John Clabe Long was born in 1938, and Clay Haley Lindsay was born in 1976.

People change as they get older. Some change for the better; others don't. Perhaps, when the sad/bad things happened, they did not feel well or had a difficult day. No one knows.

I asked John and Jesse's grandchildren to share their memories and experiences, and they did. Some experiences were positive, and some were negative but, that's life!

DADDY JOHN

James Lindsay Long wrote:

John Alva Lindsay (Daddy John) was a kind, generous, gentle man, but when he became old and senile, maybe not so kind and gentle.

He was known throughout Mason County for being a great horseman and cowboy. He was also very handsome and had the reputation of being quite a ladies' man.

He didn't marry until his late 20's and married Jesse Gamel, who was ten years younger than him. They had five children - Jack, Effie, Clay, Doris, and Peggy. They were all born and raised on the Lindsay Ranch and graduated from Mason high school.

When John Lindsay's father, Alva James Lindsay, died, John inherited the main Lindsay Ranch on Comanche Creek. The rest of the land went to John's half brothers and sisters from Alva's 2nd marriage.

John was a terrible businessman and even worse gambler. A bad combination for a successful life and family. John's gambling resulted in his losing his land and livestock. He died a poor man at Anna Lee's Nursing Home in Mason, Texas.

Despite his shortcomings, John had many good friends and was much loved by most of his family. His younger son, Clay, and oldest daughter,

Effie, were especially loving and kind to him. Clay bought out the last Lindsay acreage that John owned and took care of him in his last years.

Daddy John was an excellent butcher and cook. He could cut up cattle, sheep, goats, and wild game like a professional, and his culinary skills were remarkable. He worked at one time for Cooper's BBQ in Mason as a chef.

(When you eat at Cooper's BBQ, the sauce – dip they use is John Lindsay's recipe. Unless they made a big mistake and changed it.)

One of his specialties was a stew that he called "son-of-a-gun." It contained all matter of ingredients, including the brain. He made excellent biscuits and muffins and often carried the ingredients and frying pan in his saddlebags.

Johnny and Jimmy Long, Effie's sons, were especially fond of Daddy John and spent a lot of time with him during their youth. He bought them a horse, Tom-Thumb, and tried unsuccessfully to make cowboys out of them.

He also taught them how to play cards and dominos. Daddy John advised us at ages six and eight that we had learned all that we needed to know. We could count and add. We could read and play cards, so he told us to go out in the world and make the best of it.

After John and Jesse's divorce, John lived in a house in Katemcy, Texas. John's two sons, Jack, and Clay, also lived there at times.

(Clay's nieces and nephews called him Unk or Unkie.)

At Katemcy, Daddy John was the cook. He was by himself a lot because Unk and Jack were gone. The house burned because he left the gas stove on under a pot of beans and went to town.

Unk lost many valuable coins because he had them buried under the house, and they melted. Also, Daddy John sold the other Katemcy property without telling Unk.

Unk had put the ownership of the place in Daddy John's name so that he would not lose it in a lawsuit. Unk did not know that Daddy John had sold it until he went there to collect some tin roofing, and the new owner told him to get off his land.

Sherry Lindsay:

The reason they divorced may well be a mystery now that Unk is gone. I know it was quite acrimonious. Daddy John was not allowed back into the big house.

Daddy John was an exceptional roper besides a good rider. I remember seeing him rope all four legs of a wily goat at one throw of the lasso. He made perfect biscuits every morning in a black skillet and perfected fried chicken.

Before they divorced, I would have been around 9 or 10, I have a vivid memory of being next to him in the kitchen, and he handed his cold Pearl beer to me for a sip! Somewhere I heard Daddy John did some gambling. I don't believe that he was a heavy drinker.

Carolyn Grace Lindsay Schwartz:

He was ornery as hell and damn mean! He sure did not like kids or people in general. He made a good breakfast but stingy as hell. I guess at one time, he was a good man and not so mean!

As a young girl growing up and spending many summers at the Ranch, I was sad when I learned that Jesse threw him out, closed the door, and could care less if she ever laid eyes on him.

I figured that out quickly! I really hated when I had to visit and spend a night, it was scary as hell as he would threaten us kids with his rifle and shoot off a few shots. That is what I remember of Daddy John.

Janet Lee (Dolly) Long Hannon:

My memories of Daddy John are quite vague. About all I remember is watching him play cards.

My understanding is that Jesse divorced him (which was scandalous at that time) because he was a compulsive gambler and was going to gamble away the Ranch. I remember her talking about this several times.

I think he had already lost part of it and that Clay Lindsay had saved a large amount of it by buying it.

Deborah Dea (Debbie) Dobbs Green:

Some memories of Daddy John:
He looked all the part of a successful Texas rancher in his boots, jeans, and cowboy hat. He was handsome, like Unkie, with a little more age.

He had a twinkle in his eyes and a big smile. He was always kind to me and seemed glad to see me. He was soft-spoken and had a good sense of humor. He liked peanut butter too.

We went to see him and Unkie in the little house behind the store in Katemcy. (That was the second house.) The walls were decorated with colorful pages from color books the cousins and I had done for them. Most of them had our names and maybe a message on them.

I love that memory. How sweet those two men were to hang pictures made by all us kids on their house walls. They lived a simple life but seemed so content.

There was a party at the Ranch when Jesse lived there alone, and John was there, lots of people gathered. He was visiting with all the people in attendance, and everyone had a good time. He would tell stories and laughed a lot.

As he got even older, I remember him not shaving, having lots of stiff whiskers, and longer hair.

When he was in the assisted living center in Mason, we would visit him. He liked peanut butter, so I found a recipe and made "Peanut Butter Specials" (peanut butter, oats, vanilla, sugar, and milk rolled into balls) for him. He loved them, so I took them when we visited and even mailed him some.

Daddy John had a sister Ruby Lindsay Ellebracht. We would go north up the Brady highway in front of the Ranch and pull into a cute white house on the opposite side of the road, where she lived. She was very nice, and we all enjoyed visiting with her and her husband, Irvin.

I think Unkie and Daddy John were a lot alike. They had the same quiet but playful demeanor. Both had good personalities, got along well with just about everybody, valued hard work, and stood up for what they believed.

They resembled each other in looks; both were handsome and well dressed. They made a good team. The two of them accomplished a lot, and they enjoyed each other's company.

I think Daddy John played a significant role in making Unkie the man he became. I think Unkie's grandma, Alice Kettner Gamel, Nana's mom, also played a substantial role in Unkie's life. He loved that woman!

Alicia Lindsay Marshall:

I'm not sure of our ages, but I think it was around 1960 when I was 12.

Carolyn, John, and I were staying with Daddy John. Unkie would go out to Ranch and come back later in the day. There was this creek down from the cabin. We loved going down every day, playing, and building a dam to make it deeper!!

One afternoon, as we headed down the path to the creek, we saw a huge rattlesnake. He was lying across the path sunbathing! When he coiled and rattled, we ran back to the cabin and told Daddy John.

He grabbed a rifle, and before we knew what happened, he shot the snake! We were not allowed to go to the creek after that as Daddy John said the snake's mate would be looking for him. I will say Daddy John was extremely accurate with his rifle. He clearly wanted to protect his grandchildren.

Another story: Carolyn, John, and I were staying at Daddy John's cabin, I don't recall our ages, but Carolyn & I were 11 or 12, making John seven or eight.

The story goes like this. Every day, Daddy John would kill a chicken for dinner and cook black-eyed peas. John and I complained about the chicken.

Daddy John was livid. He got off his chair and threatened to kill John and me! We ran outside and climbed up a tree. We were thinking he was going to shoot us. He pointed his rifle at us. Unkie arrived later, and we had to tell him what happened.

I think Daddy John just tried to scare the crap out of us, and he succeeded!

The best part of the chicken story is that people just plain can't believe this actually happened when I tell this story. 😊

NANA JESSE

James Lindsay (Jim) Long:

Jesse was not one of my favorite people. I admired her for her hard work and tenacity, but she was just too selfish and intolerant for me. As Daddy John was cursing her out the back door, so was I.

She and Unk did not get along either. She was one of the few people about whom I ever heard Unk say bad words.

I think she really liked only two of her kids because they looked and acted more like the Gamel's. Jesse played bridge, but she was a terrible player.

Sherry Lindsay:

Nana kept every dress and hat over the years. The middle bedroom closets were piled high with hat boxes, and the cedar chest contained ballgowns. She kept all her nice shoes. She had shoes from the late '40s and 50s, including stilettos.

She loved to shop at Frost Brothers in San Antonio. She wore only one red lipstick by Germaine Monteil, and she used Dorothy Gray face lotions.

Jesse traveled by Greyhound bus to Connecticut to see Effie. Twice that I know of, they went on Mediterranean cruises where Effie was teaching bridge.

Nana and I went to a BBQ in Harper. There was a big crowd when we arrived, but she did not see anyone she knew. She said, "I feel like the strange dog on the farm!"

Carolyn Grace Lindsay Schwartz

I liked Jessie. She put up with me, for the most part. She had a wonderful smile and loved to share her many stories of travel.

I loved it when she would bring out all her hats and let me try them on. But she always said, "Now you be really careful, Carolyn, with my beautiful hats." I have always loved hats ever since.

Jesse always wore red lipstick, even at breakfast and when gardening! I loved her vanity. Jesse loved to garden YEP with red lips. Sherry could enter the garden sanctuary (not me), but I got to try her hats on, so I honestly didn't mind.

Oh wait, I think she let me pick a flower. It was a Peony and is my favorite to this day.

We made a lot of good fudge in the kitchen. Jessie, Peggy, Doris, Sherry, and I, took turns stirring and waiting for that wonderful vanilla to hit the chocolate; my mouth is watering. I can close my eyes and bring it all back, such a delicious memory of summers at the Lindsay Ranch.

Janet Lee (Dolly) Long Hannon:

My memories of Jesse are not very positive. We were not close, and she had definite favorites and pretty much ignored the rest of us. We could not call her grandmother, and she was never affectionate.

When I was very young, I would visit her, and she would ask me to pick out something to inherit when she passed. Whatever I pointed to, she would say, "no, no, not that, that is for...." I finally picked a very small print of a girl and a horse from her bathroom.

She was very surprised at my choice and was disdainful that I did not want anything of value.

I remember the fudge and the pecan pralines too. Yum!

I also remember riding the sway-backed horse that they had at the Ranch. "Jerry B" would come up to the pen for grain; let us ride him a couple of times around the pen bareback; then stop and refuse to move, so we would let him out and wait until he came in again. Then we would repeat the process.

I remember one meal that I had at Jesse's. It was black-eyed peas, and it had goat meat in it for flavor. Unfortunately, I cannot eat goat meat, so I was sick for a couple of days afterward.

Jesse seemed to prefer two of her children and their kids. She was not as fond of the others.

Deborah Dea (Debbie) Dobbs Green:

She was a beauty! Everything about Nana seemed in place and gorgeous. She seemed like royalty to me. She loved colorful clothes, scarves, and jewelry. Her hair was long, very long, and she sat in front of a beautiful dresser with a big mirror brushing her hair with an ornate brush. Then she would take her hair up and have the most beautiful bun I've ever seen, all perfectly in place.

She had a bed that was very high off the ground, with four tall bedposts. The bedding was beautiful. Across the room was a small antique black baby cradle that would move back and forth for rocking a baby. It had pretty bedding and a pillow. That was where Cindy Lou, her beloved little black dog slept, she would jump right up in that cradle.

Nana's house was full of antiques, old pictures, and unique items, including Chandelier lights, fireplaces upstairs and downstairs, bathtubs with claw feet, and fancy French doors.

The kitchen was adorable and had a cute breakfast nook. Jesse had an extensive collection of colorful Fiesta Ware dishes and cups. The table and benches, that Unkie now owns, were in the breakfast nook. If only that table could talk. That is where the family ate, played cards and other games, and read books, and it was also there that a lot of cussing and discussing happened.

(John had this table and the two benches made to fit that space. They were crafted in San Antonio. John wrote his name, Jesse's name, and all their children's names on the underside of the table.)

Jesse had a beautiful garden and grapevines. Her garden was huge and had many varieties of colorful flowers.

She had lots of cats and two special Siamese ones that got to come inside. One was named Ting a Ling. The "touch of grey one' was Puff. They wore bells on their collars. Nana loved those cats.

She would put sugar cubes in a sugar bowl with the lid on it, on a table, on the front porch, and raccoons would come at night, take the lid off, and eat the sugar. Scorpions would be on the bedroom ceilings in the summer.

Jesse was an entertainer, always hosting parties and attending events. She enjoyed playing bridge, getting together with friends, eating Mexican food,

Cooper's BBQ, chocolate cake, and traveling. Jesse went to New York and Connecticut to see Effie. She took many cruises; some were along the Mediterranean.

My grandmother was an interesting woman. She told me a lot of stories. Her middle name was "GO," she always wanted to do something or go somewhere. She drove to our house. When we visited the Ranch, we went to San Antonio and all the little towns around Mason to shop. We went to antique sales, and we ate out. She always had fun stuff planned for us to do.

She attended the little Presbyterian Church in Mason. We would go with her when we were there and eat at The Hilltop Cafe afterward with churchgoers and the preacher. She sold Beauty Counselor products to people and used them herself.

Nana belonged to several bridge clubs. Sometimes they would meet at a bank to play; other times, they met in members' homes. When we visited, my mom would join in, and of course, they took me.

I would play Barbies or color while the games went on. I enjoyed meeting all the ladies, seeing their homes and hearing their stories. They were all good friends and laughed a lot.

Adelia Belle "Dee" Carter White, the daughter of Julia Ann Gamel Carter, was Jesse's cousin. Everyone enjoyed going to Dee's house. Her place on the river was awesome.

My mom, Doris Dea Lindsay Dobbs, was named after this Dee. However, mom's name was spelled "Dea." I was given the same middle name, so we are all Dee's. My aunt Effie married Dee's son.

(After Effie returned to Mason, she married her high school sweetheart, Thomas Jefferson White, Jr. Nov. 15, 1978.)

Picnics were an important thing in the family back then, whether in Nana's yard, on the creek at the Ranch, or any creek or river in the area. Everyone seemed to love to picnic and to wade in the water. Sweet tea was always a necessity with the Lindsay's. If it wasn't in a pitcher or a huge plastic cup, somebody told somebody else to hurry up and get some more tea ready.

Nana and my mom could look at antiques, shop, and visit for hours. Sometimes Peggy and I would wait in the car. On one of our adventures to Wimberley, Peggy and I were tired of waiting, so Peggy hits the horn, long and loud, many times in a row.

That got my mom and Nana's attention, and they came to the car, telling us we shouldn't have been doing that. It was embarrassing. Well, Peggy told them she didn't do it, that it was me! I said no, it wasn't, it was her! We all just laughed and laughed! Peggy and I were together so much that she was like a sister or a best friend!

When Nana got older, she had her hair cut and wore a wig because she couldn't do it herself anymore.

Nana would write me letters and send birthday cards. She gave me a baton and would get little gifts for me on her trips. One gift was a small doll with blonde pigtails, white pants, and a matching blue sweater and cap.

Jesse had Stella Gipson Polk autograph her book, "Glory Girl," to me. Stella wrote, "To Debbie, I wrote this book for girls, just like you." I still have it and many other things from Nana.

I found her to be caring, kind, friendly, and outgoing. She was proud of her family history and her children and grandchildren. She enjoyed telling family stories and sharing events going on in everyone's lives. She always had family pictures out. She was especially proud of Jack and Unkie and their service to our country.

Thinking about her now, she must have been brave, strong-willed, and powerful in her own right to have lived alone as long as she did and had the life, she made for herself. Nana and Jane Dunn Sibley seemed a lot alike to me.

A person could think these two women were grandiose and over the top, but they were good-hearted women. They lived good, full lives, abundant with things and events that made them happy and allowed them to make others happy.

CONCLUSION

Thank you for sharing your memories. Like all of us, John and Jesse were flawed people, but if these two had not loved each other at one time, none of their children and grandchildren would have existed.

If we don't learn from the past, we're bound to repeat it. Be the best parent, grandparent, brother, sister, aunt, uncle, and friend that you can be. Someone is watching and learning from you.

25
Camp Verde – Camels in Texas and Beyond

In 1836 Maj. George H. Crosman urged the United States War Department to use camels in Indian campaigns in Florida because of the animals' ability to keep on the move with a minimum of food and water.

The matter came to Senator Jefferson Davis's attention, whom President Franklin Pierce later appointed secretary of war. Davis's first problem was coping with Indians and transportation in Texas, but the enormous expense of the Mexican Cession of 1848 had seriously depleted available army resources.

Davis firmly accepted the currently prevalent "Great American Desert" thesis, which held that much of the western United States was virtually uninhabitable. He urged Congress to appropriate money to test the value and efficiency of camels in the southwest as a partial solution to pressing needs.

At the insistence of the War Department, Congress passed, March 3, 1855, the Shield amendment to the appropriation bill, which made $30,000 available "under the direction of the War Department in the purchase of camels and the importation of dromedaries, to be employed for military purposes."

Davis believed that camels were critical to the country's expansion westward; a transcontinental railroad was still decades away from being built. He thought the animals could be well suited to haul supplies between remote military outposts.

On May 10, 1855, Maj. H. C. Wayne received the special presidential assignment. In command of Lt. D. D. Porter, the naval storeship SUPPLY was placed at Wayne's disposal. Wayne traveled ahead to study the continental use of camels. After trafficking down the North African coast and spending $12,000 for desirable beasts, he returned with thirty-three camels, three Arabs, and two Turks.

Thirty-two of the camels, plus one calf born at sea, arrived at Indianola, Texas, April 29, 1856, but because of severe weather and shallow water, they did not unload them until May 13. On June 4, Wayne started his caravan westward. They stopped near Victoria, where the animals were clipped, and Mrs. Mary A. Shirkey spun and knitted, the United States president, a pair of camel-pile socks.

Camp Verde is on the north bank of Verde Creek, six miles southwest of Center Point in southeastern Kerr County. It grew around the Williams community store, established adjacent to Camp Verde in 1857 to serve the soldier's needs. It is reported that the store's primary purpose was to provide liquor to the soldiers because regulations prohibited the sale of intoxicants within the camp.

When Williams's health failed in 1858, the store was acquired by Charles Schreiner, then a young rancher in the nearby Turtle Creek area, who had recently immigrated from Germany. Since the store was open only on army paydays, Schreiner, and his brother-in-law, Caspar Real, supplemented the business by contracting with the federal government to supply wood and beef to the military post.

A post office and store continued to provide irregular service to area inhabitants after the military camp was abandoned. Camp Verde's first post office was established in 1858, probably operated from Schreiner's store. It discontinued operation in 1866.

The animals were finally located at Camp Verde, where several successful experiments were made to test the camels' utility in the pursuit of Indians and the transportation of burdens. Wayne reported that camels rose and walked with as much as 600 pounds without difficulty, traveled miles without water, and ate almost any kind of plant. One camel trek was made to the unexplored Big Bend.

The first camel importation was followed by a second, consisting of 41 beasts, also quartered at Camp Verde. After a pair of successful trips to the Mediterranean and the Middle East, the U.S. Army had purchased and imported 75 camels. Within a decade, though, each one was sold at auction.

In central Texas, the camels were stationed in Camp Verde, where the Army used them as beasts of burden on short supply trips to San Antonio. In June 1857, under orders from James Buchanan's secretary of war, John B. Floyd in Washington, the herd was split.

Edward Fitzgerald Beale was directed to use 25 of the camels in his survey for a wagon road from Fort Defiance, New Mexico, across the thirty-fifth parallel to the Colorado River. Five months later, Beale's party arrived at Fort Tejon, an Army outpost a few miles north of Los Angeles.

The camels were used to transport supplies and dispatches across the desert for the Army. Some were turned loose, and some were used in salt pack trains. Others even saw Texas again after Bethel Coopwood, Confederate spy and Texas lawyer, captured fourteen from Union forces.

A California Historical Society Quarterly paper, written by A.A. Gray in 1930, noted the significance of that journey: "Beale had driven his camels more than

1,200 miles (about half the width of the United States), in the heat of the summer, through a barren country where feed and water were scarce, and over high mountains where roads had to be made in the most dangerous places. He had accomplished what most of his closest associates said could not be done."

Two private importations of camels followed the government experiment. On Oct. 16, 1858, Mrs. M. J. Watson reported to Galveston port authorities that her ship had 89 camels aboard and claimed that she wanted to test them for transport purposes. However, one port official felt that she was using the camels to mask the odor typically associated with a slave ship and refused her petition to unload the cargo.

After two months in port, Mrs. Watson sailed for the slave markets in Cuba after dumping the camels ashore in Galveston, where they wandered about the city and died from neglect and slaughter around the coastal sand dunes. A second civilian shipment of a dozen camels arrived at Port Lavaca in 1859. It met a similar fate.

The Army put the remaining herd to work at Camp Verde and several outposts in Texas. Small pack trains were deployed to El Paso and Fort Bowie, according to a 1929 account by W.S. Lewis.

In 1860, two expeditions were dispatched to search for undiscovered routes along the Mexican border. In Washington, the mule lobby did not want to see the importation of more camels, for obvious reasons.

If the mule lobby did not kill off the experiment, the Civil War did. After Texas seceded from the Union at the dawn of the war, Confederate forces seized Camp Verde and its camels. "They were turned loose to graze, and some wandered away," Popular Science reported in 1909.

"Three of them were caught in Arkansas by Union forces, and in 1863 they were sold in Iowa at auction. Others found their way into Mexico. The Confederate Post Office Department used a few." One camel was reportedly pushed off a cliff; another, nicknamed Old Douglas, became the 43rd Mississippi Infantry property. He was shot and killed during the siege of Vicksburg and buried nearby.

During the Civil War, eighty camels and two Egyptian drivers passed into Confederate hands. The camels soon were widely scattered; some were turned out on the open range near Camp Verde; some were used to pack cotton bales to

Brownsville; and one found its way to the infantry command of Capt. Sterling Price, who used it throughout the war to carry the whole company's baggage.

In 1866 the federal government sold the camels at auction; sixty-six of them went to Coopwood. Some of the California camels were sold at auction in 1863, and others escaped to roam the desert.

The camel's failure in the United States was not due to its capability; every test showed it to be a superior transport animal. Instead, the beasts' nature led to their demise; they smelled horrible, frightened horses and were detested by handlers accustomed to the more docile mules.

The Texas herd was auctioned off in 1866 to a lawyer named Ethel Coopwood. For three years, Coopwood used the camels to ship supplies between Laredo, Texas, and Mexico City, and that is when the trail starts to go cold.

Coopwood and McLaughlin sold off their herds in small bunches: to traveling zoos, to frontier businessmen, and on and on. Where did they go from there? According to Mr. Baum, a spokesperson from the Texas Camel Corps, the answers are not clear. When the Army brought its camels to Texas, private businesses imported hundreds more through Mobile, Galveston, and San Francisco, anticipating a robust market out West.

"Those commercially imported camels start to mix with the formerly Army camels in the 1870s," says Baum. The mixed herds made it increasingly difficult to track the offspring of the Army camels. "Unfortunately, it's really murky where they end up and what their ultimate dispositions were, because of those nebulous traveling menageries and circuses," he says.

That is not to say the fate of every Army camel was unknown. We know what happened to at least one: a white-haired camel named Said. He was Beale's prized riding camel during the expedition west, and at Fort Tejon, he was killed by a younger, larger camel in his herd.

A soldier, who also served as a veterinarian, arranged to ship Said's body across the country to Washington, where the Smithsonian Institution could preserve it. The bones of that camel are still in the collections of the National Museum of Natural History.

Many were used in Nevada mining towns, some were sold to butchers and meat markets, and some were driven to Arizona to aid with constructing a transcontinental railroad.

However, the railroad quickly sunk any remaining prospects for camel-based freight in the southwest. Owners who did not sell their herds to traveling entertainers or zoos reportedly turned them loose on the desert — which brings us to the story of the Red Ghost.

Feral camels did survive in the desert, although there were not enough to support a thriving population. Sightings, while uncommon, were reported throughout the region up until the early 20th century. "It was rare, but because it was rare, it was notable," Baum says. "It would make the news."

A young Douglas MacArthur, living in New Mexico in 1885, heard about a wild camel wandering near Fort Selden. A pair of camels were spotted south of the border in 1887. Baum estimates there were "six to ten" actual sightings in the postbellum period, up to 1890. A wild camel, possibly an Army camel that escaped from Camp Verde, was spotted in Arizona during the mid-1880s.

Excerpt from Arizoniana by Marshall Trimble, the state's official historian:

Most folks will tell you camels are not found in Arizona's high country. The truth is that those adaptable beasts can thrive in about any kind of terrain. The U.S. Army introduced camels to the southwest back in the 1850s, using them as beasts of burden while surveying a road across northern Arizona. But the Civil War interrupted the great camel experiment, and most of the homely critters were sold at auction. A few were turned loose to run wild—and therein lies the basis for the legend of Red Ghost.

The story begins back in 1883 at a lonely ranch near Eagle Creek in southeastern Arizona. The Apache wars were ending. However, a few renegade bands were on the prowl, keeping isolated ranches in a constant state of siege. Early one morning, two men rode out to check on the livestock, leaving their wives at the ranch with the children. About midmorning, one of the women went down to the spring to fetch a bucket of water while the other remained in the house with the children.

Suddenly one of the dogs began to bark ferociously. The woman inside the house heard a terrifying scream. Looking out the window, she saw a huge, reddish-hued beast run by with a devilish-looking creature strapped on its back.

The frightened woman barricaded herself in the house and waited anxiously for the men to return. That night they found the body of the other woman trampled to death. The next day tracks were found, cloven hoof prints much larger than those of a horse, along with long strands of reddish hair.

A few days later, a party of prospectors near Clifton were awakened by the sound of thundering hoofs and ear-piercing screams. Their tent collapsed, and the men clawed their way out of the tangle just in time to see a gigantic creature run off in the moonlight. The next day, they, too, found huge cloven hoof prints and long, red strands of hair clinging to the brush.

Naturally, these stories grew and were embellished by local raconteurs. One man claimed he saw the beast kill and eat a grizzly bear. Another insisted he had chased the Red Ghost, only to have it disappear before his eyes.

A few months after the incident with the miners, Cyrus Hamblin, a rancher on the Salt River, rode up on the animal while rounding up cows. Hamblin recognized the beast as a camel, with something tied to its back that resembled a man's skeleton. Although Hamblin had a reputation as an honest man and one not given to tall tales, many refused to believe his story.

Several weeks later, over on the Verde River, the camel was spotted again, this time by another group of prospectors. They, too, saw something attached to the animal's back. Grabbing their weapons, they fired at the camel but missed. The animal bolted and ran, causing a piece of the strange object to fall to the ground. What the miners saw made the hair bristle on their necks. On the ground lay a human skull with some parts of flesh and hair still attached.

A few days later, the Red Ghost struck again. This time the victims were teamsters camped beside a lonely road. They said they were awakened in the middle of the night by a loud scream. According to the terrified drivers, a creature at least 30-feet-tall knocked over two freight wagons and raised hell with the camp. The men ran for their lives and hid in the brush. Returning the next day, they found cloven-hoof prints and red strands of hair.

About a year later, a cowboy near Phoenix came upon the Red Ghost eating grass in a corral. Traditionally, cowboys have been unable to resist the temptation to rope anything that wears hair, and this fellow was no exception. He built a fast loop in his rope and tossed it over the camel's head. Suddenly the angry beast turned and charged. The cowboy's horse tried to dodge but to no avail. Horse and rider went down, and as the camel galloped off in a cloud of dust, the astonished cowboy recognized the skeletal remains of a man lashed to its back.

During the next few years, stories of the Red Ghost grew to legendary proportions. The creature made its last appear-ance nine years later in eastern Arizona. A rancher awoke one morning and saw the huge animal casually grazing in his garden. He drew a careful bead with his trusty Winchester and dropped the beast with one shot.

An examination of the corpse convinced all that this was indeed the fabled Red Ghost. The animal's back was heavily scarred from rawhide strips that had been used to tie down the body of a man. Some of the leather strands had cut into the camel's flesh. But how the human body came to be attached to the back of the camel remains a cruel mystery.

CAMP VERDE - a United States Army frontier post, was established July 8, 1855, on the northern bank of Verde Creek three miles outside of Bandera Pass in southern Kerr County.

In 1856 the camp was headquarters for forty camels sent by Secretary of War Jefferson Davis to be used in a system of overland communications. Albert Sidney Johnston started from Camp Verde in 1857 on his expedition against the Mormons in Utah.

The post was surrendered to the Confederate government in 1861, reoccupied by United States troops in 1865, and abandoned April 1, 1869. In 1949 a few ruins of the camel corrals and officers' quarters remained. The Texas Centennial Commission placed a marker at the site near Camp Verde, Texas, in 1936.

A second Camp Verde, two miles below old Camp Verde in Kerr County, was established March 31, 1862, by James N. Norris as a ranger station for the Frontier Regiment. It was manned by members of Charles S. DeMontel's company and served as a frontier outpost, probably until the consolidation of the regiment in March 1864.

Charles C. Kelley served as postmaster when the post office was reopened at a different location in 1887. In 1892, however, it too was closed. Walter S. Nowlin reestablished the store and post office in 1899. Both remained in operation in the mid-1980s.

26
Captain Charles Armand Schreiner

Alva James Lindsay (Clay Lindsay's grandfather) moved to Leakey, Texas, in the 1880s. After his WWII service, Alva Clay Lindsay lived in Mountain Home, Texas, for several years. Why did they go there? No one knows. The Lindsay's originally owned mostly cattle, but sheep and goats were added in the 1890s and 1900s.

The part of Texas that included Camp Verde, Leakey, Mountain Home, and Kerrville, the Edwards Plateau, was cattle country but it was exceptionally well suited for raising sheep and goats.

One of the early settlers was Captain Charles Armand Schreiner. Captain Schreiner was born Feb. 22, 1838, in Alsace-Lorraine. He arrived with his family by boat in Indianola, Texas, in 1852.

The family made their way by foot to San Antonio and north to Camp Verde, an Army outpost about 55 miles to the northwest. The land is rugged, divided between hills and valleys. (The story of Camp Verde and the camel experiment is told in another chapter).

Within four years, first, his father and then his mother would die. When he was 16, he joined the Texas Rangers and began scouting for Captain John Samson throughout the Texas Hill Country. (Charles Schreiner and Clay's great-grandfather, Franz (Francis) Kettner, served together in the Texas Rangers).

In 1857, he left the Rangers to join his brother-in-law, Caspar Real, in ranching on Turtle Creek. In 1861, he married Mary Magdalene Enderle. After the Civil War, Captain Schreiner returned to his ranch and raised sheep for the next four years.

On Dec. 24, 1869, Schreiner opened a one-room general store in Kerrville that would become Charles Schreiner General Merchandise. Captain Schreiner begin acquiring land around Kerrville and running Hereford and longhorn cattle. He brought Hereford cattle from Oklahoma to improve his longhorn herds.

In Mason, Texas, in 1880, the Captain bought a ranch and cattle from Mr. Taylor of Taylor and Clements with profits he made by driving more than 300,000 head of Texas longhorns "up the trail" to Dodge City.

The cattle he purchased were branded YO. This was the brand of Youngs Obadiah Coleman, from whom Taylor bought the cattle. Rather than rebrand the cattle, Captain Schreiner purchased the rights to the brand from Youngs Obediah Coleman and renamed his ranch the YO.

The YO (Y at the top of O) brand is currently owned through six generations of the Schreiner family of Kerrville, Texas. The YO brand now has multiple business applications, including the YO Steakhouse in western Dallas, Texas.

When Captain Schreiner divided his assets between his eight children, Walter Schreiner, the father of Charlie III, received the YO Ranch.

Who originated the famous YO brand? Youngs Obadiah Coleman was the son of Youngs Levi Coleman, who came to Texas from Tennessee. The "DeWitt Colonists of 1828 by Census" shows: Youngs Coleman: Single, 23, Male, Tennessee, 1 horse 2 cattle.

The Coleman family ranched in Gonzales and Jackson counties and moved to Goliad County in the early 1850s. The YO brand was first used on the Texas gulf coast by Youngs Obadiah Coleman of the Fulton Family Ranching Empire near Rockport.

The Laredo Weekly Times, July 27, 1919, published an article about Youngs Obediah Coleman's death by William A. Barr:

At 1:05 yesterday morning, July 20, MR Y. O. Coleman passed to his eternal reward. He was one of the last of the old-time Texas cattlemen. So far as the writer knows, there is not another of his day left.

He was born on a cattle ranch in Jackson County, March 18, 1841. He was married to Miss Herman Cox on January 1, 1868. To this union were born nine children, five sons, and four daughters.

Years ago, he told us of many of his cowboy experiences and the exciting days of long ago. Of recent years he was lived much in the thoughts of those days forever gone when the songs of the range rang out from the campfire or from where the fellows guarded the herd.

He has ridden at the front of many a stampeded herd of longhorns as they were being driven over the old trails. The men of his generation are gone. We are all better by having known and loved some of these great men."

Captain Charles Schreiner's story was published in J. Marvin Hunter's Frontier Times Magazine, November 1927:

"CAPTAIN CHARLES SCHREINER, who died at his home in Kerrville, Texas, February 9, 1927, was one of the outstanding frontier characters of the Southwest and contributed more than anyone man to the development of the region in which he lived for so many years.

Captain Schreiner was born in Alsace Lorraine, France, on February 22, 1838, and came to the San Antonio region in 1852. At that time, San Antonio was little more than a village. And the surrounding country was a wilderness infested with wild beasts and wild men.

Captain Schreiner, with keen vision, foresaw wonderful opportunities for the man with grit and determination. Although he was then but a lad in his teens, he started out with the determination to carve out a career for himself that would place him in the ranks of the state's prominent financiers and businessmen.

In 1859 he entered the stock business on Turtle Creek, Kerr County, in a small way, gradually building his herds, acquiring land holdings, and thus expanding his interests as the years passed by. Ten years later, in 1869, he engaged in the banking and general mercantile business at Kerrville, which business has continued to this good time.

In the establishment of a bank and store at Kerrville at that early date, Captain Schreiner placed himself in a position to assist the pioneers of that section and thus helped develop that favored region. He was heartily in accord with any project that was for the good of the community he had chosen for his field of operations. With the keenest of business ability, he permitted no opportunity to slip that would aid in its development.

The result was that over time, he became identified with several industrial projects, chiefly cattle and sheep raising. He was also engaged in the mercantile and banking business at Junction and Rocksprings. He also had connections with banking and mercantile concerns in San Antonio. He held stock in several railroad companies, gradually building a fortune that made him several times a millionaire.

Despite the burden of years, Captain Schreiner gave active attention to his banking, mercantile, and livestock interests until 1913, when he transferred the bulk of his property to his children.

At the age of sixteen, Captain Schreiner entered the Ranger service, serving in Captain Henry's, Captain Sansom's, and Captain McFadden's companies, from 1854 to 1859. When the Civil War came on, he enlisted in the Confederate Army and served for four years.

For many years he was in partnership with John F. Lytle in the cattle business, and the firm drove more than 150,000 cattle up the trail to northern markets. Today, Charles Schreiner's name is linked with the making of West Texas, for he was the moving, building spirit that made things possible for that region.

The town of Kerrville stands as a monument to his genius. and the substantial business and public buildings, schools, colleges, and lovely homes that thriving metropolis lend evidence to the fact that "he builded better than he knew."

For seventy-five years, he was a citizen of Texas. and when he passed away at the ripe age of eighty-nine years, he left thousands of friends throughout the state to mourn his departure."

Captain Charles Schreiner was an ordinary man who accomplished extraordinary things.

27
Alexander Kennedy Auld

Alexander Kennedy Auld was an early settler in the Kerr County, Leakey, Mountain Home area of Texas. "Alex" Auld was born Nov. 18, 1852, in Govan, Glasgow City, Scotland. His parents, Alexander and Jeane McVey Kennedy Auld, were married in Campsie, Stirlingshire, Scotland, Jan. 17, 1846.

Alex's parents were working-class small business owners in textiles; both were pattern designers for the Calico printing industry. The Auld family lived and worked just across the River Clyde from Glasgow in Govan, Scotland, a community with a long and ancient history of habitation and settlement.

Alec made his way to Scotland's eastern coast, where he was educated at the University of Edinburgh. He sailed America aboard the "Spain," arriving in New York City Aug. 26, 1878. From there, he took a steamship down to Galveston, TX.

Traveling inland from the Gulf of Mexico, he eventually settled in the Texas Hill Country. In an Oral History Interview with Joseph Marcus "J. M." Auld, Jr, Feb. 26, 2001, he answered questions about his grandfather.

"He did some surveys up here around Kerrville for a few years, or there were some surveys here that had his name on them. And they said he was educated in law, but he wasn't a lawyer. We never did find out just why he left Scotland.

My uncle Dan, who joked a lot, went over to Scotland, and spent some time looking around. He said the people told him; you had better quit asking; you might not like what you find out. You know, a lot of people either had to go to jail or leave. We supposed maybe that was my grandfather's situation, but we never did know exactly why."

Alex was 25 years old when he arrived in Texas. Two years later, according to the 1880 Census, he is boarding with the Cornelius G. Peterson family at Turtle Creek. He is listed as a farmer and as buying and running cattle. He also worked as an apprentice surveyor for Adolph Rosenthal, where he took his pay in land on the "Divide."

In 1880, Susanna Gibbens, or Susie as she was known, was a 23-year-old widow. She lived in Kerrville with her mother Leah Ann Thompson Lowrance, her daughter, Mary Ida "Dollie" Gibbens, and Susie's younger siblings.

Susie's son, James Alexander Gibbens, died March 18, 1877, when he was five days old. Her husband, William Alfred Gibbens, was only 23 years old when he died July 29, 1879, from an accident while grinding meal at a grist mill or drilling a water well.

William and his son James are both buried at the Starkey Cemetery in front of Walmart in Kerrville, Texas.

The way Alex Auld met and married his wife was not unusual in that day and time. J. M. said, "The story that I had heard was that he talked to Captain Charles Schreiner said, "I need a wife, do you know someone?" He said, "Yes, I do, by the way. I know this lady."

Captain Schreiner introduced Alex to Susanna Lowrance Gibbens. This beautiful young lady had been a widow for two years, and she had a three-year-old daughter. She was known as a reliable person who always paid on her land and didn't miss any payments.

"So, he went out, and they got acquainted." They married Sept. 14, 1881. Then they loaded up the wagon, tied the milk cow behind the wagon, and took off to the Divide because Alex had already bought land out there.

I'm not sure if they got married the day they met or the day after. He needed a wife, and she needed a husband. That's kind of the way they did it back then. They had to have married before they went off together; that would have been terrible; just not respectable, but it shows that those early people were brave and courageous."

Alex's granddaughter Mary Louise Auld Saunders Lehman told Irene Van Winkle with West Kerr Current, "Grandpa Auld came to Kerr County as a bachelor, looking for a widow and a ranch. He went out on a Thursday and came back the next Monday with a wife."

The newly married couple, and Susanna's daughter, Mary Ida (Dollie) Gibbens, moved to the Auld Ranch headquarters on the Divide, below a high bluff to the north and a flowing spring. They constructed their home of pinion pine logs cut from the ranch. It became one of the largest log homes in Texas.

They also built horse barns, a corn crib, and the Auld Ranch School. The only fences on the ranch were at the headquarters. The corrals were built of six-foot-high cedar posts, and a four-foot-high dry-stacked rock fence surrounded the cornfields, garden, and house.

In 1881, Alec Auld began to patent numerous tracts of land. He owned 3,000 plus acres by 1890. The Auld ranch was in Bandera County, about 12 miles above the town of Leakey, Texas. In 1913, the county became Real County.

On Aug. 25, 1883, 30-year-old Alexander Auld took an oath of citizenship at the Kerr County District Clerk, A. McFarland's office. The next month, Alex and his wife, Susanna, registered their brands in Bandera County for their livestock on their ranch on the Divide.

Seven children were born to Alex and Suzanna Auld:

- Maggie Mae Auld, b. June 21, 1882, was named for Alex's sister in Scotland.
- Annie Lee, b. June 10, 1885.
- John Shelby, b. May 23, 1888.
- William, b. June 5, 1891.
- Archie, b. June 20, 1894.
- Alexander Daniel, b. Aug. 2, 1896.
- Joseph Marcus, b. March 16, 1899.

J. M. Auld, Jr. said, "Alex worked and homesteaded two, or maybe three sections of the ranch sections that joined him that hadn't been taken up yet. And he had to have it in somebody's name, so he put it in the names of his daughters when they were born.

But somebody had to live on it so they'd build a little cabin and get a family or somebody who could help work, and they would live in that cabin on that section of land."

Each homesteader had to live on the land, build a home, make improvements, and farm for five years before being eligible to "prove up." A total filing fee of $18 was the only money required but sacrifice and hard work exacted a different price from the settlers.

The Auld Ranch was sprawled across parts of Bandera (Real) and Kerr counties on the Divide, which serves as the watershed for the Frio and Guadalupe rivers. The young couple raised their family there.

Alex was a hard-working, successful stockman and businessman, but nothing was easy. When you needed money, you had to sell something. To sell something, you needed a buyer of your product. So, you had to take your animals and your produce to market.

Some of the following information was taken from "Hog Drives of the Frio Canyon A Trilogy" by Linda Kirkpatrick. "This is part of a great trilogy about Alexander Kennedy Auld and his family and neighbors living and working in the Texas Hill Country in the late 1890s. It is well researched and written by Linda Kirkpatrick of Leakey, Texas, for Texas Escapes."

"The Frio Canyon suffered hard times in the late 1800s. Lipan Apache still made soirees through the area, money was scarce, and times were just plain tuff. The folks, who built up the early ranches in the area around Leakey, did what they could to get by."

They had one asset in abundance that would bring some much-needed money. They had hogs. Their problem was the same one the cattlemen had in the 1860s and 1870s. They had to round them up and drive them to market to sell them: the solution, a hog drive.

"Alexander Auld became the entrepreneur of these hog drives. He furnished the holding pens. The "pens" were large pastures, known as the East Pasture and the Maverick Camp. The oak trees supplied an abundance of acorns, which was the primary food source for the hogs.

The ranchers would bring their hogs until enough were gathered for the drive to the railhead in either Kerrville or Sabinal. The hog drives were much like cattle drives. Each rancher would bring his hogs to the holding pasture, and a tally was kept. When the hogs were sold, the ranchers were paid for the hogs he had put in the pasture.

When they had enough hogs, the drovers would drive them approximately sixty-five miles to the nearest railroad. A hog drive could contain several thousand hogs. Jake Haby, a descendant of one of the drovers, said, "As the story goes when they hit the trail with the pigs, you could see hogs from one horizon to the other."

Hogs are smart, and they can be dangerous, especially the boars with their long, sharp tusks. To round them up and get them to market, you needed good hog dogs as well as drovers. The drovers needed special leggings or chaps made from extra thick leather to protect themselves from the hog's sharp teeth and tusks.

Milton Bailey told me that his dad's "batwing" chaps were made of bull hide. The extra leather, the batwings, stuck out on the sides to better protect your legs, but they were really heavy. The few times he wore his dad's chaps, he was happy he was riding and not walking. Milton also said that his chaps were tied with a leather string in the front to break if a bucking horse caused the top of the leggings to hang up on the saddle horn.

Hog hunting continues today. Sport hunters do it for the thrill of the hunt; ranchers do it out of necessity; hogs can do considerable damage to fields, fences, and other livestock.

Alex Auld was 52 years, eight months, and nine days old when he died July 27, 1905. There are different versions of what caused his death.

1. He roped a steer and unfortunately hung up on his saddle by his chaps and was drug by the steer he had roped.
2. He was dragged by a horse when his foot got hung up in the stirrup.

The accident happened at the Grapevine Springs pens. Alex's skull was fractured. Mary Louise said. "They brought him back to the ranch, but the only way they could get him to a doctor in San Antonio was by wagon, and it would have taken them four days. He said 'No." He lingered at home for three days. "He died at his ranch in Real County," she said.

Alexander Kennedy Auld was buried in the Leakey Floral Cemetery in Leakey, Texas. His tombstone is engraved with this poem.

Another link is broken.
In our household band,
But a chain is forming.
In a better land.

Alva Clay Lindsay's grandmother, Mary E. Turner Lindsay, was also buried in the Leakey Floral Cemetery in 1890.

Susanna's oldest daughter, Mary Ida "Dollie" Gibbens, married Joseph Oliver McFanin Dec. 3, 1903, in Uvalde, Texas. She was living in Uvalde when Alex died. After Alex's death, Susanna Auld operated the ranch and raised her seven children, two daughters, and five sons. Her youngest child was five-year-old Joseph Marcus.

I had the pleasure of meeting Mr. and Mrs. Joseph Marcus Auld Sr. in 1972. Clay Lindsay of Mason, Texas, lived in Mountain Home, Texas, in the late 1940s and he knew the Auld family well. We talked about his mother raising seven children on her own. Mr. Auld said, "My mother didn't have any trouble raising us five boys. She worked us so long and so hard that we didn't have time or energy to get into trouble. When she couldn't think of anything else for us to do, she had us picking up rocks. We moved every rock on the place."

Susanna Lowrance Gibbens Auld died Dec. 25, 1925.

J. A. Auld, Jr. said, "The Auld Ranch is on the Divide south of Garvin's Store towards Leakey. My cousins still have the original home place. Uncle Dan Auld and his son, Jack, and two daughters still own the land of our original home place."

One of Alex's great-granddaughters said, "My family and I still own and ranch this wonderful land of my great-grandfather Alexander Kennedy Auld. We are blessed with his forethought and fortitude to be the first owner of this ranch. During his time, it was Bandera County. In 1913 it became Real County."

The Auld House is a featured attraction at the San Antonio Botanical Gardens.

"Located on the 11-acre Texas Native Trail, the Auld House was the 1880s family homestead of the Alexander Kennedy Auld Family. This Texas pioneer family built the piñon pine log cabin along "The Divide," the Edwards Plateau's highest point. Located near Leakey in Real County, the 14' x 47' structure is considered the largest piñon pine cabin in Texas. It was constructed of large-trunked logs from an archaic stand of piñon trees (dating from the Ice Age) on a ridge on the Auld Ranch.

Dan Auld, who bequeathed the cabin to the Botanical Garden, recalled the process of building the home, "My father and a group of young Scotchmen cut these piñon logs for this home up on top of one of the hills on the ranch. They carried them to the valley, put them on ox carts, and carried them to the present location." This Auld forebear was killed when he fell from his horse and was dragged to death.

His widow, Susanna Lowrance Gibbens Auld, stayed on the remote ranch and raised seven children by herself.

The house itself was ideally situated, located on the protected base of a 300-foot cliff where a natural spring and fern bank had formed. Mrs. Auld kept milk, butter, and eggs in a cool niche above the spring. Comanche Indians, who had long used the cliff site as a campground would still come to camp there. On horseback, they would peer down at the Auld Homestead but never bother the widow or her children.

In 1996, Dan Auld's daughter, Joan Auld Powell Hallmark, acted on her late father's bequest of the homestead to the Botanical Garden. Botanical Garden's board member, Cecil Jackson, whose avocation was log cabin restoration, proudly guided the cabin's reconstruction at the Botanical Garden. It was just the type of early Texas architecture that founders of the Botanical Garden had in mind when they planned to have structures representing Texas' geographic diversity in the 11-acre Texas Native Trail."

You can still do business with some of Alexander Kennedy Auld's descendants. If you need cedar, contact the Auld Cedar Yard LLC in Leakey, Texas. Since 1946 Auld Cedar Yard LLC has provided cedar posts for the fencing industry in and around Texas.

28
Clay Lindsay - A Good Man from Mason, Texas

The earlier chapters told the story of people who lived before Alva Clay Lindsay was born. The rest of the book will focus on the life of this extraordinary man.

Clay, the middle child of John Alva and Jesse Gamel Lindsay's five children, grew up on the Lindsay Ranch in Mason, Texas.

As an adult, he was 6' tall, slim, and athletic. His most prominent feature was his thick, bright red hair. He was a rancher and a cowboy. He dressed like most of the men at the auction barn or the feed store.

Clay was a caring, fun-loving, gentle, hard-working man with a mischievous nature and a quick wit. He loved playing games. He was an excellent winner and a terrible loser.

- Clay cared about his family and friends. His friendships lasted a lifetime.
- Clay loved life. When you choose to love life, anything feels possible.
- Clay always wanted the people around him to succeed.
- Clay didn't let failure define him. When a business venture didn't succeed, he went on to something else.
- Clay never doubted that he could do anything he decided to do. You'll never know what you can accomplish if you don't try. Just do it. His positive, can-do attitude was one of the things that I loved about him.
- Clay always had a purpose. Get up, go to work, and enjoy the life you have.
- Clay was honest, and he kept his word. He expected the same from others.

Alva Clay Lindsay lived 97 years and ten months. A total of 35,734 days. In the remaining chapters, I hope you enjoy the stories about this extraordinary man:

Clay Lindsay - A Good Man from Mason, Texas.

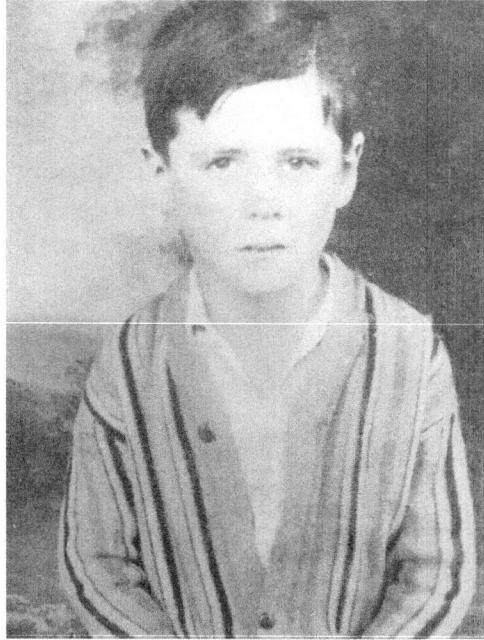

Alva Clay Lindsay

29
Clay -
Growing Up on the Lindsay Ranch

Alva Clay Lindsay was born Aug. 15, 1922, to John Alva and Jesse Gamel Lindsay. His brother, Jack, was six years old and his sister, Effie, was four years old when Clay was born. Doris and Peggy were two and four years younger than Clay.

Being too young to hang out with Jack and Effie and too old to want to be around Doris and Peggy all the time, Clay grew up a very independent person. He was comfortable in his skin, and he did his own thing.

As with most ranch children, Clay could ride a horse before he could walk. There were many animals and pets on the ranch, and his dog went everywhere with him. Clay played in Comanche Creek. He rode and worked with his dad and lived life mostly on his terms.

One of Clay's favorite people was his grandmother, Alice Kettner Gamel. From an early age, Clay looked for ways to make money. He gathered all the eggs he could find to sell to his grandmother. He could not take eggs from the chicken house, but the hens sometimes hid their nests in the barn or the pasture. Clay watched, gathered the eggs, and took them to his grandmother. She bought everyone, even though most of them were probably rotten. He saved his money.

When the Lindsay family went to Hightower's on Saturday night for skating, music, dancing, food, and fun, Clay always had the money for a hamburger, a Pepsi or an RC Cola, and candy for himself.

Doris and Peggy would beg, "Buy us one, buy us one." Clay never did. He told them, "I bought this with my money. You get your own."

Clay, Doris, and Peggy went to Behrens School. Behrens was a school community on State Highway 386, four miles northeast of Mason. It was named for Henry Julius Behrens, one of the first German settlers to move there from Fredericksburg. He arrived in January 1880, and he and his neighbors soon built a school on his land. Miss Ellen C. Hill was the first teacher.

This country school was approximately five miles from the ranch. Each school day,

Doris, Peggy & Clay Lindsay 1929

the three children either drove a horse and buggy or rode their horses to school. Clay rode his horse. Doris and Peggy rode double.

Of course, Clay did not want to hang around with his little sisters; he rode ahead. He said, "You could hear them crying for a mile." Melvin Leifeste said, "Clay would get to school, but then he would have to go back and get his sisters. One of them was always falling off."

Behrens was sometimes called the "Jackass School" because so many children rode donkeys to school. Clay, Doris, and Peggy always rode horses. One of Clay's teachers was Stella Gipson Polk.

Stella, the sister of Fred Gipson, the author of Old Yeller, also authored several books. Clay had several books which she autographed for him. When Clay introduced me to Mrs. Polk, he said, "This is my old teacher, Stella Polk." She didn't miss a beat; she quickly corrected him, "Former teacher, Clay, former."

I have an end-of-school photograph of the students and Mrs. Polk, sitting on their horses and donkeys. Clay is not in the picture, but he remembered and recognized his friends. The end of school parties included a picnic and a goat roping contest. Clay was an exceptionally good roper, and he usually won the competition.

What Texas ranchers want most, most of the time is rain. There are a few wet years, but there are many more dry years. The pastures are beautiful with green grass and colorful wildflowers when it rains. When no rain falls, it is necessary to provide feed for the cattle.

In Texas, cacti are used for food. The prickly pear tunas, or seed pods, are eaten by deer and sheep. With their thorns singed off, the pads make a substantial food for cattle. Burning pear is the ranching practice of burning the thorns off prickly pear cacti so that cattle can eat them safely. Clay and I burned pear several times. I usually did the burning. Clay would point out thorns that I missed and make sure that nothing else was set on fire.

Cattle love prickly pear, but burning pear, burning the thorns off, is not an easy task. A pear burner is essentially a flame thrower. You strap a propane tank, which can weigh as much as 50 pounds, around your waist or over your shoulder. The tank is connected to a small hose linked to a four-foot-long tube capped with a coil inside a metal bonnet.

You release the propane into the tube, drop a match, and the flame shoots out with a roar. Then you start burning pear. Waving the burner slowly back and forth, you go over the pads until the thorns curl up and turn to ash.

I usually made three passes. The first pass dried out the thorns and got rid of moisture; the second pass usually turned the thorns to ash. I would make one more pass to make sure that there were no unburned spines. It was hot, dangerous work, but it was also satisfying.

The hungry cattle run toward the noise. They know it means food. That is why two people should be there; one person to do the burning and the other to keep the cattle off you until you are ready to move to the next clump of cactus.

When Clay was 10 or 12 years old, there was a drought. His dad, John, drove his cattle several miles to a pasture with a lot of prickly pear cactus. John took a tent, camping gear, everything he needed for an extended stay. He burned pear.

The pear burner that John used was fueled by kerosene. Ranchers never get rid of anything because you never know what you might need. We still have John's kerosene pear burner. It is in the barn, somewhere.

Clay knew where his dad had gone, and he wanted to be with him. Without asking or telling anyone, Clay saddled his horse and rode the 10 or more miles to where John was camped. He stayed a week or two. I wonder what his mother thought.

After finishing classes at the Behrens country school, Clay went to school in Mason. Clay was 12 or 13 years old when he bought his first car. I never heard any stories about them riding a school bus. Did Clay drive them to school?

In 1936, when Clay was 14 years old, his class went to the Central Centennial Exposition in Dallas to celebrate the Texas Centennial, which marked 100 years of Texas independence. Clay bought a Centennial ring as a souvenir, and he kept it with his other treasure.

One of the things he liked most about going to school in Mason was going to his grandmother's every day for lunch. The school was just three blocks away, and she always had his favorite food waiting for him.

Clay played football until he broke his left wrist. He also played tennis. Mason is well known in Texas for its tennis program. Mason's tennis players have won 96 state UIL championships to date, all but one of them in the last fifty years. That is almost twice as many wins as Texas's second most successful school. Coaches Helen Tallent and Paul Smith have been inducted into the Texas Tennis Hall of Fame.

Clay said that if they had that type of program when he was playing, he would have been good. His grand-nephews, Ira and Clay Long, can attest to his prowess on the tennis court. We were visiting them in Colorado, and they decided to challenge the old man.

The two teenagers and their 57-year-old great-uncle, dressed in his regular attire, cowboy hat, boots, and jeans, headed to the local tennis courts. When they returned, about an hour later, Ira and Clay Long were incredulous. "Dad, they exclaimed, "He beat both of us, in his cowboy boots and hat." Clay Long recently added, "Yes, he beat us both, and he giggled the whole time. Quite an athlete."

Clay always kept his word, and he expected others to keep their word as well. His Aunt Nell asked Clay to drive her to Belton, Texas. He said he would if she would buy the gas. She agreed.

When they arrived in Belton, Clay drove to the gas station and filled it up, but Aunt Nell refused to pay. What did Clay do? He left her there. No one knows how she got back to Mason. Yes, with Clay, actions had consequences.

Either Clay failed a grade, or his sister, Doris, skipped a grade in school. They both graduated from Mason High School in 1940. That fall, Alva Clay Lindsay enrolled in the University of Texas in Austin.

30
Declaration of War

DECEMBER 7, 1941
A DATE WHICH WILL LIVE IN INFAMY!

The world changed for everyone on December 7, 1941. On that day, Japan bombed Pearl Harbor, and the United States officially entered World War II.

Over 16.5 million men and women served in the armed forces during World War II, of whom 291,557 died in battle, 113,842 died from other causes, and 670,846 were wounded.

Those who did not serve in the armed forces worked tirelessly to support the war effort. With their men at war, women worked at jobs they had never done before. Rosie the Riveter was the star of a campaign to recruit female workers for defense industries during World War II.

Based in part on a real-life munition worker, the strong, bandanna-clad Rosie became one of the most successful recruitment tools in American history and the most iconic image of working women in the World War II era.

The campaign brought thousands of women into the workforce. Women did things that they had never done before, and they did their jobs well. The lives of their husbands, brothers, boyfriends, and sons were in their hands. They supplied the troops with airplanes, ships, and munitions, without which, we would not have won the war.

WACs

In addition to factory work and other home front jobs, some 350,000 women joined the Armed Services, serving at home and abroad. At the urging of First Lady Eleanor Roosevelt and women's groups and impressed by the British use of women in service, General George C. Marshall supported the idea of introducing a women's service branch into the Army.

In May 1942, Congress instituted the Women's Auxiliary Army Corps, later upgraded to the Women's Army Corps, which had full military status. Its members, known as WACs, worked in more than 200 non-combatant jobs stateside and in every theater of the war. By 1945, there were more than 100,000 WACs and 6,000 female officers.

WAVES

In the Navy, members of Women Accepted for Volunteer Emergency Service (WAVES) held the same status as naval reservists and provided support stateside. The Coast Guard and Marine Corps soon followed suit, though in smaller numbers.

WASPs

One of the lesser-known roles women played in the war effort was provided by the Women's Airforce Service Pilots or WASPs. These women, each of whom had already obtained their pilot's license before service, became the first women to fly American military aircraft.

They ferried planes from factories to bases, transporting cargo and participating in simulation strafing and target missions, accumulating more than 60 million miles in flight distances and freeing thousands of male U.S. pilots for active duty in World War II.

More than 1,000 WASPs served, and 38 of them lost their lives during the war. Considered civil service employees and without official military status, these fallen WASPs were granted no military honors or benefits. It was not until 1977 that the WASPs received full military status.

DECLARATION OF WAR
WWII TIMELINE IN THE PACIFIC

Mr. Vice President, Mr. Speaker, Members of the Senate, and of the House of Representatives:

Yesterday, December 7th, 1941 -- a date which will live in infamy -- the United States of America was suddenly and deliberately attacked by naval and air forces of the Empire of Japan.

The United States was at peace with that nation and, at the solicitation of Japan, was still in conversation with its government and its emperor looking toward the maintenance of peace in the Pacific.

Indeed, one hour after Japanese air squadrons had commenced bombing in the American island of Oahu, the Japanese ambassador to the United States and his colleague delivered to our Secretary of State a formal reply to a recent American message. And while this reply stated that it seemed useless to continue the existing diplomatic negotiations, it contained no threat or hint of war or of armed attack.

It will be recorded that the distance of Hawaii from Japan makes it obvious that the attack was deliberately planned many days or even weeks ago. During the intervening time, the Japanese government has deliberately sought to deceive the United States by false statements and expressions of hope for continued peace.

The attack yesterday on the Hawaiian Islands has caused severe damage to American naval and military forces. I regret to tell you that very many American lives have been lost. In addition, American ships have been reported torpedoed on the high seas between San Francisco and Honolulu.

Yesterday, the Japanese government also launched an attack against Malaya.

Last night, Japanese forces attacked Hong Kong.

Last night, Japanese forces attacked Guam.

Last night, Japanese forces attacked the Philippine Islands.

Last night, the Japanese attacked Wake Island.

And this morning, the Japanese attacked Midway Island.

Japan has, therefore, undertaken a surprise offensive extending throughout the Pacific area. The facts of yesterday and today speak for themselves. The people of the United States have already formed their opinions and well understand the implications to the very life and safety of our nation.

As Commander in Chief of the Army and Navy, I have directed that all measures be taken for our defense. But always will our whole nation remember the character of the onslaught against us.

No matter how long it may take us to overcome this premeditated invasion, the American people in their righteous might will win through to absolute victory.

I believe that I interpret the will of the Congress and of the people when I assert that we will not only defend ourselves to the uttermost but will make it very certain that this form of treachery shall never again endanger us.

Hostilities exist. There is no blinking at the fact that our people, our territory, and our interests are in grave danger.

With confidence in our armed forces, with the unbounding determination of our people, we will gain the inevitable triumph -- so help us God.

I ask that the Congress declare that since the unprovoked and dastardly attack by Japan on Sunday, December 7th, 1941, a state of war has existed between the United States and the Japanese empire.

"Reflections on Pearl Harbor" by Admiral Chester Nimitz.

I found this story while researching WWII. Admiral Chester Nimitz from Fredericksburg, Texas, about 40 miles south of Mason, in the Texas Hill Country, was in the right place at the right time.

"Tour boats ferry people out to the USS Arizona Memorial in Hawaii every thirty minutes. We just missed a ferry and had to wait thirty minutes. I went into a small gift shop to kill time. I purchased a small book entitled "Reflections on Pearl Harbor" by Admiral Chester Nimitz."

Chester William Nimitz was born Feb. 24, 1885, near a quaint hotel in Fredericksburg, Texas, built by his grandfather, Charles Nimitz, a retired sea captain. Young Chester, however, had his sights set on an Army career.

While a student at Tivy High School, Kerrville, Texas, he tried for an appointment to West Point. When none was available, he took a competitive examination for Annapolis and was selected and appointed from the Twelfth Congressional District of Texas in 1901.

He left high school to enter the Naval Academy Class of 1905. Many years later, after becoming a Fleet Admiral, he was awarded his high school diploma. At the Academy, Nimitz was an excellent student, especially in mathematics, and graduated with distinction -- seventh in a class of 114.

He was an athlete and stroked the crew in his first-class year. The Naval Academy's yearbook, "Lucky Bag," described him as a man "of cheerful yesterdays and confident tomorrows.

Sunday, Dec. 7, 1941, Admiral Chester Nimitz was attending a concert in Washington, DC.

He was paged and told there was a phone call for him. When he answered the phone, it was President Franklin Delano Roosevelt on the phone. He told Admiral Nimitz that he (Nimitz) would now be the Commander of the Pacific Fleet. Admiral Nimitz flew to Hawaii to assume command of the Pacific Fleet. He landed at Pearl Harbor on Christmas Eve, 1941.

There was such a spirit of despair, dejection, and defeat; you would have thought the Japanese had already won the war. On Christmas Day, 1941, Adm. Nimitz was given a boat tour of the destruction wrought on Pearl Harbor by the Japanese.

Big sunken battleships and navy vessels cluttered the waters everywhere you looked. As the tour boat returned to dock, the young helmsman of the boat asked, "Well, Admiral, what do you think after seeing all this destruction?"

Admiral Nimitz's reply shocked everyone within the sound of his voice. Admiral Nimitz said, "The Japanese made three of the biggest mistakes an attack force could ever make, or God was taking care of America. Which do you think it was?"

Shocked and surprised, the young helmsman asked, "What do you mean by saying the Japanese made the three biggest mistakes an attack force ever made?"

Nimitz explained:

Mistake number one:

The Japanese attacked Sunday morning. Nine out of every ten crewmen of those ships were ashore on leave. If those same ships had been lured to sea and been sunk--we would have lost 38,000 men instead of 3,800.

Mistake number two:

When the Japanese saw all those battleships lined in a row, they got so carried away sinking those battleships, they never once bombed our dry docks opposite those ships. If they had destroyed our dry docks, we would have had to tow every one of those ships to America to be repaired.

As it is now, the ships are in shallow water and can be raised. One tug can pull them over to the dry docks, and we can have them repaired and at sea by the time we could have towed them to America. And I already have crews ashore anxious to man those ships.

Mistake number three:

Every drop of fuel in the Pacific theater of war is in top of the ground storage tanks five miles away over that hill. One attack plane could have strafed those tanks and destroyed our fuel supply. That's why I say the Japanese made three of the biggest mistakes an attack force could make, or God was taking care of America.

"I've never forgotten what I read in that little book. It is still an inspiration as I reflect upon it. In jest, I might suggest that because Admiral Nimitz was a Texan, born and raised in Fredericksburg, Texas, he was a born optimist. But any way you look at it, Admiral Nimitz was able to see a silver lining in a situation and circumstance where everyone else saw only despair and defeatism.

President Roosevelt had chosen the right man for the right job. We desperately needed a leader that could see silver linings in the midst of the clouds of dejection, despair, and defeat."

There is a reason that our national motto is, IN GOD WE TRUST.

Why have we forgotten?

PRAY FOR OUR COUNTRY!

In God We Trust!

This is the WWII timeline in the Pacific.
- Dec. 7, 1941: Japanese bomb Pearl Harbor, Hawaii.
- Dec. 8, 1941: Japanese bomb the Philippines, destroying many aircraft at Clark Field.
- Dec. 22, 1941: About 43,000 Japanese troops begin the main invasion of Luzon; American and Filipino troops begin to amass on Bataan.

- Dec. 24, 1941: Manila declared "open city."
- End of December 1941: Ground war in progress on Bataan.
- Feb. 8, 1942: Japan decides to regroup after its forces are repelled.
- March 1942: Having received reinforcements, Japanese strengthen attacks.
- March 12, 1942: Gen. Douglas MacArthur evacuated to Australia from Corregidor.
- April 9, 1942: Gen. Edward King surrenders Bataan; death march begins.
- March 1, 1942: Final Japanese assault on Corregidor begins.
- May 6, 1942: Gen. Jonathan Wainwright asks to surrender Corregidor.
- October 1944: MacArthur returns, coming ashore at Leyte in the southern Philippines.
- Feb. 3, 1945: Battle of Manila begins.
- March 4, 1945: Manila officially liberated, but the city is devastated by bombing and the Manila Massacre, in which about 100,000 people were killed.
- Aug. 6, 1945: U.S. drops atomic bomb on Hiroshima, Japan.
- Aug. 9, 1945: U.S. drops atomic bomb on Nagasaki, Japan.
- Aug. 15, 1945: Japanese Emperor Hirohito announces Japan's surrender.
- Sept. 2, 1945: Japan officially surrenders aboard the Missouri.
- December 1945: Japanese Gen. Tomoyuki Yamashita sentenced to death for the Manila Massacre and other war crimes.
- Feb. 23, 1946: Yamashita hanged in the Philippines.
- April 3, 1946: Japanese Gen. Masaharu Homma, who directed the battle for Bataan, is executed for his role in the death march and atrocities committed in prison camps. American and Filipino forces make up the firing squad.

Alva Clay Lindsay, Merchant Marine Corp. WWII

31
Clay's World War II Diary

Nov. 2, 1942 – June 12, 1946

"A Daily Reminder of IMPORTANT MATTERS,"
Cadet A. C. Lindsay.

In one way or another, World War II changed the lives of everyone at that time. 16.5 million young men and women served in the military. Over one million were killed or wounded. Their lives and the lives of all who knew and loved them were never to be the same.

These brave Americans went places, saw things, and did things, both good and bad that they would not have done if not for the War. Some things happened that they did not want to remember, many things happened that they could not forget.

If you know someone who lived during those years, talk to them, ask questions, and listen to their stories. You may not have another opportunity. When all of that "Greatest Generation" is gone, few will remember what they did.

A young man from the Hill Country of Texas joined the Merchant Marine. During his training and service, he traveled all over the U.S. and all over the world. Without these Mariners, America would have lost the War. "We Deliver the Goods" is a Merchant Marine motto, and they did.

Before World War II, there were about 55,000 civilian sailors employed in the U.S. Merchant Marine. This number increased. As many as 250,000 men were serving in the U.S. Merchant Marine by the end of the War.

Clay was one of those men, and he kept a diary. He was 95 years old when I transcribed it. His mind was still sharp, and he elaborated on many of the entries. I included some of the stories he told.

I hope you will feel that you are there and that you will experience where he was and what was happening. There were dull, boring days, scary days, sick days, and many rough sea days.

Clay graduated from Mason High School in 1940. He enrolled in the University of Texas in Austin that fall and was working toward a law degree. Clay was a "keeper." He kept his Algebra and English textbooks and a Geology notebook containing 91 written pages and six typed pages of notes.

Clay's cousins, Kathleen Crosby (St. Clair) and Jane Dunn (Sibley), were also enrolled at U. T. These three always enjoyed each other and remained lifelong friends. Clay wrote his address, 2315 Nueces St. Austin, Texas, and his phone number 3798, in his books.

Then came Pearl Harbor. During World War II, over 6,000,000 men enlisted, and 10,110,104 were drafted. Clay Lindsay, Melvin and Paul Leifeste, and several other young men from Mason, Texas, went to San Antonio to sign up. When they returned to Mason, Melvin and Paul were in the Army, and Alva Clay Lindsay was in the Merchant Marine.

Clay and his nephew, James Lindsay (Jim) Long, took a drive a few years ago and visited Melvin and Paul. The "old guys" were reminiscing about that day. They remembered going to San Antonio and being given some tests and things to fill out. Melvin said, "The next we knew, Paul and I were given a gun and told, 'You're in the Army now.'"

Why did Clay, a young rancher from the Texas Hill Country, join the Merchant Marine? Jim had a possible answer to that question. "Unkie was a smart man. I bet that when they tested him, they recognized that there was something special about him." Other young men from Mason served in every service branch, but Alva Clay Lindsay was the only Merchant Mariner.

U.S. Merchant Marine Cadet Corps was established in 1938. The Academy's permanent site in Kings Point, NY, was acquired in early 1942. Construction of the Academy began immediately, and 15 months later, the task was virtually completed.

The Academy was dedicated Sept. 30, 1943, by President Franklin D. Roosevelt, who noted that "the Academy serves the Merchant Marine as West Point serves the Army and Annapolis the Navy."

World War II required the Academy to devote all its resources toward meeting the emergency need for merchant marine officers. Enrollment rose to 2,700, and the course of instruction was reduced in length to 24 months.

Shipboard training continued to be an integral part of the Academy curriculum, and midshipmen served at sea in combat zones the world over.

Clay was one of the first to attend the Academy. He arrived Feb. 10, 1943, seven months before the official dedication.

Clay kept a daily journal in a little pocket-sized book. The first page is titled:

"A Daily Reminder of IMPORTANT MATTERS,"
Cadet A. C. Lindsay.

He enlisted "enrolled" at the E.O. (Enrollment Office) in San Antonio, TX, on Nov. 2, 1942. He went to New York in February 1943.

* * * * *

His diary begins in late 1942.

Went to Oklahoma (where his sister, Effie, lived)*, back to Texas to San Antonio to a dance.*

He went to two places in San Antonio to dance with the ladies; Our Lady of the Lake College, where Shirley Beth Grote Lyles attended, and the University of the Incarnate Word to visit Jackie Richardson.

Shirley Beth and Clay were friends all their lives. She said that the college required the girls to mail their friends engraved invitations to the dances. The men had to bring their invitation and show identification at the door to be admitted.

Signed up with MM (Merchant Marine). Went to New York with 16 other boys. Cold and cloudy.
February 10, 1943 - Identification issued by Captain of Port, New York to Alva C. Lindsay, Seaman, U.S.M.S. Training Station, Sheepshead Bay, New York, by Stanley Parker, Rear Admiral.

On Feb. 10, 1943. Cadet Alva C. Lindsay was age 20, height 5-11, weight 145, color eyes Green, Color hair, Red. (He never changed. He was the same size all his life.)
"The military was very strict about the age limits. Being drained by the battle in the North Atlantic against U-boats, the Merchant Marine was often less careful.
"Richard Stephens tells how in 1943 that he had just turned 17 and graduated from high school. He showed up at a Merchant Marine recruiting office with obviously doctored documents.
"The only problem was that he weighed 129 pounds, 1 pound below the 130-pound minimum weight. He was sent to the corner grocery to buy some bananas that he could eat to gain an extra pound."
These young Cadets enjoyed liberty and exploring the Big Apple. Clay tells two stories of their adventures with the subway. A group was going somewhere, and when a car stopped, one of the young men said, "That's it!" and jumped inside. It was the wrong car. He realized it as the door closed. Clay said the last they saw of him; he was trying to pry the door open. It took him two days to get back to base.
Another time, when they got off the subway, they were in the middle of Harlem. Those young white men in their white uniforms did stand out. He said they walked down the middle of the street and got out of there as fast as possible.
A Seaman Passport was issued to Clay Lindsay March 17, 1943. Cordell Hull, Secretary of State, sign it. He is rated as a Merchant Seaman. "This passport is not valid for travel in to or in any foreign state for the purpose of entering or serving in the armed forces of such a state.

This passport is valid only while the bearer thereof is following the vocation of Seaman or is proceeding to or from the vessel upon which he is or will be employed."

Finished (training). (Clay studied to be an engineer and was an oiler on some of the ships.)

CERTIFICATE OF SERVICE.

This certifies the Alva Clay Lindsay, having taken the oath required by law, is hereby qualified to serve aboard American vessels of 100 Tons gross and upward in the Steward Department in a rating of Messman F.H. Feb. 10, 1943, Port of New York,

Seaman Certificate New York Feb. 10, 1943, United States Maritime Service

Regular enrollment: This is to certify that Alva Clay Lindsay 4214-08965 has satisfactorily completed the course of training at the Maritime Service Training Station Sheepshead Bay, NY, and has been accepted for regular enrollment with the grade of Mess Attendant, second class.

Dated Feb. 14, 1943, at New York, NY. Original enrollment at San Antonio TX Nov. 20, 1942

WM Fitz Gerald Comdr U.S.N.R. Executive officer

Released from active duty at U.S.M.S. graduate station, N.Y. on Feb. 13, 1943.

February 13 Went aboard the S.S. Ohio. Very sick.

The S.S. Ohio was an oil tanker built for the Texas Oil Company (now Texaco). April 20, 1940, the ship was launched at the Sun Shipbuilding & Drydock Co. in Chester, Pennsylvania. The Allied forces requisitioned her to re-supply the island fortress of Malta during the Second World War.

The tanker played a fundamental role in Operation Pedestal, which was one of the fiercest and most heavily contested of the Malta convoys, in August 1942.

Epilogue: The last ship built for the Texaco fleet was Star Ohio, in honor of the famous Second World War tanker. Northern Marine Management operates her on behalf of Chevron.

The nameplate, ships wheel, ensign, and several other Ohio objects are preserved in Malta's National War Museum in Valletta.

April 9 -Port Houston, TX April 9, 1943, endorsed for Deck department and qualified to serve in the rating of ordinary Seaman.

Clay was a member of the Seafarers' International Union of North America Atlantic & Gulf District. Joined June 9, 1943, paid dues July 9, 1943, Nov. 17, 1943, and Dec. 10, 1943.

Alva C. Lindsay Linen Man 7/11/43 to 11/14/43 to and from New Orleans LA on the S.S. Wm. M. Evarts, The Wm M. Evarts was a steamship, nature of voyage Foreign, he was at sea for four months. The Wm M. Evarts was a troopship. Troopships used during World War II were operated by the Army Transportation Service, with "civilian" mariners, the U.S. Navy, and the War Shipping Administration.

July 11, 1943, to Nov. 14, 1943, onboard the U.S.A.T. Wm. M. Evarts.

William Maxwell Evarts (Feb. 6, 1818 – Feb. 28, 1901) served as U.S. Secretary of State, U.S. Attorney General. He was a U.S. Senator from New York. He was born in Boston, Massachusetts, the son of Jeremiah Evarts, an author, editor, and Indian removal opponent, and the grandson of Declaration of Independence signer Roger Sherman.

On March 6, 1943, construction began on a United States Maritime Service liberty ship in Evarts' name. The SS William M. Evarts (hull identification number MS 1038) was launched April 22, 1943, and served during World War II in the European theater. It transported troops and supplies from its homeport in Norfolk, Virginia, to various ports on the Atlantic and Mediterranean coasts. After World War II, the ship was decommissioned and finally scrapped in 1961.

Insert 1943 July – November

Went to Texas City, then to Portland, Maine. Took train home. Went to Houston on to N. Y. Sea going tug, went to Panama, then to Oakland by train to Brownwood, Texas Home.

Went to New Orleans, SS Russ Evosita (not sure of the name), to Cuba, British West Indies, to Recife Brazil, to San Lorenzo to Falkland to San Juan to Cuba to Panama to New Orleans.

Went home

The above entries cover his activities for five months. Clay always was a man of few words.

1944

Recalled for active duty at U.S.M.S.U.S. New Orleans Jan. 3, 1944

United States Department of commerce bureau of marine inspection and navigation

Release from Active Duty as Steward's Mate 2 class on Feb. 21, 1944, at U.S.M.S. Upgrade School, New Orleans. L.A.,

Port New Orleans Feb. 21, 1944, Endorsed for Steward Department and qualified to serve in the rating of 2nd Cook, Baker (F.H.)

Went to school New Orleans.

This was a Baker's school. It lasted several weeks. This is where he met Claude Harkins, also from Texas. He and Claude remained friends.

One thing that made a difference to these military men and women was the USO. Clay tells stories about the canteens in New Orleans and at the Palace Hotel in San Francisco. He and his friends went to the USO at every opportunity. They had a good time in New Orleans. They went to the USO dances, ate, drank, and visited with the pretty girls.

The girls were not supposed to go out with any of the Cadets, but sometimes things happened. One night, a couple of young ladies agreed to let Clay go with them after they finished at the Club.

They were to get their car and drive around to the door and pick him up. They left to get their car, and Clay went outside to watch for them. A car came around the corner. Clay ran to it and tried to open the door, but it would not open. It was the wrong car.

Of course, I asked, "Did the right car ever come around the corner?" A sly smile and a "yes" was his only answer.

After finishing school in New Orleans, Clay went home to Mason, Texas, on his way to report to the Merchant Marine base in San Mateo, CA.

In January 1942, the Maritime Commission purchased 10 acres on Coyote Point, San Francisco Bay, hastily built 11 buildings among the eucalyptus trees, and formally dedicated the facility on Aug. 29, 1942.

Coyote Point was home to a U.S. Merchant Marine cadet school, which eventually became the first campus of the College of San Mateo.

March 23, 1944 - 5 a.m. left Mason on bus to San Angelo, hitchhike on to Pecos, Bus to El Paso. Caught a ride to Stockton with a lady in a 41 Conv. Arrived in Frisco at 5 p.m. March 25.

Clay said that this was a very nice car. He does not remember where they slept. They probably just changed drivers and kept going. The lady told Clay that her husband told her not to pick up any hitchhikers. He was glad that she did. He made good time traveling from Mason to San Francisco.

Stayed at Palace Hotel.

The Palace Hotel is on Market Street in San Francisco. Originally established in 1875, the Palace was San Francisco's first premier luxury hotel. It was destroyed in the San Francisco earthquake and fire. It was rebuilt, and the current hotel opened Dec. 19, 1909. The "Garden Court" (also called the "Palm Court")— which occupies the same area that the Grand Court did in the earlier structure—

has been one of San Francisco's most prestigious hotel dining rooms since the day it opened. Clay was impressed. The room rate a few years ago was $500.00 per night.

Clay said that there was a USO dance at the Palace every Saturday night. He and his friends went there every weekend.

March 27 reported to 262 California St. Went to base at San Mateo. (This base was located on Coyote Point in San Mateo, California. You can read more about it in another part of this story.)

Notice of Classification. Clay Alva Lindsay has been classified in Class 1A May 23, 1944. (He had already been serving for more than a year.)

June 25 finished at San Mateo. Identification Card United States Naval Reserve. "This is to certify that Alva Clay Lindsay, Midshipman, MMR USNR is a member of the Naval Reserve of San Mateo, California 6/25/1944

July 6 - left base had party at San Francisco

San Francisco, Calif July 6, 1944, rating of cadet.

July 8 – Left by train to Seattle.

July 15 – Went to Vancouver

July 21-23 Went to Victoria

July 27 – 1:00 a.m. left Seattle, foggy and rain

July 28 – Foggy, rough sea. (You will see a lot of "rough sea" entries. These ships were cargo ships and were hauling a lot of cargo. Clay said that sometimes 4 – 5' waves would wash over the deck. He said that you really had to hang on.)

July 29 – Cloudy

July 30 – CLEAN & WARM

July 31 – Warm and rain.

August 1 – Warm

August 2 – Arrived in Port of Honolulu at 10 a.m. 8 p.m. Starting unloading. Went ashore.

August 3 – Unloading. Went ashore.

August 4 – Unloading

August 5 – Unloading

August 6 – Unloading went to Pearl.

August 7 – Unloading went to Waikiki Beach

August 8 – Still unloading.

August 9 – Still unloading.

August 10 – Still unloading

August 11 – Still unloading.

August 12 - Getting ready to leave 2:54.

August 13 – At sea.

August 14 – At sea.

August 15 – At sea. (Clay's birthday.)

August 16 – Arrived in Frisco Pier 44

August 17 – Move to Oakland

August 18-26 - Loading

August 19 - Cadet Harps to San Mateo to dance.

August 21 – San Mateo with Gypsy.

August 24 – Dinner at Arnold's. (This was George Arnold, one of Clay's best friends. His mother was Rose, and they lived in San Mateo. Clay said that Rose came to see him when he was in the hospital after his appendix ruptured.)

August 28 – Left Oakland (On the Beloit Victory. He sailed several times on this ship.)

August 29 – Rough. Coal. (Unreadable activity at 30-minute intervals.)

August 30 – Cabin

August 31 – Pretty calm, warm.

September 1 – Calm and hot.

September 2 – P.A....?

September 3 – Made my first (driving, diving, or dancing) *in S. F.*

September 4 – Army Transport Ship about 5 miles away. Chief Steward, ship going to put him aboard the A.T.S. Zigzag.

September 5 – Big rain.

September 6 – Sept. 6, 1944, on the Beloit Victory. Took Steward back aboard. Crossed the equator. Lost most of my hair. Lost a day Wednesday to Thursday. (There was a hazing ritual that happened to every young man who had never crossed the equator before. They were thrown overboard, hair cut etc. Clay has the certificate that he was given to the Domain of Neptunus Rex.)

September 8 – Friday. Back on course again. Thought we had found the (plane) but it was a red flag on back. 100% advanced a day off some island.

September 9 – Saturday. Received message from Frisco last night. Rain.

Sept. 10 – Seasick last night. Zigzagging.

September 11 – Still feel bad. Cool. 30 minutes (I do not know what these entries are referring to but there are a lot of notations of 30 minutes.)

September 12 – Cool, still feel bad. 30 minutes. Just passed a C-2 Zigzagging.

September 13 – Orders changed last night at 11:05. Not going to Brisbane, Australia. But to Moreton Bay only 125 miles from Brisbane. Zig Zagging. 9 p.m. Received message???

September 14 - Going on to New Guinea. Zig Zagging

The New Guinea campaign of the Pacific War lasted from January 1942 until the end of the War in August 1945. According to John Laffin, the campaign "...was arguably the most arduous fought by any Allied troops during World War II."

September 15 - 13:00 sighted land. 3. Going up through China Straights. Really a jungle. Few small huts. 5 p.m. Anchored out. 10 p.m. Just got orders to move. Dock number 21 at 6 a.m.

Sept. 16 - 8 o'clock waiting to go in. Rain. 9 a.m. going ashore, Raining.

September 17 – 7 a.m. Leaving Marianas going out the Guston Straight. 8 p.m. Anchored, have to wait morning to go on. Reefs bad.

September 18. 5 a.m. Getting underway 1 p.m. Pulling into New Guinea 4 p.m. anchored out Finekheaven.

New Guinea is a large island in Oceania. After Greenland, it is the world's second-largest island, covering a land area of 303,381 sq mi, and the largest wholly or partly within the Southern Hemisphere and Oceania.

Australian territories were invaded in 1942 by the Japanese. The Australian territories were put under military administration and were known simply as New Guinea. The highlands, northern and eastern parts of the island became key battlefields in the Southwest Pacific Theatre of World War II. Approximately 216,000 Japanese, Australian, and U.S. soldiers, sailors, and airmen died during the New Guinea Campaign.

September 19 Still anchored out. Hot

September 20 Rain and Warm

September 21 Rain Another ship hit us last night.

September 22 Rain and warm

September 23 Rain - 5 hours.

September 24 5 a.m. M. Ps came aboard to search ship. Went ashore. 7 p.m. moving into dock

September 25 Rain 10 a.m. moving back out into bay

September 26 Rain and Hot.

September 27 Hot Rain

September 28 Hot rain

September 29 Hot Rain

September 30 11:30 Received orders to get up steam. Orders canceled; New orders canceled.

October 1 7:15 Standby 9:00 In a dock unloading No. 3 hatch

October 2 8 a.m. out in bay again 3 p.m. back along dock.

October 3 Along dock

October 4 along dock

October 5 6 p.m. moving out into bay

October 6 Rain

October 7 Unloading

October 8 Unloading

October 9 Rain

October 10 Unloading

October 11 Unloading

October 12 Rain H.O.T.

October 13 Rain H.O.T.

October 14 Rain H.O.T.

October 15 Rain hot went to (navito don)?

October 16 loading and unloading

October 17 same

October 18 same

October 19 same

October 20 Same

October 21 Same

October 22 Leaks, 11 a.m. finished loading, Taking on water. 6 p.m. leaving Finnschafen about 300 troops

Finschhafen is a town 80 kilometers east of Lae on the Huon Peninsula in Morobe Province of Papua New Guinea. The town is commonly misspelled as Finschafen or Finschaven. During World War II, the town was also referred to as Fitch Haven in the logs of some U.S. Navy men.

Finschhafen was occupied by the Imperial Japanese Army March 10, 1942, during World War II. Australian forces recaptured the town during the Huon Peninsula campaign Oct. 2, 1943.

October 23 12 midnight docked at Milne Bay unloading troops.

October 24 unloading cargo

October 25 Unloading

26 unloading

27 unloading

28 finished unloading taking on mail

29 9 p.m. Ready to leave Milne Bay; 9:50 a.m. Leaving

30 Windy. Off Guadalcanal Rough

Guadalcanal is the principal island in Guadalcanal Province of the Solomon Islands nation, located in the south-western Pacific, northeast of Australia. The island is mainly covered in dense tropical rainforest and has a mountainous interior.

After six months of hard combat in and around Guadalcanal and after dealing with jungle diseases that took a heavy toll on troops on both sides, Allied forces managed to halt the Japanese advance. They finally drove the last of the Japanese troops into the sea Jan. 15, 1943. American authorities declared Guadalcanal secure on Feb. 9, 1943.

October 31 Very windy and rough

November 1 Windy

November 2 Rain windy

November 3 cross International Date Line

November 3 extra day, cross equator.

November 4 very rough (Clay says that when the seas were very rough, that meant that there would be 4- to 5-foot-high waves crashing over the deck of the ship. As a man of few words, he said, "You really had to hang on.")

November 5 had to cut down speed

November 6 still rough

November 7 still rough

November 8 still rough

November 9, 1,200 miles from Frisco cold

November 10 Cold, rain 766 off coast of California

November 11 cold rain

November 12 anchored in bay at Frisco.

November 13 going to Oakland.

November 14 same

November 15 Market Street

From 11/15/44 to 4/2/45, Clay sailed to and from San Francisco on the S.S. Beloit Victory - Foreign. Five months. He was a Cadet Midshipman, Engine.

November 17 arriving base

November 27 leaving army base, for sea

November 28 Very rough and rain

November 29 Very rough. Standing watch

November 30 Rough Sea

December 1 rough

December 2 calm rain

December 3 warm rain

December 4 warm rain

December 5 warm

December 6 cross equator

7 Buelin Torsible (?)

December 9 few miles off Ellice Island. Calm and Hot.

December 10 off Ellice Island

Tuvalu, formerly known as the Ellice Islands, is a Polynesian island nation located in the Central Pacific Ocean just below the equator and about 1,000 km north of Fiji. It is approximately 2,000 km east of the Solomon Islands. The Ellice Islands were part of the British Western Pacific Territories from 1892 to 1916.

Tuvalu is the world's fourth-smallest country; the archipelago of six coral atolls and three islands covers an area of just 26 km. The island nation has a population of about 11,000 people. The island of Funafuti serves as the capital.

Dec 11 Off Guadalcanal, (?) music.

December 12 Running on 1 B (battery)?

December 13 Arrival at French (Polynesia) France.

When the United States entered World War II on Dec. 8, 1941, it was determined that Australia, New Zealand, and the "Far East" had to be supplied with personnel and equipment.

One mistake that the Japanese made was their inability to grasp the Pacific Ocean's immense size, one-third of the planet or 64,186,300 square miles (about twice the area of the Atlantic Ocean), and Americans would not make that mistake. Another mistake the Japanese made was to believe that the Pacific's size made them immune to attacks from the United States of America.

Both mistakes proved to be flawed and fatal for the Japanese. It was difficult, if not impossible, for various Japanese forces in the Pacific and on the Asian mainland to lend mutual support to one another across large land and sea areas.

The initial successes of the Japanese required their supply lines to become that much longer. American military personnel were aware of the problems faced by the Japanese and planned accordingly.

United States planners realized that the Pacific Ocean's size could be a problem in transporting personnel and material. They looked at two routes from the United States into the Pacific: one route would be from the West Coast of the United States, via Hawaii, and one from the East Coast of the United States, via the Panama Canal.

By the end of December 1941, Operation Bobcat was created and put into action. It would be the first joint United States Navy-United States Army effort to send troops and supplies to the Pacific to build a military base. The plan called for constructing a refueling station for ships crossing the Pacific from the Panama Canal. It would be established in French Oceania on the Polynesia Island of Bora Bora.

The ships for Operation Bobcat departed the East Coast of the United States in two stages: some from New York harbor Jan. 20, 1942, and some from the Charleston, South Carolina, Navy Yard. The assembled convoy departed Charleston Jan. 27, 1942, and the five transports and accompanying escort vessels arrived in Bora Bora Feb. 17.

When they arrived, personnel began to unload the 20,000 tons of supplies necessary to establish the base. A major problem developed: the equipment, including heavy tractors, trucks, and bulldozers essential for unloading the ships, had been loaded first back in the United States and were at the back of the vessels when the convoy arrived in Bora Bora.

As a result of this error, it took 52 days to get everything unloaded. A lesson was learned about how to load cargo vessels, which explains that "logic" is an essential part of the term logistics.

The Japanese never attacked Bora Bora. The fuel facilities established there proved vital for the ships crossing the Pacific. Some of the eight coastal defense 155mm guns installed around the island are still visible and somewhat accessible to residents and visitors to Bora Bora.

Numerous events had to occur for World War II to end with the ceremonies formally and finally in Tokyo Bay Sept. 2, 1945. Operation Bobcat in French Polynesia contributed to the successes in the Pacific. The Pacific is vast. The War was brutal. Many aspects of the Pacific war are visible to this date and the effects on the cultures of the islanders.

December 14 rain

December 15 rain

December 16 rain anchored.

December 17, 4 a.m. leaving French (Polynesia) 10: a.m. only a few miles away from Japan. Met two big conveys. 13 transports, 7 troops (ships), 7 destroyers.

December 18 on way to beach, tin fish mess bar

There was a Merchant Marine Tin Fish Club. With an initial membership of 142, this exclusive Club was limited to Cadets who had been forced to abandon ship because of enemy action. "Tin Fish" was also another name for torpedoes.

December 19 arrived at beach, mail, rain

December 20 rain, Unloading main worked cargo all night no sleep

December 21 Hot worked cargo 5 hours had an alert last night, but nothing happened.

December 22 Hot worked, rain.

December 23 rain, alert

December 24 went ashore received some mail

December 25 (Christmas day) worked all day unloading cargo.

December 26 worked cargo

December 27 West Hinting

December 28 unloading

December 29 loading

December 30 unloading

December 31 loading

January 1… 1945 Unloading, rain

January 2 going into dock

January 3 Loading

January 4, I have done things these last two weeks I wouldn't want to do again. Munitions S.H. (Clay did not elaborate.)

January 5 Rain. Finished loading, taking on water

January 6 Move out into stream 11:15 on way again

January 7 7 a.m. arrived at Howland Island about 100 ships there and more arriving. 9 p.m. looks like big city tonight.

Howland Island is an uninhabited coral island located just north of the equator in the central Pacific Ocean, about 1,700 nautical miles (3,100 km) southwest of Honolulu. The island lies almost halfway between Hawaii and Australia and is an unincorporated, unorganized United States territory. Geographically, together with Baker Island, it forms part of the Phoenix Islands. For statistical purposes, Howland is grouped as one of the United States Minor Outlying Islands.

Howland was occupied by a battalion of the United States Marine Corps in September 1943 and known as Howland Naval Air Station until May 1944. All attempts at habitation were abandoned after 1944. No aircraft is known to have ever landed there, although anchorages nearby could be used by floatplanes and flying boats during World War II.

For example, July 10, 1944, a U.S. Navy Martin PBM-3-D Mariner flying boat (BuNo 48199), piloted by William Hines, had an engine fire, and made a forced landing in the ocean offshore of Howland.

Hines beached the aircraft, and although it burned, the crew escaped unharmed, was rescued by the USCGC Balsam (the same ship that later took Unit 92 to Gardner Island), transferred to a sub chaser, and taken to Canton Island.

January 8 convoy of about 30 left out - hot. 20 ship convoy, 3 L.S.T., 1 L.C., 14 transports, 2 helicopters, 9 knots, 2 freighter, 2 destroyers

January 9 at dock taking deck load, truck, and jeeps.

January 10 9 a.m. leaving Howland Island.

January 11 4 a.m. sub reported over starboard, dropped 3 depth charges, crossed equator.

January 12 hot going very slow

January 13 off Palau Islands picked up 2 more destroyers.

January 14 hot, rain

January 15 1 p.m. land sighted pursuit planes out. Anchored a few off Leyte

January 16 going to Leyte, anchored, around 300 ships.

January 17 hot, anchored. 10 p.m. 1st air raid, dropped bombs 5:30 a.m. Strafing. 6 a.m. Air raid

January 18 rain Plane just came in with wounded 10 aboard 6 time before landed

8 p.m. air raid, bomb, air raid

January 19 Okinawan boat along side

January 20 rain

Jan 21 3 a.m. Air raid slept all day 6:30 p.m. air raid.

January 22 1:30 a.m. air raid, a lot of firing

January 23 5 a.m. air raid 6:30 a.m. going into dock, 9 a.m. at dock

January 24 rain, hot 9 p.m. air raid a lot of firing.

January 25 3 a.m. air raid 7 p.m. Air raid 8 p.m. Alert, radio reception off air. The day was long, hot, just waiting.

January 26 2 a.m. dropped bombs

January 27 10:30 p.m. air raid, 2 zeros shot down

January 28 9 a.m. to 11:30 five air raids

January 29 10:30 air raid, 4 damaged ships in here

January 30 8 a.m. air raid, working cargo.

31 2 a.m. air raid 7 p.m. air raid

February 1, 1945, Unloading, mail run

February 2 11 p.m. air raid, big fire by airport.

February 3 Fire still burning

February 4 hot unloading mach (machines, machinery)

February 5 Americans entered Manila

February 6

Feb 7 War - arrived here Tacloban Samoa

Tacloban (pronunciation: [tɐkˈloban]), or simply referred to as Tacloban City is in the Philippines. The city is located 360 miles (580 km) southeast from Manila. Tacloban was briefly the capital of the Philippines, from Oct. 20, 1944, to Feb. 27, 1945.

On May 25, 1942, Japanese forces landed in Tacloban, signaling the beginning of Leyte's two-year occupation. They fortified the city and improved its airfield. Since San Pedro Bay was ideal for larger vessels, the Japanese Imperial Naval Forces made Tacloban a port of call and entry.

This time was considered the darkest in Tacloban's history and the country due to the incidences of torture among civilians, including the elderly. In response, guerrilla groups operated in Leyte.

Leyte was the first to be liberated by the combined Filipino and American troops. General Douglas MacArthur's assault troops landed in the Tacloban and Palo beaches (White Beach and Red Beach, respectively) and the neighboring town of Dulag (Blue Beach) Oct. 20, 1944. (Clay Lindsay went to Red Beach Feb. 19.1945)

These landings signaled the eventual victory of the Filipino and American forces and the fulfillment of MacArthur's famous promise: "I Shall Return."

February 8 Air raid 10 p.m. air raid 2 a.m.

February 9 getting water

February 10 hot

February 11 going into dock

February 12 unloading

February 13 unloading

February 14 Unloading

February 15 unloading

February 16 unloading

February 17 went to Dahlay

February 18 unloading, air raid

February 19 Moving to Red Beach. (See above.)

February 20 Unloading anchored by docks, sick.

February 21 sick and hot

February 22 sick and hot

February 23 sick and hot

February 24 going to Tacloban City

February 25 loading fuel oil air raid 10 p.m.

February 26 8 a.m. leaving Tacloban waiting convoy

February 27 waiting convoy

February 28 waiting convoy no cook stove, out of eggs etc. 9 p.m. air raid.

March 1, 1945, air raid dropped several bombs

March 2 11 p.m. air raid

March 3 3 a.m. air raid

March 4 rain - still waiting convoy. 8 p.m. air raid

March 5 Rain, orders to go into Tacloban

March 6 7 a.m. going to Tacloban taking water. 4 p.m. run aground, 10 p.m. still trying to get off. Tugboat here now.

March 7 3 a.m. off aground. 12 p.m. received orders to leave the 8th at 12 noon. 6 p.m. changed orders to leave 10 a.m. the 9th.

March 8 1 a.m. air raid, a lot shooting.

March 9 10 a.m. Leaving Tacloban canceled. Greenville Victory, 4 destroyers. 6 p.m. very seasick

(The Greenville Victory was laid down under U.S. Maritime Commission contract by California Shipbuilding Corporation, Los Angeles, California; March 21, 1944; launched May 28, 1944; sponsored by Miss Mary J. Vukov; and delivered to the War Shipping Administration (W.S.A.) July 8, 1944.

During the remainder of World War II, S.S. Greenville Victory served as a merchant ship under charter to Sea Shipping Company of New York City. She served in the Pacific War, participating in the Battle of Okinawa. In Okinawa, from May 27, 1945, to June 19, 1945, she supplied goods as a cargo ship and used her deck guns to defend herself and other ships from attacks.

Following World War II, she transported cargo in the Atlantic Ocean and the Pacific Ocean as the U.S.A.T. Greenville Victory. She was transferred to the Army Transportation Service in the spring of 1948. Acquired by the Navy March 1, 1950, she was assigned to MSTS as a (T-AK-237).

March 10 Seasick. Slow down as something is wrong with G.V. 6 p.m. picked up S.O.S. from lifeboat. About first cargo ship to go this way. Lots of mines through here.

March 11

March 12 7 a.m. Arrival at W. (Litehouse)? Saipan broadcast? About one day run from here. Lots of ships here. 11 a.m. AT Anchor 3 battle ships, C.N.C., Iowa 7th 16 (companies)? 6 p.m. leaving.

March 13 Some faster ships, so rough last night that I couldn't sleep. Have a sty on eye. 2 escorts

March 14 still rough windy don't feel very good

March 15 still rough

March 16 3 a.m. at Antuch ? breaking convoy 9 a.m. Greenville Victory ahead.

March 17 still rough 2 p.m. even with Greenville 3 p.m. just passed a flat top.

March 18 no ship in sight

March 19 Sub warning. So far, we keep track … 35560

March 19 Extra day, cross date line standing 12-4 watch.

March 20 running on one battery?

March 21 going to Honolulu

March 22 arrival at Honolulu 4 p.m. 4:30 going into Pearl Harbor. 6 p.m. docked at Pearl Harbor

March 23 docked right back of where Arizona was sunk

March 24 took on D (diesel) oil. Finished working on fueling. Also took on enough food to get to Frisco.

Dinner best meal we have had in a long time. Tomatoes, lettuce, steak, tough, potatoes, green beans cake and ice cream. Orders to leave 8 a.m.

March 25 8 a.m. leaving Pearl Harbor 2 p.m. seasick, rough

March 26 rough feel a little better

March 27 rough very sick

March 28 rough very sick

March 29 sick

March 30 sick 6 p.m. arrived at hospital.

Clay was on the Beloit Victory. The reason Clay was so sick was that he had a bad appendix. His appendix ruptured while he was on the ship. So, what to do? When they reached San Francisco, they lowered him over the ship's side in a canvas sling and put him in a speedboat. The speedboat took him into the harbor. Finally, he got to the hospital.

March 31 very sick.

April 1 to 16, 1945 in hospital.

As Clay wrote, he was "very sick." He said, "I had tubes sticking out from me in all directions."

While he was in the hospital, Clay had some visitors. George Arnold's mother, Rose visited him. One of the ship officers and his wife came and brought all his things from the ship. He was in the hospital in San Francisco for over two weeks.

April 17 on my way home.

Clay traveled by train from San Francisco, Calif. to Brownwood, Texas. He was on the train for most of four days.

April 20 Effie met me Brownwood. at home. (He was in Mason for about three weeks.)

April 21 - May 13 at home in Mason.

May 14 Left for Galveston to be operated on (He was in Galveston two weeks.)

May 28 arrived home from Galveston.

May 29 – June 16 at home in Mason. (He was in Mason a little over two weeks.)

June 17 left for New York

Clay went to Kings Point, New York.
There were two loose pages where Clay kept notes. The year is 1945, after his operations and before he was discharged from the Merchant Marine.

Monday - Sept 12 or 13 left Kings Point, Raining.

Tuesday – Left for Baltimore, MD.

Wed. went down to coast guard office to see about Jr. Ensign.

Thurs took exam AND PASSED (Alva Clay Lindsay, just an enlisted man, become an officer, which, according to his nephew James (Jim) Lindsay Long, was very unusual.)

Friday – 1 p.m. Left for Leonardtown.

Saturday - At Bill Brubaucker's home.

Sunday morning left for Baltimore.

Tues - Bill took exam for Jr. Ensign

Wed. - went down to S A

Thursday - Reported aboard J. C. Donnell

Fri J. C. Donnell

Sat. J. C. Donnell

(Clay Served on the J. C. Donnell /from 9/27/45 to 10/13 45 to and from Baltimore, Md. 2 weeks, as an oiler. Coastwise.)

Thursday Reported aboard J. C. Donnell

Fri J. C. Donnell

Sat. J. C. Donnell

U.S.S. Pasig (AO-89) was a fleet replenishment oiler in the service of the United States Navy. In her class, the lone ship was the first of only two U.S. Naval vessels to be named for the Pasig River, which flows through Manila on the Philippine Island of Luzon.

Originally built in 1917 by the Newport News Shipbuilding & Drydock Company of Newport News, Virginia, she served the Atlantic Refining Company of Philadelphia, Pa. as S.S. J. C. Donnell. Acquired by the U.S. Navy through the War Shipping Administration Jan. 22, 1943, and commissioned the same day, as U.S.S. Pasig (AO–89).

Pasig was intended for use as a storage tank in the South Pacific near New Caledonia but was replaced by concrete barges. She decommissioned and was delivered to W.S.A. Sept. 25, 1943, and was struck from the Naval Vessel Register Oct. 11, 1943.

J. C. Donnell statistics: Displacement: 7,165 long tons (7,280 t) light, Length: 516ft. 6 in. Beam: 68 ft. Draft: 30 ft. 10 in. Propulsion: Triple expansion reciprocating engine, 3 single ended Scotch boilers, Single shaft, 2,400 shp (1,790 kW), Speed: 10.5 knots; 12.1 mph) Armament: 1 × 4 in (100 mm) gun. Returned to her owner, Pasig reverted to her original name and served as S.S. J. C. Donnell until scrapped in 1947.

Thurs October 1 went to Leonardtown, Left Leonardtown on 5th.

Went to Wash.

16 Went to Philadelphia

17 Left Philadelphia for Baltimore and reported aboard S.S. Henry Van Dyke

Launched as HENRY VAN DYKE, lease lend to Britain. (Liberty Ship) Scrapped Kynosoura, Greece, 1971.

18 Van Dyke

19 Van Dyke

20 5 a.m. left Baltimore for Philadelphia

21 9 a.m. Aboard the W. C. Yeager

The W. C. Yeager was a custom build tanker ship. It held about `140,000 barrels of oil and had a typical 42-45 Merchant seamen crew and 17 Navy personnel. The Navy A.O. designation indicates Fleet Oilers.

Tankers were developed around the turn of the century to carry liquid cargo: gasoline, oil, or molasses. During World War II, American tankers made 6,500 voyages. They delivered 65 million tons of oil and gasoline from the U.S. and the

Caribbean to the war zones and our Allies. They supplied 80% of the fuel used by bombers, tanks, jeeps, and ships during the War.

Sailed on the W. C. Yeager Oct. 21, 1945, to Oct. 24, 1945, to and from Philidelphia, Pa.

It was a steamship; Clay was an Oiler. The trip was 3 days. Coastwise.

22 Aboard W. C. Yeager

13 Same

24 Left Yeager 1 p.m. and went aboard Atlantic Range (Another tanker ship.) Alva C. Lindsay Oiler Oct. 25, 1945, to Nov. 6, 1945, on the S.S. Atlantic Ranger, to and from Philadelphia, Pa. Coastwise. 2 weeks.

25 Went to Wilmington, Del.

26 12-12 left Chester Pa. for Texas

27 at sea

The WAR SHIPPING ADMINISTRATION certified that Alva C. Lindsay has been awarded the Pacific War Zone Bar, confirming active service with THE UNITED STATES MERCHANT MARINE in that war area.

Clay and the other men of the Merchant Marine traveled all over the world and delivered the goods. Without them, the Allies would not have won the War. Percentagewise, the Merchant Marine lost more men during the War than any other service.

The rest of the story is that he returned to the Lindsay Ranch in Mason, Texas, where he lived the remainder of his life, stating that he NEVER wanted to get on a ship again.

There were a few other notations in his little black book.

Cash Account June …

June 9, 44 Traveler check 60.00

June 20, 44 Traveler check 50.00

June 27, 44 cash and check 118

July 1, 44 Cash and Travelers 104

This address is listed: Cpl. C. S. Long 18076107 (Was this Effie's husband, Clabe Scott Long?)

878 Bombing Squad

499th Bombing Group

% Postmaster, San

There are lists of money that I assume people owed him as well as a list of five things he was to purchase before June 1944: Notebook paper, toothbrush, ruler, flashlight, and gloves.

The other addresses are R. H. Richards, 775 42nd. Ave. San Francisco, CA. Phone Skyline 3896. Correspondence after August 1, 44. % Napa State Hospital, I.M.O.L.A., Napa County, Calif., and H. Brown, 180 BonView St. S. F. Cal.

The last entry proves that he was at home. He has a listing June 12, 1946, of 4 cows and calves, 3-4 years old, 6 cows and calves, 12 dry cows, 1 yearling heifer, 1 2-year heifer and 1-3-year heifer. He is back home and counting cows. Clay was a good rancher, and a good rancher knows his stock.

The merchant sailors' vital and undisputed role in the war effort was hailed by presidents, generals, and admirals alike. Roosevelt pushed for veterans' benefits for them. Time and again, the seamen returned to face intense perils, Roosevelt declared, "because they realized that the lifelines to our battlefronts would be broken if they did not carry out their vital part in this global war."

Re-read the entries in Clay's diary from January through March 1945. Was he in danger? Was he in a warzone? The men who served in the Merchant Marine were called "the forgotten heroes." They were considered an Auxiliary Service. They were not considered to be veterans and were ineligible for any benefits until 1988. After 42 years, these brave men were deemed worthy of receiving a flag and a headstone.

Clay's headstone, including an inscription acknowledging his WWII service in the Merchant Marine and the Navy, was placed on Mason Mountain overlooking the land he loved.

His memorial service was held March 27, 2021, at the Lindsay Ranch in Mason, Texas. His son, Clay Haley Lindsay, created and erected a magnificent cross on Mason Mountain. At the end of the celebration, Mendy Beaty Lindsay played "Taps." It was the perfect ending to a moving celebration of his life. Thank you, Clay & Mendy. Well done.

Lindsay Family Military Service, WWII and Beyond

Jack Gamel Lindsay was in the Army and the US Army Air Corps, WWII. He was inducted into the Army in 1942. He chose Paratrooper School, qualified as "Expert Rifle." He transferred to the Air Corps, where he qualified as a flight officer of B-26 bombers.

Jack told a few stories of his time in Tunisia, North Africa.

While there, he bought a beautiful silver bracelet for his wife, Jean.

Jack completed his overseas missions doing low aerial bombing over Central Europe. He said he brought his plane back with gaping holes. He broke his neck and was discharged in 1946. He was in the service for just over four years.

Clabe Scott Long (Effie's husband) – Sergeant, US Army Air Corps, Spring 1942 through Summer 1945, WWII.

Alva Clay Lindsay was in the Merchant Marines, WWII 1943-1946.

Louie Raymond Dobbs (Doris's husband) was in the Air Force, WWII. Enlisted 1941: Fort Bliss, El Paso, Texas. Grade: First Lieutenant, Area of Service: Air Corps, Stationed: England.

He was a bombardier in heavy bombers, B17's & B24's. He served in the European Theater and Germany. He made many successful missions, "Spirit of 44".

His plane "Boston Bombshell" was shot down over Germany Feb. 22, 1944. It crashed; some crew members died. Louie was taken prisoner.

He was held in camp Stalag Luft 1 Barth-Volsang Prussia 54-12. He was liberated at the end of the war.

Ernest Davis (Peggy's husband) was in the US Army and later the 8th US Army which became the US Air Force. Ernie was a Cavalryman in the Army and a B17 Bomber Pilot in WWII.

"Formaldehyde" was the name of his plane. He was shot down over Bad Hall, Austria, and the Germans machine-gunned off his arm as he was parachuting down. Unbelievably, the Germans saved his life. He was in a POW Nazi hospital for one year before being repatriated to the United States.

Second generation:

John Clabe Long (Effie's son) served in the US Marine Corps from 1960 until 1966. He was an infantry officer and served in Vietnam, where he earned a Bronze Star for his platoon's accomplishments. He was promoted to Captain in 1966 before his enlistment ended.

James (Jim) Lindsay Long (Effie's son) was a 1st. Lieutenant in the US Army from 1962- 1964.

Clay Haley Lindsay (Alva Clay's son) was in the US Marine Corps 1995-2000. Corporal Lindsay's specialty was Aviation Electronics. He was stationed at the Marine Corps Air Station, Cherry Point, Havelock, N.C. for most of his tour.

Third generation:

Jason Geis (Peggy's grandson, Lindsay Davis Geis Trapp's son) served 20 years in the Army:

I served in the US Army as a medic with the light infantry airborne and five overseas deployments.

JASON M. GEIS, MBA Sgt. Maj. (Ret.), USA
Former President, (2008 - 2018), Wounded Heroes Fund
SERVICE, SUPPORT, APPRECIATION

It has been an honor to have served my country!

32
The USO -
They Made a Difference

13 Things You Probably Did Not Know About the USO in World War II:

1. USO clubs were everywhere. Several estimates put the number at roughly 3,000 USO clubs worldwide during World War II. Some were run out of established or newly constructed buildings; some were run out of homes, barns, museums, railroad sleeping cars and churches. Today, the USO has about 160 locations worldwide.

2. Pugilist's welcome. Some USO locations had boxing rings and punching bags, as the sport was far more popular than it is today.

3. Smokes, but not booze. USO snack bars sold cigarettes to troops but didn't sell liquor. Today, alcohol and tobacco are forbidden, but all snacks at USO locations are free to troops and their families.

4. Celebrity waiters. Stars of the stage and screen weren't just entertainers back in the 1940s. They would also bring you coffee and a doughnut. At New York City's famed USO Stage Door Canteen, troops could meet the stars of the day, watch them perform, and even be waited on by them. At the USO Hollywood Canteen, some stars worked shifts in the anonymity of the kitchen.

5. To keep uniforms spiffy, some World War II-era USO centers offered a button-sewing service.

6. The woman in charge. In keeping with the era's gender roles, many USO clubs had the position of Senior Hostess. An esteemed woman from the local community, the Senior Hostess, coordinated the junior hostesses and large-scale activities at USO clubs.

7. No slacks allowed. Junior hostesses were arguably the most famous feature of stateside USO's during the World War II era. These young women catered to and danced with troops, among other upkeep duties. They also had a somewhat formal dress code—no slacks allowed—compared to today's volunteers.

8. Things junior hostesses were forbidden from doing. Smoking inside most USO areas, drinking alcohol on the job, dancing with other women when troops were present, refusing to dance with a serviceman unless he was "ungentlemanly" and dancing "conspicuously."

9. Mobile USOs are not a new thing. Mobile USOs started circulating in the lower 48 states in 1942. They consisted of trucks with generators, screens, and projectors to show film reels, and many were equipped with a public address system, turntables and records, sports gear, board games, books, and snacks. And because no World War II USO experience was complete without a dance, the local USO would often organize carloads of junior hostesses, with chaperones, to meet at Mobile USOs.

10. $33 Million. That is the approximate amount of money the USO raised from its inception in 1941 through 1945. Thomas Dewey and Prescott Bush spearheaded the fundraising campaign. Factoring in inflation, that is the equivalent of $433.7 million today.

11. USO tours were dangerous. Thirty-seven USO entertainers died during World War II. The most famous entertainer who didn't make it back was legendary Big Band leader and then-Army Major Glenn Miller, whose plane disappeared over the English Channel on the way to France. (One of the Big Bands that Clay remembered was the Ted Weems' Orchestra.)

12. The world's largest producer of banana splits? The USO's Honolulu center became famous for making banana splits for troops during World War II. According to the book, "Always Home: 50 Years of the USO," the center went through nearly a ton of bananas and 250 gallons of ice cream a day at the height of its operation.

13. Helping start the modern childcare industry. Today, millions of working families drop children off at daycare. That was not the case entering the 1940s. However, with many women working to support the war effort, and their husbands often deployed, select USOs started their own daycare operations.

33
Mountain Home, Texas

After Clay returned home from WWII in 1946, he stayed in Mason and worked on the Ranch for a short time, but he decided that he wanted his own place.

Marcus Auld, the youngest son of Alexander Kennedy Auld, owned a lot of property on the "Divide" in Kerr County. The closest community to where he and his family lived, was Mountain Home. Marcus was a frequent visitor to the Lindsay Ranch. No doubt, he talked to Clay about Mountain Home and the need for young, hard-working men to settle there.

At the intersection of State Highway 27 (which runs here along the Old Spanish Trail) and State Highway 41 in north-central Kerr County, Mountain Home was settled about 1856. Ranching has always been the principal business.

Garven's Store was built in 1932 along Hwy. 41, which originated in Del Rio and ended at Mountain Home. It was an old-fashioned general store that handled all types of merchandise. There was a gas station out front, and they sold dry goods and groceries, and other supplies. It is still the most popular attraction in Mountain Home.

In 1946, the population of Mountain Home was 150. In 1949, local ranchers added another welcome feature to the Divide landscape, the Garven Community Center, built on Garven family land, just across U.S. 83. "All the ranchers would meet here once a month on Friday nights. There was music, and many bands played, including the Texas Top Hands.

Many families had their own tables where they would sit outside and enjoy the evenings. In 1952, Highway 83 came through. The original site of Garven's Store was on an old wagon road that cut around from the old Auld ranch across Hwy. 41, and over through the Bushong's Ranch. Before the road crews and surveyors came in, they had 'cedar choppers' working ahead of them clearing the land."

Mountain Home is a few miles north of Leakey, Texas, where Clay's grandfather, Alva James Lindsay, lived in the early 1880s. Clay's father, John Alva Lindsay, was born in Leakey. His grandmother, Mary Ellen Turner Lindsay, died in Leakey May 12, 1890. Her grave is the oldest grave in the Leakey Floral Cemetery.

Clay borrowed money from his mother's cousin, Francis Kettner, and moved to Mountain Home, Texas. He bought or leased some land, bought sheep and cattle to stock it, and began his new life.

The small, older home on the property had two bedrooms and a living area that opened onto a screened-in front porch. A back porch led into the small kitchen. The house had electric lighting, an icebox instead of a refrigerator, and no bathroom.

There was a large barn, pens, and an outhouse on the property. There was a lot of cedar in the area that Clay cut and sold for fence posts. He stocked his ranch with sheep, goats, cattle, horses, chickens, and a cow.

The milk cow was named Elsie. Knowing Clay, I'm sure he named his cow after Borden's famous Elsie. Elsie the Cow, a cartoon cow developed as a mascot for the Borden Dairy Company in 1936 to symbolize the "perfect dairy product."

Elsie's mate, Elmer the Bull, was created in 1940. He was the mascot for Elmer's Glue. The pair were given offspring Beulah and Beauregard in 1948 and twins Larabee and Lobelia in 1957.

Elsie has been bestowed such tongue-in-cheek honorary university degrees as Doctor of Bovinity, Doctor of Human Kindness, and Doctor of Economics. The City of Bridgeport, Conn., presented her with their P. T. Barnum Award of Showmanship.

Clay often named animals for his favorite people. In the 1960's, he named a ewe for Jill Larimore. Jill rode in the truck's floorboard like a dog and traveled with Clay on his 260-mile trips to White Top Package Store.

In the 1970s, he named a lamb Lyndee for my niece, Lynna Dee Haley, and a handsome bull calf for my nephew, Hutch Haley. He also called a pretty heifer calf Pam for his favorite sister-in-law, Pamela Haley Bruce. When "Pam" the cow had a calf, he proudly pointed out that she was a really good mother.

Clay's older sister, Effie Lindsay Long, and her two young sons, John, and Jim, lived in the Gamel house in Mason, with her Aunt Nell, while her husband, Clabe Long, was overseas. When the war ended, they moved. Clabe was traveling, looking for work, Clay had a house and needed a cook, so Effie, John, and Jim moved to Mountain Home. John had attended first grade in Mason, but the closest school to Mountain Home was sixty miles away; he missed second grade.

James (Jim) Lindsay Long shared his memories about that time and place.

Two of Clay's horses were Jerry B. and Tom Thumb. Jerry B. (who you will hear more about in another chapter) was a big sorrel horse. Sorrel is a reddish coat color in a horse lacking any black. It is a term that is usually synonymous with chestnut and one of the most common coat colors in horses. Some regions and breed registries distinguish it from chestnut, defining sorrel as a light, coppery shade, and chestnut as a browner shade.

Clabe Judson Long gave Jerry B. to John Alva Lindsay when their children, Clabe Scott Long and Effie Mary Lindsay, married. Tom Thumb was a gift from John Alva Lindsay to his grandsons John Clabe and James Lindsay Long. They learned to ride, but if the intent was to make cowboys out of them, it didn't work.

Jim also remembered a horse that John Lindsay gave Clabe Long. Jim said that this horse was very unusual. If it was startled by a loud noise, the horse would run backward. 😊

"Effie, Unkie's sister, John and I lived with Unkie at his Ranch in Mountain Home, Texas after WW II while our dad, Clabe, was looking for a job.

One afternoon, John and I were out on the screened-in porch, trying to stay cool. Unkie came in from the barn. On the way, he noticed a big Texas red wasp nest on the eaves of the porch. He decided to eliminate it.

In those days, you rolled up a newspaper, set it on fire, and then put the torch to the nest. You had to move fast because red wasps can sting! Anyway, Unk went out the screen door with his torch burning and attacked the nest. John was seven years old, and I was five. We immediately locked the screen, fearing a wasp bite of our own.

Unk ran for the door with the wasps close behind, but he couldn't get in. The door was locked! John and I trembled behind the screen. Unk went running off behind the house, wasps in close pursuit. He got several bites, but he didn't spank us, he never did, he was a kind, gentle, yet mischievous man."

Clay had two pet deer. A newborn or a baby deer is called a fawn. When a deer is one year old, it is no longer called a fawn, it is then known as a yearling, and after they reach their second year, the males are called bucks, and the females are called does.

Jim remembers when Clay brought a fawn in the house and kept it there overnight. John and Jim named her Faline, and they slept with her. The following day, they were covered with fleas. Their mother, Effie, was not happy. Clay's pet deer that was a buck, was named Bambi.

Bambi is a 1942 American animated drama film produced by Walt Disney and based on the 1923 book Bambi, a Life in the Woods by Austrian author and hunter Felix Salten. The film was released Aug. 13, 1942.

The main characters are Bambi, a white-tailed deer; his parents (the Great Prince of the forest and his unnamed mother); his friends Thumper (a pink-nosed rabbit); and Flower (a skunk); and his childhood friend and future mate, Faline.

Both Bambi and Faline became full-grown deer. They would still come up to be fed. After Faline had a fawn, she didn't come up anymore. Clay put a collar and bell on Bambi, who grew to be a handsome 8-point buck. He also quit coming up to be fed. One day, Clay found the collar and bell in the pasture. The hunter probably didn't see the collar and bell until after Bambi was killed.

After Clay's death, I sorted through his treasures, and I found fifteen letters from Marie Nutter. Cedric and Josephine Reed Nutter owned a ranch in Mountain Home and a home in Navasota, Texas. Josephine Marie Nutter, born in 1932, was the youngest of their two daughters.

In Mountain Home, Texas, population 150, the arrival of a handsome, friendly, hard-working young man with bright red hair didn't go unnoticed. Marie and Clay met at the post office, where everyone went to get their mail.

The Nutter Family lived on one side of Mountain Home, and Clay's property was twenty miles away, in the other direction, on a very rough dirt road. Marie said that Clay was well-liked by her mother and dad and others in the community.

Clay was pleasant to be around, and he never turned down a chance for a home-cooked meal. He visited the Nutter home frequently, and they welcomed him as a member of their family. Clay enjoyed all kinds of card games, dominoes, and "42". He also enjoyed Mrs. Nutter's food.

Marie said that he was ready and willing to help everyone. He helped her dad work sheep. What does "working sheep" involve? Read on.

Sheep require more attention than some animals. Like any other profession, it takes work to be a successful sheep rancher. During the year, you make sure that they have enough forage, grass, legumes, weeds, etc. They also need minerals and salt. There are mineral blocks and salt blocks that they can lick, or you can buy fifty-pound bags of loose salt and minerals and put them in a low trough. Sheep also need a supply of clean water. A sheep can drink from one-half to five gallons of water a day.

You also need to check the flock at regular intervals to make sure that they are healthy, and in times of drought, you need to make sure that they are not bogged down in a water hole. If they must wade through mud to get to the water, their wool can get wet, and they may be unable to get to dry ground without help.

In Mountain Home, at that time, ranchers checked their stock by saddling up and riding the pastures each day to make sure that the sheep, goats, and cattle were OK.

I don't know how many sheep and goats Clay, Mr. Nutter, Mr. Auld, and their neighbors owned, but Texas's sheep population numbered 10,800,000 animals in 1943. Many of these were raised on the Edwards Plateau.

Sheep ranching includes busy seasonal activities, of which lambing is the preeminent one. In the early days in the Southwest, particularly on the Edwards Plateau, range ewes were bred in the fall; the gestation period is about 150 days, to lamb between February and May. At higher elevations, a later lambing time was preferable.

The rancher or his sheepherder, acting as a midwife, carefully watched over the ewes in his flock, assisting at a difficult birth and forcing indifferent mothers to nurse their offspring. They also feed and care for orphaned lambs or lambs born to "dry" ewes and do everything necessary to get the lambs through their critical first weeks.

One man called the lambing season a "month-long hell of worry and toil." Some of the larger ranchers hired special crews, hijadores ("lambers"), composed of three or four men, to handle the task.

Shearing season was another intense time. The first chore was the round-up. On the Lindsay Ranch, getting all the sheep and angora goats into the trap, a holding area, sometimes took several days. The night before the shearing crew arrived, we brought the sheep and goats to the barn and put them in separate pens. We separated the ewes and lambs the following day.

The shearing area was raked and cleaned of debris, the wool rack set up, and the first wool bag attached to it by long metal pins. We placed additional bags within easy reach.

There were special needles and strong cotton sacking twine to tie ears in the sack and sew the bags closed when they were full. To ensure that the wool was not contaminated with non-wool fibers, we used paper twine to tie the fleeces.

221

The shearers brought their shearing boards and shearing rigs into the pen. They placed the boards on the ground to keep the wool as clean as possible. The gasoline motors powered the "drops." These were the shafts to which the machine shears, known as handpieces, were attached. These operate similarly to human hair clippers. A power-driven toothed blade, known as a cutter, is driven back and forth over the comb's surface, and the wool is cut from the animal.

Many shearing crews were local, and others went from ranch to ranch each shearing season. They wanted to have a good reputation so that they could go back to the same ranches year after year. Shearing was an art, but it was also hot dirty work.

From early morning until they were finished, shearers bent over their animals. They kept a tally of the sheep they sheared, and they were paid by the head. Since the bucks were larger, stronger, and more difficult to handle, a shearer was paid double or sometimes triple for each buck or ram that he sheared.

There were times when some of the sheep were accidentally cut. A friend shared this story. "I remember one year on the ranch, where I grew up, a sheep shearing team ended up nicking the sheep so badly that it made them bleed and tossing them so hard that several of them were injured.

Jake told his boss, and his boss threatened to fire them and get someone else to finish shearing the sheep. The team boss apologized for his men and said it wouldn't happen again, and it didn't. They were a well-known and well-respected sheep shearing outfit, but that year they had a few employees that were in training."

Usually, a young boy tied the fleece with twine and put it into the woolsack. The eight to ten feet long sack was fastened to the rim of the wool rack. When filled, it weighed about 360 pounds.

Bending over and shearing the sheep was hard on the back, and tromping the wool was a dirty job. On the Lindsay Ranch, someone, times that someone was me, would climb up the rack and jump down into the empty sack. As each fleece was thrown in, I would jump and tromp on it to compress it as much as possible.

When the sack was full, the top was sewn shut with heavy twine and a large needle. "Ears" were created on the two corners for handholds to help load the packed bags. It was dirty work, but the lanolin from the wool was good for my leather boots. We usually had twelve to fourteen bags of wool.

When all the sheep were shorn, Clay paid the crew boss. The crew boss paid the individuals on the crew. The shearers loaded their equipment and moved to another ranch. When they were gone, the tags, the dirty bits, and wool pieces left on the ground were gathered and put in a tow sack. You didn't waste anything. Even tags brought a little money.

The full bags of wool were loaded onto the truck and trailer to be taken to the wool warehouse in Ingram, Texas. There, the wool was unloaded and graded to determine the quality.

An expert grader examines the wool for length, diameter, fineness, crimp, pliability, color, luster, and other qualities before giving each bundle a grade. There are 200 total possible points. Correct checks receive 4 points for fineness, 3 points for length, and 3 points for shrinkage.

The rancher was paid when the wool sold. The day the check came was a "red-letter" day. We used our wool money to make the annual payment to the Federal Land Bank.

The production of wool is the oldest trade commodity known to man. The wool industry is mentioned in the Old Testament of the Bible and was the first widespread international trade throughout ancient civilizations.

While the grown sheep were being shorn, the rancher and his helpers, on our Ranch, that was usually me, worked the lambs. That included castrating, docking, and marking.

To castrate the male lambs, one person held the animal's back against his chest with all four legs elevated. The other person cut the end of the scrotum, pulled out both testicles, and cut the cords. Castration produced better mutton and ensured that only the prize rams would breed the ewes.

Clay delighted in throwing one or more of those "mountain oysters" at anyone who would scream and holler and make a fuss about it. As some consider them a delicacy, most were put into a bucket and given to anyone who wanted them.

Each lamb was caught and held while the tail was "docked." Docking, cutting off all but two inches of the tail, was done for sanitary and reproductive reasons. If the tails are left on wool sheep, such as Rambouillet & Merino, they get covered in excrement. The odor attracts blowflies, and the flies lay eggs on the sheep.

When the eggs hatch, the maggots eat the flesh of the lamb, and in the process, poison the sheep, resulting in an illness called Flystrike. It is far worse than anything that takes place during the docking process.

Someone else did the catching and holding, and Clay did the cutting. He was skilled, fast, and efficient. Two or three extremely sharp knives and a good whetstone were always at hand. There is a joint on the tail where the cut was to be made. Clay quickly found it and usually performed the operation with one cut. Later we counted the severed tails to determine the number of lambs that had been marked.

Marking was done for identification. On the Lindsay Ranch, we branded sheep with red paint. The "2" was Clay's mark, and his mother, Jesse's mark, was a red "O."

Some ranchers also earmark the animals by notching one or both ears with distinctive combinations of cuts and slashes known as "crops," "lance points," or "downfalls." By using a slightly different mark each year, a rancher could tell the age of his sheep.

1. The sheep also had to be "drenched" for worms. Gather the sheep. Herd the sheep into an enclosed pen or yard.
2. Measure out the drench. Load the drench gun with the correct dosage. Double-check that the dosage is correct before continuing.
3. Restrain the sheep. Approach each sheep from behind and place your hand under its neck to hold it securely in place.
4. Insert the nozzle into the mouth. Slip the nozzle of the drench gun into the corner of the sheep's mouth, far enough in so that the sheep can't spit the drench out.
5. Squeeze the trigger of the drench gun to deliver the medication into the mouth of the sheep.
6. Use colored chalk to paint a mark on the head of the animal when it has been drenched.

Once a year, you also need to pour a small amount of medication on the sheep's head and backs to kill external parasites. As you can see, "working sheep" is easily said but not easily done. It is a lot of work.

Many ranchers have cattle, sheep, and goats. Commercial goat ranching in Texas primarily involves raising Angora goats, from which the textile fiber mohair is obtained. They are shorn at the same time and in the same manner as the sheep. The United States ranks as the second leading producer of mohair in the world. As much as 97 percent of the domestic product is grown in Texas.

Goats, both Angoras and Spanish goats, are good in brushy pastures. Their browsing destroys small shrubs and prunes taller bushes and trees to a height of four or five feet, thus permitting more grass to grow. Many ranchers have developed a mixed ranching system of raising cattle, sheep and goats that fully utilize the region's varied vegetation resources.

Our friend, Milton Bailey, managed some very large ranches. One ranch in Concho County ran 5,000 sheep, 5,000 angora (hair) goats, and 300 cattle. I asked how many men helped with the round-up when it was shearing time.

He said, "We had some good dogs. All I had to say was, "Get 'em" and those dogs would bring in every head on the place. The boys and I just rode along to check on things."

Marie's letters gave an insight into Clay's life in Mountain Home. She mentioned some of the animals. She asked about Elsie (the cow), Marie, Pal (her favorite horse), Feline (the doe), Louis Jr, Blackie, Betty L, and Betty S. In a letter dated 1948, Marie asked about the black colt. "Did she try to pitch you? Have you named her yet?"

Clay mentioned Marie often. After his death, I wrote about some of the correspondence that he kept, including those from Marie Nutter. My comments prompted the following response from Effie's son, John Clabe Long.

"This brought back memories of the times when Jim and I were on Marie Nutter dates. Clay and Marie in the pickup cab, and we boys were supposed to be quiet in the back. Well, you know how that went! Sneaking, looking, whooping, and wondering what all the fuss was about up there. It was fun for the boys.

It was also a life lesson. It made us wonder about our future and the mysteries of what was to come in a pickup of our own one day."

After a year or so, Clabe Long found work, and Effie, John, and Jim left Mountain Home and moved to Canton, Texas. Clay stayed in Mountain Home a few years longer. No one knows when or why he moved back to Mason.

Joe Dickey, his brother, and his father lived in Mountain Home. Mr. Dickey cut cedar for a living. Clay always liked children. He took Joe and his brother to Garven's Store and bought them Pepsi's and candy.

A few years ago, a strange pickup drove up the road. Joe Dickey got out and came to the door. Joe and Clay reminisced about old times for an hour or so. Joe told Clay how much his kindness meant to two young boys who had nothing.

When you have an opportunity to do so, be kind. What seems insignificant to you may mean the world to someone.

When I researched Mountain Home for this book, I decided that I would try to locate Marie. I found her through an inquiry that I posted on Facebook. A friend of a friend recognized the name, and a few days later, Marie called me. She was happy to learn that Clay had children, both a daughter and a son and that his daughter and grandson had red hair. Marie said, "Clay was a really good man. Everyone in Mountain Home liked him."

She said that they were never seriously romantic but that they were very close friends. After our visit, I put 15 letters into an envelope and mailed them to her.

Marie, I enjoyed our conversation. I hope you enjoy the memories of good times in Mountain Home, 70 years ago.

34

Family Stories, Katemcy, Lindsay Ranch

Clay left Mountain Home, Texas, and moved back to Mason and then to Katemcy, Texas. John and Jesse, his father and mother, were having serious difficulties. John's gambling problem resulted in Jesse divorcing him. Clay purchased the Mason Mountain portion of the Ranch.

On April 29, 1950, when his younger sister, Peggy, married, Clay, who was very handsome in his tuxedo, gave the beautiful bride away. The Mason County News published a photo and the following story.

"In one of the most impressive ceremonies of the season, Miss Peggy Lindsay, daughter of John A. Lindsay and Mrs. Jesse Gamel Lindsay, became the bride of Ernest Davis, of Odessa, on the evening of April 29 in the garden of the Lindsay Ranch home near Mason. Following a wedding trip to the Davis Mountains, the couple will be at home in Odessa."

Clay's niece, Sherry Lindsay, recalls, "That was a beautiful wedding on the lawn. I was a bride's mini-maid, and my sister Carolyn was the flower girl (who did somersaults down the lawn after the ceremony)." Sherry was six years old, and Carolyn was three.

Katemcy, Texas

Some of the early settlers in Katemcy were the Coots, Turner, Dobbs and Cowan families. The community was initially named Cootsville for Andrew Jackson Coots who was an early settler.

This man was mentioned in the first chapter. After she was twice widowed, Clay's 2nd-great-grandfather, James Buchanan Lindsay, married Margaret Allen Coots Smith. Margaret's first husband, Andrew Jackson Coots, Sr. died Dec. 19, 1849. Their oldest son was Andrew Jackson Coots, Jr.

These names may sound familiar. All except the Cowan family have been mentioned in other chapters. Clay's grandmother, Mary Ellen Turner, was probably related to the Turner family. Clay's sister, Doris Dea Lindsay, married Louie Raymond Dobbs from Katemcy. I have Cowan ancestors.

The first house built on the land which became the town plot of Katemcy was a picket building located on the creek's west bank and occupied by a man from

Burnet, who had driven several hundred hogs from Burnet to Katemcy to eat acorns and pecans.

When the hogs were fat, men came from Burnet in wagons, butchered the hogs, cured the meat, and rendered the lard. They took the finished products to Austin and sold them for a good price.

Some of the first settlers lived along the creek about two miles north of the old Katemcy post office, almost to Camp San Saba, Texas. Probably the first to come to this vicinity were the families of Andrew Jackson Coots and William Turner.

In 1874, John Cowan settled at Devil Springs just south of Katemcy off the old Katemcy/Mason Road. This location was a former Indian camp called Devil Springs because the Indians gave the settlers so much trouble.

While the Cowans were clearing the land for a field and orchard, they discovered some Indian graves. Many arrowheads were found around the springs, also two small leather pouches that contained white and blue Indian beads.

The Cowan brothers, John, Elias, and Alfred built and operated a sawmill, gristmill, and cotton gin on the east bank of Katemcy Creek.

Doctor William Flemon Cowan, and his wife, Mary Ann Primm Cowan, who was a midwife, moved there from Limestone County. The Cowan family cut oak and sycamore timber from Katemcy Creek, sawed it into lumber, and built the first house in Katemcy. It was a frame house located on the west side of the creek across from the gin. It served as a residence, store, and post office for W. F. Cowan.

In 1883, W. F. Cowan applied for a post office; he submitted the name of the Comanche chief Ketemoczy, who had his winter camp in the granite rock near the head of Katemcy Creek at one time. The Postal Department shortened this name to Katemcy. Eventually, the rocks, creek, village, and community for miles in every direction were called Katemcy.

Many people moved to the Katemcy Community between 1900 and 1910. The main attraction was cheap land and an abundance of water. At one time, Katemcy had two dry goods and grocery stores owned by Houston Dobbs (husband of Lavinia Pernesia Watts) and Felix Jordan. Dr. Hicks Martin was the physician, and he operated a drugstore.

Henry Custer's blacksmith shop, Dennis Turner's barbershop, a chili joint, pool hall, and domino room were also in Katemcy. N. Z. Bethel's telephone exchange served the Katemcy and Peter's Prairie Communities.

The change in the mode of farming, from manual labor to tractors, and school consolidation, contributed to Katemcy's decline. Today there is little left of that active community.

After John and Jesse's divorce, Clay, his dad, and occasionally his brother, Jack, lived in Katemcy. They first lived in a small house on the creek. Many of Clay's nieces and nephews remember being at that house.

"There was this creek down from the cabin. We loved going down every day, playing, and building a dam to make it deeper.

One afternoon, as we headed down the path to the creek, we saw a huge rattlesnake. He was lying across the path sunbathing! When he coiled and rattled, we ran back to the cabin and told Daddy John. John shot the snake."

Clay also bought a property on the north side of the road, behind the store. That house burned when John left a pot of beans on the fire when he went to town. The fire destroyed Clay's papers, photographs, and some of his coin collection.

John Alva Lindsay, age 75, Katemcy, Texas, c. 1962

When Clay purchased the property, he put it in his dad's name, and without consulting or letting Clay know, John sold it. Clay found out when he went to get some materials, and the new owner told him to "Get off my land."

At some point, Clay added two rooms to the small hunting cabin that was on the Mason Mountain portion of the Ranch. That is where he probably lived after he left Katemcy.

As we will see, Clay was a traveling man.

35
Clay's Business Adventures

Clay's nephew, James (Jim) Lindsay Long, shared this story.

Unkie and his brother Jack were very enterprising. After WW 2, they both had several schemes for making money. One of the ventures they got into, along with their brother-in-law, L. R. (Stony) Dobbs (Doris Lindsay's husband), was a ranch in Evergreen, Colorado.

John and I happened to be in Mason in the summer of 1952 when the Colorado venture was going full steam. Unkie was in Mason preparing to haul a load of hogs to the ranch in Evergreen. Unkie decided to bring us along so we could help with the menial work in Colorado.

We took off in a pickup pulling a trailer full of hogs. On the 1st day, we got to somewhere in the Oklahoma panhandle. It was late, and Unkie pulled off to the side of the road, and we all fell asleep in the front seat.

I vaguely remember it being dawn, and two burly-looking hombres were walking up to the pickup. Unkie was awake, and he quickly reached into the glove compartment and pulled out a loaded 45 pistol. The two intruders saw the weapon and immediately fled. Unkie simply said, "Glad I brought the pistol."

We went ahead on and arrived that day in Evergreen with the hogs. The Evergreen venture failed. There was a bad drought in Colorado between 1952 and 1955, and the ranch was auctioned to pay the debts. Stony Dobbs never got into a partnership with the Lindsay's again.

Jack and Clay were involved in a sheep-raising enterprise in New Mexico which did not end well. Jack went to town, and Clay stayed with the sheep. A blizzard blew in that lasted several days. When it was over, there was nothing left. Clay survived, but the sheep did not. They had frozen to death.

Jim remembered a blizzard that killed a lot of sheep in Hereford, Texas. John and Jim helped drag the frozen bodies out of the pasture. They were stacked in a big pile and doused with gallons of kerosene. Jim said, "It was a huge fire."

"Jack and Unkie went into a new venture a couple of years later and opened a feedlot in Omaha, Nebraska. John and I worked there for one summer, but it also failed."

After Clay's death, I found some love letters. Yes, he saved everything. Was I jealous? Not at all. Clay was good-looking, personable, and all man. I had no illusions about his life during the 49 years before I met him. He had dated every eligible young woman in Mason County, at least twice, and other pretty women all over the country.

Two letters were from a lady who signed her name "Lucky." They were written in February and March 1957 from Omaha, Nebraska. From Clay's niece, Sherry, I learned that "Lucky" was probably a blonde (go figure) named Pat. Her father probably had some connection with the feedlot.

According to her long letters, one was 14 pages, she was divorced from George and had children. One daughter, Stephanie, missed Clay. "Lucky" probably had horses and may have brought some of them to the ranch.

In her letter, she asked Clay if he had talked to his sister Peggy and what Peggy thought of him getting involved with a "darn" Yankee? After reading her letters, I concluded that Clay was the one who was "lucky" because he did not become more involved with her.

Clay returned to Texas, but he never gave up his quest for a successful enterprise.

36
White Top Package Store -
The Winkler Family

Clay was always driving somewhere, and 99.9% of the time, he was towing a trailer. He pulled horse trailers, cattle trailers, and flatbed trailers. He was always hauling, feed, lumber, watermelons, horses, cattle, sheep, hogs, or some of his family's belongings.

He went to Muleshoe, Texas (a town in north Texas that some laughingly call Jenny Slipper). Muleshoe, the county seat of Bailey County, is on U.S. Highway 84 in the Blackwater Valley. It was founded when the Pecos and Northern Texas Railway laid tracks across the county in 1913 and was named for the nearby Muleshoe Ranch.

Clay traveled to New Mexico, Colorado, Iowa, Nebraska, and all over Texas. Many times, his nieces and nephews were with him. John and Jim Long, Mike Davis, John, Tom, and Jay Lindsay, had many memorable experiences while traveling with their Uncle Clay.

Sherry, Carolyn, Alica Lindsay, and Lindsay Davis also remember their adventures with Clay. For several years, Clay would drive to Council Bluffs, Iowa, after school ended and bring three or four of Jack's children to the Ranch for the summer. He took them back to Iowa before school started.

Sherry Lindsay traveled with her red-headed Uncle more than the rest of Jack and Jean's children. She came to the Ranch every time she could. These are some of her memories. Snapshots of a unique man:

Setting – Before the interstate highways, driving from Iowa to Texas. It is Hot! I remember Clay quaffing an ice-cold Pepsi-Cola in one smooth continuous swallow. His eyes didn't even water. Then, gas up and move on South.

Setting - The Oklahoma/Texas border. Clay stopped at Turner Falls. I headed to the water and was soon soaked. He didn't scold me. I think he wished he could join me! We pulled into an orchard that had a sign advertising "Homemade Cherry Cider." It was superb. There were so many gems along the highways.

Pre 1966 and the eradication of the screw worn. Clay was in a constant battle treating his sheep. Up close and personal doesn't describe the lessons learned on a ranch of life and death.

During the 1950-1957 Texas drought, Clay and Daddy John moved up to Nebraska. I went down to the Ranch with my trusty red-headed driver. One night "we" drove off the road. We were close to Post, Texas, it was pitch black, and there was a 90-degree bend in the road. We ended up in a field.

Clay and I both had to return to Nebraska as it was time for school to start. I was bereft. I didn't want to leave. I was sobbing as we drove across the creek and turned North. I looked over at him, and his face was wet with tears. I loved that man.

Alica Gamel Lindsay Marshall recalled one experience:

> This incident probably took place in 1962 when I was about 14 years old. As I got older, I chose not to go to Texas. We had been at the Ranch during the summer. Unk was driving us back to Council Bluffs, Iowa because it was nearly time for school to start.
>
> When he stopped for gas, he realized that all the luggage he had tied onto the car roof was gone! He turned around and headed back a few miles. We found our clothes scattered all over the median and the highway!
>
> We all picked up what we could find. You can imagine how upset Mom was. Unk gave her money to buy some of the things we lost.

In the 1960s, Clay, ever resourceful, began working for the Pouncey Fixture Exchange, 103 Main, Brownwood, Texas. The company, owned by Clifford Lake Pouncey, sold commercial refrigeration equipment. Clay traveled all over Texas delivering and installing refrigeration units, walk-in coolers, and Scotsman Ice Machines.

He delivered and installed a walk-in cooler and possibly an ice machine at the White Top Package Store on Highway 651 between Crosbyton and Post, five miles from Kalgary and 260 miles from Mason, Texas.

One of the partners wanted to retire, so Clay bought into the business. Clay's partner, W. T. Scott, known as "Scotty," was born in Kalgary, Texas. He served in the Navy during World War II. He was stationed aboard the USS Utah at Pearl Harbor. Mr. Scott's in-person account of the bombing is recorded at the Nimitz Museum, National Museum of the Pacific War in Fredericksburg, Texas.

For years, Clay and W. T. worked one week on and one week off. Later they changed to working two weeks on and two weeks off. Clay owned the store and drove 520 miles round trip for twenty-five years.

Clay made friends everywhere he went, and Kalgary was no exception. The Winkler family more or less adopted him: Boney, Doylene, their daughters Carla and Nan, Boney's mother and dad, Roy and Sue Winkler, and Boney's younger brother, Roy Don Winkler.

Clay always made it to their house in time for a meal, and Doylene fed him well. He worked with them. Boney had several large chicken houses and sold eggs. Clay helped in the chicken houses and with the ranch work.

He enjoyed every minute he spent with them, with one exception. One day Boney, Clay, and two or three others were rounding up cattle. Clay always wore the best "dress" hat and the worst "work" hat. Boney rode by, snatched Clay's beat-up old hat off his head, and dropped it into the burn barrel, which was burning. Clay was furious. You never mess with a cowboy's hat! Never!

Clay played with them. He double-dated with Roy Don Winkler and Barbara Young. They married in 1966, but Clay remained single. Clay, an excellent dancer, was a member of the Crosbyton square dance club. He and Boney were also members of the Spur and Ralls Cowboy Polo teams.

The Spur team won the Cowboy Polo World's Championship in 1970. Cowboy polo is a variation of polo played mainly in the western United States. It differs from traditional polo in that five riders make up a team instead of four. Western saddles and equipment, a rodeo arena or other enclosed dirt area, indoors or out, and a large red rubber ball were used. The mallets had long fiberglass shafts and hard rubber heads.

Cowboy Polo reached its peak of popularity during the 1970s. The riders wore cowboy hats, jeans, boots, and a shirt in the specified club color. Clay kept both his Ralls and Spur team shirts. After winning the championship, there was an outbreak of equine encephalitis, which prevented them from transporting their horses across state lines.

Clay was the oldest in most groups, but you couldn't tell it by his looks or actions. On what turned out to be his last visit with Roy Don Winker, he and Clay remembered their fun times. Roy said, "I didn't realize how old you were!" Clay was 19 years older than Roy.

"Anyone who knew the Winkler's knew that when they dropped by the house, they would be welcomed and well-fed." That was true. Clay was always there for Sunday morning breakfast and many other meals as well.

This special friendship lasted more than 40 years. Clay outlived everyone except Boney and Doylene's youngest daughter, Nan Winkler McCloy. Nan wrote:

I have so many fond memories of Clay growing up. Clay was part "second Dad" and part big brother and friend. He was always just part of the family always.

Clay was working at the White Top Package store in 1970 when my mother and stepfather, Zella, and Howard Ellis, met him. Mother was very impressed with Clay.

Howard was there to buy beer, but Mother was not a big beer drinker. Clay asked, "What would you like to have?" Mother replied, "What I would like is a big glass of cold water." Out the back door, Clay went. Mother said that the water he brought her was the best she had ever tasted. That glass of cold water sealed our fate.

37

Clay and Dee - Leo and Virgo

CLAY - LEO

Clay was born Aug. 15, 1922, so he was a "Leo." I found these traits listed for his "sign," and I think they describe him very well.

Generous and big-hearted – Clay was. "Do you have a friend who would give you the shirt off their back if you needed it? If you do, there's a good chance that person is a Leo."

"Leos have a lot of love to give. If a Leo finds a place for you in their heart, consider yourself lucky. (I did.) Leos tend to be extremely generous with their time, attention, affection, and money. As a result, Leos tend to attract people to them, so don't be surprised if the Leos in your life have a considerable entourage!"

Well, now, let's discuss that "money" part. Clay could be generous, but he also watched every penny. He knew exactly how much money he had and where it was. One day, when I was going to town, I picked up a $20.00 bill and took it with me just in case I needed it.

When I got home, Clay confronted me. "Did you take my money?" "I had $20.00 laying on that dresser. Did you take it?" Why would you take MY money?" I responded, "I was going to town and thought I might need it, but I didn't." I took it out of my pocket and handed it to him."

He continued, "I don't know why you would take MY money! If you wanted money, all you had to do was ask!" That was the last straw! I said, "Take a good, long, hard look at me. Do I look like a six-year-old who needs to ask for her allowance, or do I look like a sixty-year-old woman who works here just like you?"

He didn't have a clue. He said, "Well, you have the checkbook, and you can write a check." "Yes, I can, and I will." I wrote a check for $500.00, and I've never been without cash since that day.

After that, when I would be getting ready to go to town, Clay would ask, "Do you need any money?" "No, I have plenty, but thank you for asking." After Clay died, I found $126.00 in his wallet. I smiled and said, "Yes, Clay, I'm taking YOUR money!"

Leos have self-confidence. They aren't afraid to like what they like, and they carry themselves with such incredible confidence that they can convince other people to like it, too.

Leos are persevering and determined, making them pretty much unstoppable considering how much self-confidence they have. When Leos set out to achieve something, they will not stop until it's done (and done right). Their determination is usually fueled by an unflappable optimism, which carries them through even when the road to achieving their goals gets rocky.

Leos are often naturally gifted leaders. Self-confidence, determination, and big-heartedness are traits that most people admire and desire, so it's no surprise that Leos are usually well-suited to lead others.

Their charisma draws people to them, and their self-confidence inspires trust in their abilities. Additionally, their generosity and optimism breed loyalty! But Leos can be quickly disappointed when their generosity is met with ingratitude.

Leos work hard to achieve their goals and honor their commitments, and they typically pursue their goals and ambitions with great determination. They aren't likely to be phased when the going gets tough, either, since Leos are also known for their physical and mental fortitude.

Leos are consistently honest. A Leo's desire to give gifts (pecans and lemon drops anyone) or pick up the check shows their generosity. Accept their gifts, express gratitude, and have a good time.

Leos respond well to kind words. And feel most loved when they hear you say it. Clay was usually the best pitch or domino player in the room. Everyone knew he loved to win and hated to lose. He was the worse loser in the world!

Clay was compassionate, and he had a good memory. He remembered from visit to visit a problem you might have had, and he would be concerned and ask about it. Clay had many life-long friendships. Am I attempting to describe the perfect man? No, but this does illustrate the man I married.

DEE- VIRGO

Dee was born Sept. 8, 1936.

Virgos are practical, logical, thoughtful, well-grounded people. Virgos know that hard work pays off. They aren't afraid to throw themselves into a project, no matter what it takes. They can also be creative.

You'll be hard-pressed to find someone more responsible and reliable than a Virgo. When left in charge, Virgos are sure to take their responsibilities seriously, and they'll always show up when you need them.

Virgos are patient. They're willing to see the best in people and to give them time to shape up their act. (I did put up with Clay for 49 years.)

Virgos are also humble and affectionate and are willing to help others. But Virgo's high standards can also make them overly judgmental and critical towards others. Really? Stubborn, no, not me. ☺ Virgos can be set in their ways. Since they're so dedicated, they often think that they know best. (And most times, we do.)

As critical thinkers, Virgos can also be over-thinkers. Their minds are so busy all the time, thinking about things they need to do or their next project.

Picky? Virgos are pretty set in their ways. Many Virgos are what we'd think of as type A personalities. Part of the Virgo personality is their intensity; They thrive on deep and intellectual connections. They are supportive and loyal romantic partners.

Virgos are perfectionists. They want everything done according to their standards. Exactly! To me, there are three ways to do something. The right way, the wrong way, and my way! I also think that you should "Lead, follow or get out of the way!"

Most of these traits describe Clay and me well. We both were honest and caring, and we worked hard. We worked most of the time. Someone asked me, "What do you do for fun?" I thought about it and then answered, "I work."

Clay was never idle. In the last few years, when his health worsened, he shelled pecans, stripped electrical wire, and kept busy. When I would clean one of the houses, he would say, "What took you so long? I could do that in thirty minutes!" But of course, he never did. ☺

I loved Clay's wit and his quick comebacks. I could hold my own in that department most of the time. Once, we were discussing wages and how much people made now compared to years ago. I said, "Well, I've worked here a long time; when do I get paid?" Clay said, "You get room and board." My instant response, "Yes, sometimes really, really bored!"

One thing about doing something and doing it well is the sense of accomplishment you have when you finish. Clay married me because I didn't mind hard, dusty, dirty, exhausting work. Did we always agree? Of course not. I was amazed at how we approached an issue from different viewpoints, but we came up with the same result.

Once when we were building the Cabin on Comanche Creek, Clay, in complete frustration, said, "Why don't you just do it the way I told you to?" Without hesitation, I shot back, "If I wanted to do it wrong, I'd do it your way, but I don't want to do it over, so I'll do it right the first time."

Clay and I built things. We worked for five years building fences on the ranch. Now, our son can do what we did in a couple of months. We built salt sheds and sheep feeders, cattle pens, and houses. We never thought about it; we just did it.

We also tore down a lot of things. We tore down houses and sheds and barns and salvaged everything. You never knew when you might need something. We have two barns full of now worthless things that we might have needed.

We recycled. We used lumber and materials from things we tore down to build other things. The lumber and windows in the Cabin on Comanche Creek were once part of the Lindsay Country Store.

Mason Mountain Manor is constructed from part of a WWII barracks building from Post, Texas. The Manor's bunk beds are made from the rafters of Doris Kasper Grote's house, which was built in 1925, as is the shiplap in the living area. You can't buy good lumber like that these days.

The 2x8's that we used to build the tables at the Creek were once a porch. I enjoy making something new out of something old. Clay and I didn't hesitate to take on any project. We were proud of our accomplishments.

We remodeled houses. Clay bought at least three that "just needed a little work." Yes, some of those "famous last words."

I needed current income to collect my social security, so I worked for Nolan and Helen Donop at the Donop Feed store for several years. I told Helen, "I may make mistakes, but I won't cheat you. It is your business, and I'll do things the way you want them done, even if it is wrong." We got along just fine.

Clay and I respected, trusted, and loved each other. We were both strong, independent, honest, truthful, and faithful. We never regretted our decision to marry.

Even the experts say that we were compatible. "Leo gives off a radiant warmth and optimistic spirit, which is something that Virgo admires. Virgo is an organized, hard worker, and that quality is very sexy to Leo."

Was Clay perfect? No, and neither was I, but we had a good time together. A card I gave him says it best, "Clay, lots of women marry a guy and then try to change him, but not me. I love you just the way you are. Just don't get any worse!"

38
Mason Friends

Clay grew up in Mason, and nearly everyone was either a friend or a relative. Clay was self-confident, generous, and loyal. His friendships extended to many different types of people. If Clay didn't know a group of people, he wouldn't say anything, but he was outgoing and friendly with people he knew.

I will tell you about three Mason families who knew Clay at different times in his life. The Larimore family, when he was young, the Parker family when he was middle-aged, and the Hudson family, who knew him when he was older.

Clay was born Aug. 15, 1922, so he was a "Leo." I think these words describe him perfectly, "Leo's are known for being committed to an unchanging set of values; if you're lucky enough to be their friend, you'll find that loyalty and dependability in their relationships are two of them. You can also expect your Leo friend to be in your corner no matter what."

Clay was usually the oldest person in any group, but you never thought about his age. He had fun with old and young alike. One of our friends, Carlton Watson, said, "Listening to Clay and my grandsons playing games, it was hard to tell which one was supposed to be the adult."

THE LARIMORE FAMILY

The Lindsay and Larimore families were friends for years. Jesse and Clay played bridge with Willard and Hilda Larimore. When their son, Kenneth Larimore, married Ruth Slusser Sept. 18, 1957, the friendship and bridge playing continued.

Kenneth and Ruth had one son, Mark. Ten months later, Ruth delivered twins named John and Jill. Eleven months later, another son, Joe, was born. They had four children in three years.

Ruth's older brother, Buba, loved to tell the story of how one Mother's Day Ruth did not have any babies and the next Mother's Day she had three. They were not expecting twins with the second birth.

Clay would laugh and say that everyone around the table had a handful of cards and a baby on their lap when they played bridge. As the children grew, Clay and Jill, one of the twins, became remarkably close. He would pick her up and take her with him to the ranch. She spent every minute with him that she could. She said, "Clay saved my life by getting me away from all those boys!"

The friendship lasted a lifetime. Jill Larimore Merritt named her daughter Lindsay.

THE PARKER FAMILY

Clay spent many hours with Ravis Arnold (Cotton) and Elizabeth "Betty" Parker and their family when he was in Mason. At their home, it didn't matter that he was the oldest one there. Clay was one of the family.

When Clay was in town, there was usually a poker game or a domino game at the Parker's. Work to be done. Give me a call. Want to play poker? I'll be there! Supper time, count me in. One of the main reasons that he was such a frequent guest was Betty's cooking.

Clay said, "She makes the best cornbread in the world," and she often sent the left-overs home with him. I watched as she threw things in a bowl, stirred them up, and put the batter in the oven. It was always perfect. When I made it for him, he always said, "It doesn't taste like Betty's."

Clay never said anything about what he did for Cotton and Betty's daughter, Angela. When he was 92, Clay had a heart attack. Angela wrote him a letter. What she wrote was news to me.

We returned to Mason one week after the surgery. A few days later, Oct. 26, 2014, Angela sent Clay a letter. She had heard what happened to Clay, and she wanted to thank him for what he had done for her.

I dreamed about Clay Lindsay last night. As a little girl, I remember going to your store and running around and getting a coke. I remember watching you and Dad play poker. I remember fishing in your pond. There are other things that I have forgotten, but I'll never forget the way you trusted me and believed in me.

You loaned me money to buy a car. I drove that car to my classes on the first day of beauty school. As I didn't have any money, I also slept in that car in the school's parking lot.

You believed in me and trusted in me. If not for you, Clay Lindsay, I wouldn't be where I am today! I will always be grateful for what you did for me. Thank you for believing in that young girl that didn't believe in herself at the time.

Angela worked hard and graduated from Conlee's College of Cosmetology in Kerrville, Texas. Later, she bought Conlee's and established a barber school as well. She sold both those businesses and opened "2 Shops" in Kerrville. Texas.

Angela, a mother, and grandmother strives to be the best that she can be. She continued her education and has never stopped learning. In addition to owning "2 Shops" in Kerrville, Texas, Angela owns A&B Cabin Rentals and Photography @ Angela Parker Beam.

Help someone if you can. What you do might make a difference.

THE HUDSON FAMILY

The Hudson family became friends with Clay in his later years. Wendy Hudson rented the Gamel House, Clay's grandmother's former home, in Mason. Wendy's son Treg and daughter-in-law, Natalie, had two young sons, and of course, Clay made friends with them right away.

The friendship continued as Natalie, and Treg's family grew to seven children. All of them thought that Clay "hung the moon." He kept track of their school activities, visited them at their home, gave them gifts and candy. They were happy to see him coming around the corner.

Clay kept the thank you notes the older boys wrote.

January 12, 1999,

Dear. Mr. Lindsay.

I really like the calf. It is very fun to play with. I love it very much, and it is very healthy.

Love, Jared

James' letter included a drawing of two spotted calves and the name Ferdinan.

Dear Mr. Lindsay,

Thank you much for the calf. It is much better than any cat or dog. It will follow us everywhere. It will frolick and run a lot. In the morning, it will butt the rope and run about, and the girls are in love with it. Thank you!

Love, James.

All the Hudson children grew to be fine young men and women. Some are married, with children. Their grandmother, Wendy Hudson, owns and operates Market Square in Mason, Texas. Stop in and tell her that Clay said hello.

Clay at Buzzin Cousins. Clay on the right, brother Jack with eye patch across from him.

39
Our Lives
1972 - 1999

Clay and I married Oct. 30, 1971. Clay's father, John Alva Lindsay, died March 30, 1974. Our daughter, Alica Kay Lindsay. was born Jan. 7, 1975, and our son, Clay Haley Lindsay, was born Nov. 6, 1976.

We lived on the Ranch and drove 260 miles to our business in Garza County every week until 1980, when Alica started school. For the next twelve years, the children and I stayed at our home, next to the store, so they could attend school in Crosbyton, Texas. They rode the bus 20 miles each way, each day.

Clay continued to commute from the Ranch to the store each week. Clay's mother, Jesse Gamel Lindsay, died March 23, 1987. Her daughters held a large auction and sold most of Jesse's things. Clay kept three pieces of furniture and a few items that had belonged to his grandmother, Alice Kettner Gamel.

Clay's sister, Effie Lindsay Long, died June 1, 1989. A few days later, there was a large estate sale. I worked the day and night before to make sure that everything was ready for the auction. The yard at the Gamel House was covered with tables and tables of Effie's treasures.

Eighteen days later, June 19, 1989, Clay's brother, Jack Gamel Lindsay, committed suicide. Jack usually went to his friend, Robert Bow's house each morning. When he didn't arrive, Robert came to the Ranch to check on him and found him dead on the step.

Jack's six children lived worldwide: Sherry in New Zealand, Carolyn in New Jersey, Alica in Arizona, John in Iowa, Tom in Australia, and Jay in Illinois.

I authored a poem entitled "The Shot in the Dark."

> The June night was quiet, the man all alone
> As he sat on the step by the door.
> What were his thoughts? What made him decide,
> "I don't want to live anymore?"
> Was it sadness, sorrow, depression, despair?
> Were his burdens too many, too heavy to bear?
> Or could it have been, "I just don't care!"
> Why we wonder, we ask, but the answers aren't there.
> We loved him, but we couldn't stop him,
> We didn't know the thoughts of his heart.
> No ear heard the sound, but it spread the world 'round,
> The sound of the Shot in the Dark.

The big house burned. Arson was suspected. After Jack's death, his former wife, Doris Anderson, claimed the entire property. After a lawsuit, the day before the case was to go to the jury, we reached a settlement. Clay bought out Jack's former wife, and then he bought each of Jack's six children's share of the Ranch.

After that, Clay moved from the Mason Mountain portion of the ranch to the house where Jack had lived. We sold our share of White Top and moved to a new location about ½ mile south of the store.

Alica and I lived there until 1993, when she graduated from Crosbyton High School, finishing second in her class. She was the salutatorian. That fall, Alica attended college at Southwest Texas State University, now Texas State University, in San Marcos, Texas.

Our son, Clay Haley Lindsay, moved to Mason in 1992 and lived with his dad. He joined the Marine Corps when he was a senior, and upon graduation from Mason High School in May 1995, he immediately went to the Marine Corps Recruit Depot in San Diego, Calif., for thirteen weeks of recruit training.

Alva Clay and I, and Mendy Beaty, Clay Haley's future wife, drove to San Diego and attended his graduation ceremony in September 1995. It was very impressive.

Clay's specialty was Aviation Electronics. He attended school in Tennessee. He worked on the Harrier Jet, and where his plane went, he went, and that was sometimes Yuma, AZ. Clay was stationed at the Marine Corps Air Station, Cherry Point, Havelock, N.C. for most of his tour.

Neither Clay nor I had attended regular worship services for many years. When I decided to get back where I belonged, the children and I worshiped with the Church of Christ in Crosbyton and Post. When we moved to Mason, Clay joined us. One Sunday, when the invitation was given at the end of the worship service, Clotilda Arrowsmith, a feisty, beautiful young lady in her 80's, went forward and said that she wanted to be baptized. She was immersed that morning.

On our way home, Clay said, "I'm ready." I didn't know what he was talking about, so I asked, "Ready for what?" He replied, "I'm ready to be baptized. If she can do it, I can do it. But I don't want a big crowd." I immediately called the preacher, Don Norwood, when we got home and shared the good news. We drove back to Mason, and Clay was immersed that afternoon." Of course, I shed tears of joy.

Thank you, Clotilda, for your courage, your example, and your love for the Lord.

40
Our Lives
2000 – 2019

L etters to family and friends give an idea of what was happening in our lives.

2000

The year 2000, Y2K, was a busy year for the Lindsay's. Yes, we two worked a lot. In February, we tore down the old hunting cabin in the back pasture. We started building another at the base of Mason Mountain. I worked part-time at Donop's Feed and Hardware Store. We worked on the Cabin until the middle of June.

In June, we went to North Carolina to help Clay H. move his accumulation of stuff, including two trucks and four cars, back to Mason. We had a good time, saw some Louisiana plantations, met many friendly people, and made new friends.

We also brought a ditch digger back with us, and we used it to dig a water line from the windmill to the Cabin. We dug a ditch approximately 3,000 feet long. Getting water and power to the Cabin site was a BIG job, and Clay H. was a big help.

We remodeled a rent house on Westmoreland into the Townhouse, our second B&B, in August and September.

On Labor Day, we went to the South Llano at Junction and spent the day floating

Clay – always a working man.
Photo by: Betty & Gene Elders,
April 2009

on the river with the Cross and Weaver families. Everyone had a good time. Then, it was back to work.

Mason Mountain Manor, the new hunting Cabin, is a work in progress. It was livable when hunting season started. It will be finished next year and will be our third B&B.

We watched the grass burn up for the first nine months of 2000 and the tanks dry up. Then, after five years of drought, things changed in October. The Lord blessed us with more rain in October than we had all year. The tanks are full, the creek is running, the grass is green, and it looks like spring.

FYI: I am still a slave laborer on the Ranch. Daddy Clay supervises a lot.

2002

We never made a big fuss over birthdays, but in 2002, when Clay would be 80 years old, I decided that a party was in order. That was the most significant event of 2002. Clay's nieces and nephews, plus old and new friends, came to Mason to celebrate with him.

I wrote an article about this party, and it was published in the Mason County News Aug. 28, 2002.

ALVA CLAY LINDSAY'S 80TH BIRTHDAY

Mason County News August 28, 2002

"Around Town and County"

Alva Clay Lindsay Celebrates 80th Birthday.

Clay Lindsay was born on August 15, 1922. Family and friends from around the world came to Mason on August 2 and 3 for a family reunion and celebrated Clay's 80th Birthday.

The Picnic in the Park Friday, August 2, was attended by 150 friends and family members who enjoyed sandwiches, watermelon, brownies, memories, and Wendy Hudson's wonderful Lemon Drop cake.

After shopping, swimming, and throwing Unkie in the pool, the party continued Saturday, August 3, with the Bash in the Barn. James and Shannon Worrell hosted the Lindsay family at their beautiful new barn. Shannon Worrell and her dad, Glen Grote, who brought his big rig from Oklahoma, cooked and served steak, potatoes, and salad to 60 guests.

After dinner, several nieces and nephews told stories of growing up with Clay. This roast was the highlight of the evening. The Bash ended with Shannon's Chocolate Earthquake Cake, ice cream, and fireworks.

Sunday's activities included breakfast at Willow Creek Cafe, church, a trip to Fredericksburg, swimming, ranch tours, and a special work project at the Lindsay Cemetery. Several nephews cut weeds, fixed the fence, and learned more about their ancestors buried there. The day ended with BBQ, dominoes, pitch games, and visiting at the Cabin on Comanche Creek.

Zavala's, Crosby Cemetery, Old Yeller at the Mason County Library, the Gamel House, White's Crossing on the Llano River, and the Eckert James River Bat Cave were points of interest on Monday, August 5.

More than a dozen guests traveled to Padre Island, where the party continued at the home of Mike, Jennifer, and Peggy Davis. The weeklong celebration ended Friday, August 9, with a tour of the River Walk and lunch at Mexican Manhattan in downtown San Antonio.

Clay has always loved children. He had 12 nieces and nephews before he had children of his own. These excerpts from his "Memory Book" tell why so many came from so far to wish Unkie Happy Birthday.

"Clay - Thanks for giving us a home after WW II, for trying to teach me to work, for teaching me how to save money, and for being a fine Man. We love you." John Long

"When summer came, Mom would tell us kids that our Uncle Clay, better known as Unkie, would be driving up from Texas to pick up whoever wanted to spend the summer there. I didn't go often, but I vividly remember one trip.

Less than a half-hour after arriving at Daddy John's house, I stepped on a nail! It went all the way through my shoe and out the top of my foot! Needless to say, Unkie did not rush me to the hospital.

Instead, he had me soak my foot in kerosene for hours; then, he carried me around for a few days until I was better. My foot healed just fine with no infection. I guess Unkie knows more about kerosene than I gave him credit for. Thanks for taking care of me." Love, Lisa Marshall

"When I was a little girl, Unkie would always bring me lemon drops! Thanks for the memories!" Love Debbie.

"Thank you for being you! Thanks for being there for me whenever I needed it most. Knowing you were only a phone call away has always been a comfort. Thanks for everything." Love, Pam

"I did not get to be with Unkie as much as Tom and John. Mom kept me at home, and I didn't get to come to the ranch as often as I would have liked. I will always remember Unkie knee grabbing and Pitch playing.

At the time, I thought that was incredible due to my not understanding the art of the game. I will also never forget some of the chairs breaking at the Spoons game. Unkie, you will always be remembered by my family at the Ultimate Cowboy." Jay Sam Lindsay

"In the late '50s and '60s, I read the Burma Shave signs from Iowa to Mason County every summer. I loved traveling with Unkie. He would come in the Rambler, pick me up, and deliver me to the Ranch. Unkie knew how much I loved being at the Ranch, and I still do.

A person needs a pivot point - a point of return - for me, that point is five miles north of Mason on US 87, across Comanche Creek. My Uncle hugging me and saying, "If you ever need help, call me." That's what makes me strong. Thank you for being there for me." I love you dearly. Sherry

Lindsay family members in attendance included:

Alva Clay, Deloris, and Clay Haley Lindsay, Mason, Texas; Alica Lindsay, Richardson, Texas.

Doris Lindsay Dobbs, Debbie, Lance, and Tiffany Green, Canyon, Texas.

Peggy Lindsay Davis, Mike and Jennifer Porter Davis, Padre Island, Texas; Lauren and Jordan Davis, New Albany, IN; Gary and Lindsay Davis Lyons, Heltonville, IN; Kevin and Erin Trisler, Bloomington, IN.

Sherry Lindsay, Phoenix, AZ; Olivia Baker, Auckland, NZ.

Joe and Carolyn Lindsay Schwartz, NJ.

Bill and Alica Lindsay Marshall, Phoenix, AZ.

John Clay Lindsay, Council Bluffs, IA.

Tom and Janet Lindsay, Blaxland, NSW Australia.

Jay, Maurine, Carrie, Jaime, and Brian Lindsay, Chicago, IL.

John and Ruth Long, Irving, Texas; Bryan Long, San Francisco, CA. Christy Long, Washington, DC; and Barbara Long, Fairway, KS.

Jane Dunn Sibley, Austin, Texas; and Kathleen Crosby St. Clair, Eldorado, Texas.

Other family and out-of-town friends who made the party a great success were: Zeph and Pamela Haley Bruce, Lubbock, Texas.

Carroll and Alan Johnson, Hurst, Texas.

Jerry, Donna, Hannah and Jordan Weaver, Wolfforth, Texas.

Lana and Cody Cross, Wilson, Texas; Leland Brieger, Fredericksburg, Texas; Juanell Brieger McMillan, Slaton, Texas.

Dennis, Kaitlin, and Shannon Murphy, League City, Texas; Cody Boyle, League City, Texas.

Bill and Gloria Woodard, San Antonio, Texas; and our newest friend, Dennis Gorski, Mission Viejo, CA.

Thank you for coming. It was a wonderful reunion."

After the festivities, it was back to everyday life on the Ranch. Daddy Clay moved cattle, shelled pecans, played dominoes, and waited for hunting season to end. I managed to stay busy.

2002 brought both joy and sorrow. Clay's 80th Birthday was a great success, but Peggy Lindsay Davis's death saddened us on December 2. There was a celebration of her life in May 2003. At her request, Peggy's family scattered her ashes on Mason Mountain.

Peggy's son-in-law, Gary Lyons, a talented stonemason from Bedford, Indiana, crafted the perfect monument, brought it to Mason, and installed it on Mason Mountain. This beautiful spire with a vertical engraving of the name "LINDSAY" is a work of art. Well done, Gary, well done.

A second monument now stands atop Mason Mountain. On March 27, 2021, family and friends came to the Lindsay Ranch to say goodby to Alva Clay Lindsay. To honor his dad, Clay Haley Lindsay created an impressive eight-foot-tall metal cross of 8" channel iron and installed it on the southern tip of Mason Mountain. It is visible from many parts of the Ranch.

When I asked a recent Mason Mountain Manor guest to describe it, Mr. Brown responded, "It is inspirational."

2004

Clay Haley Lindsay and Mendy Lanise Beaty, the daughter of William and Patricia Garrett Beaty, were married Oct. 23rd. More than two hundred guests attended the wedding. Lindsay family and friends from Texas, Colorado, Indiana, and New Zealand came to celebrate with them. Shannon and James Worrell hosted the events.

Their new show barn was the site of the rehearsal dinner. Deloris Lindsay, the groom's mother, served beef stew, cornbread, pecan pie, chocolate chip cookies, and a cheesecake with jalapeno jelly topping.

Many Mason friends donated their time and toil to transform a hillside in the pasture into a beautiful outdoor wedding venue. The show barn and wedding area were decorated in fall colors with pumpkins, corn stalks, and gourds. Chairs were provided for the wedding party dressed in formal attire. The invitation suggested casual dress for the guests as they would be walking across the pasture and sitting on bales of hay.

The plan was to have a short ceremony and a good party. That is what happened. It was a real shotgun wedding. The invitation read, "Bring your shotgun and shells. A skeet shoot will follow the ceremony."

 A beautiful horse-drawn carriage, driven by Mr. Chuck Bearden, transported Mendy and her dad, William, from the dressing area to the wedding site. To the bride's chagrin, her dad carried his shotgun as he escorted her down the aisle. The bride's uncle, Cecil Rice, a Baptist minister, performed the ceremony. When he asked, "Does anyone have any reason why these two should not be joined in marriage?" The crowd erupted in laughter because the carriage horse neighed and shook his head.

Driscol Draper, Heather Hudson, and Ashley Scantlin photographed the event. Their photographs provide lasting memories of that special day. Mendy won the skeet shoot that followed the wedding ceremony. Watch out, Clay, don't mess with her!

The reception was held in the Worrell's show barn. Roddy Stockbridge and Randy Kruse prepared a delicious BBQ meal, and a live band supplied music for the event. It was a wonderful party.

When I asked what people remembered about that day, they said, "It was a great party. We had a lot of fun." Well done, Beaty family.

2006

The severe drought of 2006 covered several states, including much of Texas.

We're still in a drought, but we didn't have any grass fires. We didn't have enough grass to burn.

Comanche Creek and three tanks (ponds to those who live north of the Mason-Dixon Line) went dry. We asked everyone to pray for tank water. A few days later, God blessed us with 1 ½" of rain, and the following week He finished filling the tanks with another 2". Thank you, Lord!

Instead of going places this year, we stayed at home and, you guessed it, fed cows. Last week we sold 33 head. No rain, no grass, no option! Since Clay is a pet farmer instead of a rancher, this was long overdue.

He always keeps some "replacement" heifers, but he doesn't sell any old cows, so the herd keeps growing and growing and growing. We still have TOO MANY. We're burning prickly pear and feeding cattle cubes to get them through the winter.

FYI this is how you burn pear. First, buy a Reeves Pear Burner. It is a propane tank with a flame thrower attached to it by a hose. Next, fill it with propane, strap it on. When filled, it weighs a little over 40 pounds. Set a feed sack on fire so you can get the flame thrower working.

Then you try to avoid being trampled by 40 or 50 hungry cows as you burn the stickers (thorns) off the prickly pear pads. The thorns turn bright red, then make an ash of themselves and fall off. The cattle love them. Want to taste it? Go to the Mexican Food section of the grocery store and buy a jar of Nopalitos.

When we're not feeding cows, we are taking care of B&B guests. We also allow people to walk around the Ranch and look for rocks for a small fee.

We've been blessed with good health, and of course, we'll brag about our children. Alica enjoys living in the big city of Richardson. Clay H. is busy with his business, Lindsay Electric. When he has any free time, his dad manages to find something for him to do.

With cows, guesthouses, rock hunters, and our dear deer hunters, to care for, we are never bored. One day Clay was sitting on the porch, looking out the window at the little hole of water and the brown ground, complaining about it being so DRY. I asked, "Where would you rather be?" He couldn't think of any place better than right here. That sums up our situation in 2006. God has blessed us, and we are content.

2007

The outstanding event of 2007 occurred June 21 in Fredericksburg, Texas, when our one and only grandchild, Garrett Clay Lindsay, was born. Garrett, your grandpa Clay was proud of you, and he loved you very much, even though he yelled at you when you beat him playing Pitch.

2008

Clay was 86 in August. He is healthy and he exists on peanut butter, sweet tea, Pepsi, lemon drops, milkshakes, brownies, and anything that has sugar in it. He doesn't go to the doctor, but he has been going to the back pasture for six hours or so each day, checking cows and cutting brush the old-fashioned way, by hand.

The price of feed is up, cattle prices are down, and we need rain. Other than that, all is well. We need to repair fences next year. We have the equipment to clear the right-of-way and to rake the brush. When son Clay comes out and uses it, it makes a difference in a hurry.

We repaired the fence we were working on in 1975 when Alica was a baby. Now, son Clay H. is working on it. Thirty years from now, Garrett Clay Lindsay can do it. Oh yes, speaking of Garrett, our brilliant grandson, He is a joy.

We had company this year, and Clay put them to work. Sherry cleaned up inside and out while she was here. When Zeph Bruce, our nephew from Lubbock, came, he and I built new front steps to the porch and built shelves in the Manor.

Clay's 2nd cousin, Jack Alan Lindsay, died Nov. 10, 2008. If you have received any Lindsay family history from me, it is due to Jack and Peggy's work. (Yes, they have the same name as Clay's brother and sister) Jack's grandfather, John Hamilton Lindsay, and Clay's grandfather, Alva James Lindsay, were brothers.

Jack Alan and Peggy Bue Lindsay worked for years compiling Lindsay family information. They shared it with me, and I have shared it with you. Jack was planning to publish a Lindsay Family History. Jack, I hope you approve of what I have done with your invaluable information.

Clay and I are blessed and thankful that we can do what we need to do.

2009

The outstanding events of 2009 were related to Alica's wedding.

June 2009 – Mason

In June, family and friends came to the Lindsay Ranch to celebrate Alica and Taylor's upcoming wedding and Garrett Clay Lindsay's second Birthday.

Debbie and Tiffany Green brought everything they needed and decorated the Cabin on Comanche Creek. Since the wedding was to take place in Las Vegas, Mendy Beaty Lindsay created a beautiful cake in the shape of a roulette wheel.

Lindsay's know how to party, and everyone had a good time. We played cards, toured the Ranch, Mason, and Fredericksburg, and went to a private pool party to celebrate Garrett's Birthday.

October 2009

Alica spent months planning her wedding, and everything went as planned. Alica Kay Lindsay and Taylor Porter were married Oct. 10, 2009, in the Mandalay Bay Wedding Chaple in Las Vegas, NV.

Our nephew, Mike Davis, picked us up at the Ranch in his black Cadillac, and we drove to Las Vegas. Mike was impressed when I started loading our beautiful black soft-side luggage into the car. Well, I put almost everything in garbage bags, but the color matched the car, and everything fit perfectly.

Mike and I took turns driving, and of course, Clay was the passenger. He paid particular attention to the big rigs on I-10. In true Lindsay style, we only ate at the best places, Taco Bell and McDonald's. Mike tried to vary the Mexican restaurant choice in El Paso, but they didn't measure up to Taco Bell.

To say that Clay was a picky eater would be putting it mildly. When I first met him, he would only eat a grilled cheese sandwich at a restaurant. He said, "They can't mess that up too bad." After we had children, I got him to drink a McDonald's milkshake and eat some French fries.

I prepared a food bag for Clay when we traveled. I took a jar of peanut butter, crackers, instant tea, sugar, lemon drops, and Pepsi. I enjoy breakfast out, so I would order my food and a cup of hot water for Clay. He would prepare his hot tea and eat peanut butter and crackers, and he was well satisfied.

When we arrived in Vegas, we stayed two nights at the South Point Hotel, Casino & Spa, a new resort located just minutes away from the famous Las Vegas Strip. Mike and Clay enjoyed the Casino.

Alica rented a spacious four-bedroom guesthouse for the event. Not only did we have nice bedrooms and kitchen facilities, a game room and pool table, but the patio and outdoor area were large and well equipped. Some guests enjoyed the swimming pool.

Family and friends from Texas, California, and Colorado joined us Friday night for a cook-out. After the meal, visiting and playing Pitch, the youngsters went out on the town. Reports are that the bachelor and bachelorette parties were enjoyable. We old folks went to bed.

Saturday morning was busy. The women made sure that their hair, make-up, dresses, and accessories were perfect, and the men went to be fitted with their formal attire.

At Mandalay Bay, the ceremony in the Wedding Chapel was well done. Alica's 87-year-old Dad, looking very handsome in his tuxedo, proudly walked his beautiful daughter down the aisle.

I was the designated family photographer. I couldn't take photos in the Chapel, but I took many pictures after the main event. Our last stop was at the iconic "Welcome to Las Vegas" sign. I was the last to hear about Clay being propositioned while I was performing my photographic duties.

"What happens in Vegas stays in Vegas!"

After the wedding, Mike Davis' job was to take care of his Uncle Clay and get him back to the guesthouse. Mike recently told me this story. "There were several events at Mandalay Bay that day, and I had to park a few blocks away.

After the wedding, we were leaving, and Unk, still dressed in his tux, was having trouble walking in those fancy shoes, so, to save him a long walk, I told him that I would get the car and pick him up.

I settled him by the door of a bar. "I'll get the car. When you see me drive up, come on out." About ten minutes later, I drove up in front, but no one came out. "I'm sorry, sir, but you can't park here." a doorman said. I asked, "Did you see an old guy sitting here?" "Oh, yes, he's inside at the bar." My Uncle Clay doesn't drink anything stronger than Pepsi or iced tea, so I knew something was up. I gave the guy a tip to let me park long enough to get my uncle.

Sure enough, Unk was sitting on a barstool, surrounded by beautiful women. Two blondes and a brunette. They were talking and laughing and having a good time. I went up and said, "Unk, we have to go. He replied, "I'm not going anywhere!"

Clay was extremely hard of hearing, but instead of wearing hearing aids, he would usually smile and nod when someone talked to him. A few minutes later, I said, "Unk, these ladies are Pro's!" "Pro's he said, pros at what?" I told him. He looked at one of the blondes and when she nodded her head, Unk, a man of few words, said, "Let's go!" An old guy wearing a tuxedo probably has money. If you are a working girl, it never hurts to ask.

The wedding reception was held at the guesthouse. To end the day's festivities, the wedding party and guests went to Caesar's Palace. We ate at the TREVI Italian Restaurant on the mezzanine level overlooking the fountain and the surrounding plaza.

TREVI is named after the Fontana di Trevi in Rome, one of the world's most famous fountains. Legend holds that if visitors to the fountain throw a coin into the water, they are ensured a return trip to Rome. TREVI staff believes the same is true here in Las Vegas: throw a coin into the 'Fountain of the Gods,' and you'll be sure to return.

After dinner at TREVI's, the young people continued partying on the Las Vegas Strip. The older ones went back to the guesthouse. Of course, there was more visiting and Pitch playing.

Thanks to months of meticulous planning by Alica, everything went well.

On our way back to Mason, Mike, Clay, and I drove to Scottsdale, AZ. Mike had planned to meet a friend there. When we had difficulty finding a place to spend the night, I called my sister, Pam Bruce, in Lubbock, Texas.

She found a motel in Scottsdale that was not far from the highway and made our reservations. We arrived, settled in, went to bed but about midnight, the power went out in a twenty-block area. Power was restored at about 7 a.m.

We three spent a hot night in Scottsdale. Even though they had no control over the situation, the motel comped our stay. On top of that, Mike's buddy didn't show! It was a night to remember.

We had been gone nearly a week when we drove through the Lindsay Ranch gate at midnight. It was good to be home. Thank you, Mike Davis, for everything.

November – Dallas

After we recovered from the Las Vegas trip, Clay and I drove to Richardson, Texas, in November.

A wedding reception was held for Alica and Taylor Nov. 7 at the Tower Club in Downtown Dallas. It was a sit-down dinner for 100 guests.

Guests from the Lindsay family included Clay and Mendy Lindsay, Mike and Jennifer Davis, Janet Lee (Dolly), Hannon, Pam, Zeph Bruce and Carroll, and Alan Johnson.

Alica did it again. The party could not have been better. Alica, Pam, Zeph, Clay, and I spent most of the day making sure that everything was like she wanted it to be.

Most of the guests had arrived, but Mike and Jennifer Davis were missing.

Jennifer's Birthday was November 7, and she and Mike had been in Dallas for a few days. They were staying in a nice hotel a few blocks from where the reception was to be held. On Saturday, they took a cab to the Tower and asked for directions to the Lindsay Reception.

A young lady led them to a nicely decorated room. Even though neither Mike nor Jennifer recognized anyone, someone said, "I'm so glad you're here You can tell us what needs to be done." There was a nice bar and smoked salmon appetizers. Mike made Jennifer a Martini and fixed his drink, and they settled in to enjoy the evening. They still didn't recognize anyone, but perhaps these were Taylor's friends and family.

After half an hour, Mike noticed a card reading, "Congratulations, Lindsey and Steve" or something like that. Lindsey and Steve? Who were they?

Mike and Jennifer found another Tower employee and said, "We are looking for the Lindsay-Porter party. "Come with me, the employee said. Finally, the Davis Wedding Crashers arrived at the right party, which was already in full swing.

Janet Lee (Dolly) Long Hannon was the last to arrive, and everyone had a good time. After the party was over, Mike, Jennifer, Clay, Mendy, Alica, Taylor, Dolly, and a few other friends continued celebrating at the Karaoke Bar.

As a gift to the out-of-town guests, I rented rooms for several of them on the hotel's fourth floor. There was a 25-year high school reunion in the suite next to our room. Pam and Zeph's room was at the other end of the hall.

The party continued all night long with people coming and going, laughing, singing, partying, and having a wonderful time. The music was so loud that the headboard of my bed was shaking. I called the front desk at 2 a.m. and it was quiet for thirty minutes or so. 87-year-old Clay, who was practically deaf, and 13-year-old Zeph Bruce were the only two people on the fourth floor who slept that night.

We cleaned up and took everything back to Alica's house, and her dad and her cousin Zeph were thrilled with the leftover candy from the Candy Bar. Clay went home with full pockets plus two or three bags of candy. Zeph made many friends on the flight back to Lubbock by sharing candy with everyone on the plane.

Well done, Alica.

2010

On Aug. 10, 2010, we celebrated Clay's 88th Birthday with a party at the Richard P. Eckert Civic Center in Mason. Over one hundred friends and family members came to wish Clay a happy birthday. Some wrote comments in the guest register.

"Clay, Wow, it looks like I am the first to get to sign your book. I just wanted to say "Thank You" for everything you did to help me during the past years. If it wasn't for your help, I might not be where I am today. You are a great and wonderful man. We are all better people because we know you. Happy Birthday." Love, Angela Parker Wollman

"Happy Birthday, Bolivar. Of my 56 years, you have been my favorite Uncle and person. I cherish all of our time together. You're taught me a lot that I apply every day. I love you and wish 88 more birthdays with you." Nephew Mike

"Dad, Happy Birthday! You are a great dad and friend. I appreciate all you have done for me throughout the years!" Love, Alica

"Dear Unkie, I have always loved you. You mean the world to me and everyone who knows you. Thanks for the memories!" Love, Debbie (Your niece.)

"Clay, I hope you have a great 88th. Birthday! I figure it must be pretty important since we got in a day and a half prior to the party." Lance

"Unkie, we are so glad we were able to come to your 88th Birthday. We love you so much!" Tiffany and Canon

"Happy, Happy Birthday, Clay! Love you lots!" Donna, Jerry, Jordan, and Hannah Weaver

"Clay, you have been a blessing (sometimes in disguise) to my entire family. God bless your old bones and young heart." Wendy Hudson

2011

The most significant change in our lives this year was brought about by the drought. We received about 4" of rain in 15 months. Son Clay used our bulldozer and cleaned out five earth tanks while they were dry. He also put a water trough in each pasture. We hope to drill a new well soon.

(We drilled three dry holes. Several months later, we did get water about ten feet from the last dry hole.)

In August, we received 3 ½" of rain; now we have tank water but still have no grass and won't have any for another year, if then. We sold all our cattle except for 19 calves.

Many ranchers, large and small, have been forced to sell or ship their cattle out of Texas. Clay's grandfather, John Gamel (You can read the story of his life in previous chapters.), drove cattle north in the 1870s and 1880s.

Son Clay helped us haul our cattle. We had no truck, we used his, no trailer, we borrowed a big one from a neighbor, bad pens, bad gates, and we couldn't load them by ourselves. We had no grass and no water. We had no business being in the cattle business.

This year we built a new fence on the east side of the Ranch. Now we have the best fence we've ever had, water in the tanks, and only five donkeys and deer in the back pasture.

2012

The major event of 2012 was Clay's 90th Birthday party.

Clay H. rebuilt the fence along the highway and the south side of the property with his dad's supervision. Clay also designed and built the new entryway. He completed it just in time for his dad's party.

The 90th Birthday was a big three-day affair, and many families and friends attended. On Friday, we met at the Gamel House for food, visiting, and pitch playing. The guys played all night. Clay came home with his pockets full of quarters.

Everyone was invited. The invitation was also published in the Mason County News.

"The family of Alva Clay Lindsay invites you to join us as we celebrate his 90th Birthday, Sat., August 11, at the Richard P. Eckert Civic Center, 1024 McKinley St., Mason. Texas.

We will be in and out all day, and we will try to have the birthday boy there at 4 p.m. Come and go or come and stay. There will be tables set up for cards, dominoes, Skip-Bo, and visiting. We hope that you will join us for BBQ at 6 p.m."

It was a repeat of Clay's 88th Birthday, only larger. More than 100 people attended.

Clay's longtime friend Charles Perry (C. P.) Ray and his family drove 350 miles from Etoile, Texas, to Mason. Even though his health was not good, C. P. told his daughter, Teresa Welch, "I want to go to Clay's party," and she made it happen. What a wonderful surprise. Thank you for coming. It made Clay's Day.

Sunday, the family got together and played cards. What, you ask, did I do all that time? I worked, and so did everyone else that I asked to help. Thanks, everyone, for everything.

2013

In 2013, Clay wanted to take a trip, so he made a list of people and places he wanted to visit. I started making plans and plans and plans. I was to be the tour guide and chauffeur.

Everyone we visited were working people, so I planned to be at their homes over a weekend and find something to do during the week that Clay would enjoy. He enjoyed playing poker, so I added casinos to the list.

Our niece, Sherry Lindsay from New Zealand, was visited in early June. After her departure, we loaded the Jeep Liberty that I rented and started driving west June 14, 2013. (Seven years later, June 14, 2020, Clay would leave this world and begin his eternal journey.)

Our first stop was Phoenix, Arizona. We visited Clay's niece, Alica Lindsay Marshall, and her family. They were having a pool party when we arrived, and all had a good time.

Alica and Sherry spent the next day, Father's Day, with us. We played cards (of course). Monday morning, we headed to Las Vegas, Nevada, to play poker (Clay won). Then on to Bakersfield, California where we visited great-nephew Jason Geis and his family (we saw 17,000 oil wells). The next stop was Sacramento, California to see Frances and Oscar Chroust, the Railroad Museum, and another casino (Clay won again).

From Sacramento, we drove to Nevada City, California, and visited with David and Tonya Lindsay. We played cards and dominos and went to Lake Tahoe.

Reno, Nevada was our next stop. Clay played more poker (he broke even). Our daughter, Alica, flew out from Dallas and joined us for a few days. From Reno, we went to Salt Lake City, Utah. We played tourist and went to Temple Square. The drive through Utah was beautiful.

In Durango, Colorado, we visited with great-nephew Clay Long and family and rode the narrow-gauge railroad to Silverton. After a picnic lunch, we went back to their home for more visiting and (of course) card-playing.

We left Durango on Sunday morning and drove toward Santa Fe, New Mexico. We visited an old Spanish church in Chimayo, New Mexico, and the Loretto Chapel on the Santa Fe Trail in downtown Santa Fe. There we saw the miracle staircase. Google it. It is amazing. We would not have found these places if not for my trusty Garmin Nuvi 50 GPS.

From Santa Fe, we headed toward Texas. We drove and drove and drove through New Mexico; not much to see but long flat roads. We stopped in Clovis at Taco Bell, Clay's favorite place to eat, and called my sister Pam. She reserved a room for us at a Holiday Inn in Lubbock. We checked in at 10 p.m.

This trip was Clay's idea, but every morning, I could hear him whispering, "I wish I were home; I wish I were home!" We were back in Texas, and we were getting closer and closer to home.

We had planned to stop in Canyon, Texas, to see our niece Debbie Green and family, but they were on vacation in San Antonio! Our final party was at my sister's home in Lubbock. Pam Haley Bruce invited Debbie and her family, Lana Cross, Donna and Hannah Weaver, Juanell McMillan, Theron, and Carlton Tanner, and Don and Sherry Byers to meet at her house. It was a grand finale to our trip.

The next day, Clay finally got his wish. He was HOME on July 9. He said he didn't think he would ever leave home again! We traveled 4,876 miles through seven states without any problems. Thank you, Lord!

Since July, we have had some rain but, we are still in a drought. We have not restocked the Ranch with cattle. I drove every mile of our trip, and Clay looked out the window. Every state we traveled through needed rain. Clay said, "I've never seen so much worthless land in all my life!"

We have a new south fence and a new road to the back of the Ranch. Son Clay did an outstanding job, even with his dad's supervision. If you haven't visited in a while, come on down, it is great!

To finish out this year of first's, we are looking forward to a visit from Clay Long and his family during Christmas week.

Clay's great-niece, Erin Geis Trisler, shared some of her memories from 2013. "Christmas Wishes, submitted by Erin Trisler.

While I appreciate the reason for the season, generally speaking, Christmas isn't usually my schtick. Indiana Decembers equates to short days with bone-chilling cold; the month is busy but too long for me. Thank goodness my immediate family loves it because they keep me in good spirits.

Now and again, some gifts top all other gifts. In 2013, my niece Maddie Marie Geis was born (and shares my middle name!), and Dee and I exchanged the following emails. What follows is a fun summertime nugget of history.

From: Erin Trisler
To: Deloris Lindsay
Sent: Wed., Dec. 18, 2013, 9:43 a.m.
Subject: Re: Merry Christmas

I loved reading about your travels! Next time, please tell Unkie he needs to head north to Indiana.

My kiddos need to learn how to play Pitch so they can beat up on him, in cards, that is. 😊 Love galore from the Hoosier state to the Lonestar state!

From: Deloris Lindsay
To: Erin Trisler
Sent: Wed., Dec. 18, 2013, 11:36 a.m.
Subject: Great minds!

Erin. You won't believe this, but yesterday Clay said, "Well, maybe after the first of the year, we can take another trip and go to Indiana. I'd like to see Erin and her family!"

2014

Last year we went west to visit family and friends. This year Clay decided to see his friends and family who live east of us, so I planned another trip.

We rented a car and drove first to Center, Texas, where we visited the Watson and Koonce, families. Then we went to a Casino in Shreveport.

I promised Clay that he could stop at every Casino we passed. If he saw a billboard or a sign, we would stop, and we did. Our first visit with family was in Indiana.

In Indiana, we visited Clay's niece, Lindsay Davis Trapp, and her husband, Brian, in Seymour. We played a few games of cards, of course, and enjoyed the food and friendship. From Seymour, Clay, Lindsay, and I drove to Indianapolis.

We visited with Lindsay's daughter, Erin Geis Trisler, her husband Kevin, daughter Georgia and son Grant in Indianapolis. Everyone joined in the card games; the usual Lindsay family trash talk flew around the table along with the cards and quarters. Laughter, tall tales, and teasing added to the fun. Clay loved every minute of it.

Erin wrote, "Come June 2014, Indiana didn't know what hit it. There was a lot of Skip-Bo, Pitch, laughs, memory-making, lemon drops, iced tea, lap-sitting for the kids, and long sunny days with beloved Texas family in our midst.

(If we'd had a pool, Unkie would've pushed us all in, no doubt!) I could never have dreamed that Aunt Dee and Unkie would head north. I am so grateful to this day that they did."

After Indiana and Chicago, we worked our way back home through Iowa, Kansas, Oklahoma, and Texas. We visited Alica in Garland and then a few more friends in East Texas before returning to Mason.

We saw green, beautiful, bountiful crops, and water everywhere on this trip.

We had no trouble of any kind. The rented VW handled beautifully, and Clay came home with so many quarters and nickels that he could hardly carry them. He was a happy, happy man.

Our trip, by the numbers:

- Three weeks four days
- 4040 miles
- 11 states
- 23 cities (some twice)
- 51 family and friends (some twice)
- 15 casinos
- Many stops at Taco Bell and McDonald's.
- Card games, Pitch, Skip-Bo, and poker, too many to count.
- Dominoes, at least ten games, Jim Biefeldt didn't win any!
- My jobs: Tour guide, chauffeur, porter, maid, and butler.
- Clay's job: Passenger.

Thank you, Lord. We are happy to be home.

2014 - FIRST FLIGHT

A couple of weeks after we got home, we received an invitation to David Alan Lindsay's 60th birthday party. It was to be at their home in Nevada City, California, on July 26. David, Clay's 2nd cousin 1x removed, had traveled to Mason many times to see him. I thought we should go,

I told Clay that I would not drive another 4,000 miles but that we could fly. Reluctantly he agreed. Clay had never flown commercially. Once, seventy years before, he flew in a small private plane, and he never wanted to repeat that experience.

I sweetened the pot by adding an incentive. We would fly to Reno, Nevada, where he could play cards for a day, go to David's party and then spend another day in the Casino before returning home. He reluctantly consented.

We drove to Austin-Bergstrom International Airport Thursday, July 24, and boarded US Airways flight 523 at 3:25 p.m. We arrived in Reno at 6:30 p.m.

Clay sat in a window seat. It was a clear sunny day. He said, "I've never seen so much water!" What looked like large, dark pools of water were cloud shadows.

Clay dressed as he always dressed. He wore his best boots, jeans, belt, pearl-snap shirt, and Stetson. When we arrived in Reno at 6:30 p.m., I informed the flight attendant that this was Clay's first flight. She exclaimed, "He is my first "virgin" passenger!"

She told the flight crew, and they invited Clay into the cockpit. They treated the 92-year-old cowboy like royalty. He also got a couple of hugs from the beautiful blonde flight attendant.

I collected our luggage, rented a car, and drove to our downtown Hotel/Casino. As we were checking in, a taxi drove up and out stepped the flight crew. Of course, they recognized Clay. You couldn't miss that Stetson.

Clay played cards Thursday night and Friday. On Saturday, July 26, we drove to Nevada City, California to celebrate David Alan Lindsay's 60th Birthday.

Tonya worked very hard to make this a special event. It was David's first birthday party. Tonya knew we were coming, but David didn't. We wanted to surprise him. The guests were scheduled to arrive at 11 a.m. Tonya asked us to arrive before the festivities began so that David and Clay could visit.

We drove up to their gate and pushed the buzzer at 9 a.m. Tonya said, "David, someone is at the gate; go let them in." David uttered a few choice words about people arriving so early as he came out of the house. Yes, he was surprised. He and Clay had a good visit, and we enjoyed David's party.

We drove back to Reno Saturday night. Clay played cards all day Sunday. The plan was to arrive in Austin at 4 p.m. Monday to avoid driving after dark. But things didn't work out as planned.

Monday morning, we checked out of the hotel, turned in the rental, ate breakfast at the airport, and boarded US Airways flight 418 for a 9:30 a.m. departure. We didn't depart. We sat and sat and sat. There was something wrong with one of the instruments. After an hour or so, a technician arrived, fixed the problem, and we flew to Phoenix, where, of course, we had missed our connecting flight. We arrived in Austin at 9 p.m.

I avoided hitting any of the suicidal deer that graze along the Hill Country roadside, and we drove through the Lindsay Ranch gate a little after midnight.

Home again! When I asked Clay what he thought of the trip, he said, "You spend more time waiting than you do flying!"

2014 - SEATTLE TRIP

For my Birthday, Clay suggested that Alica and I take a trip. We traveled to Seattle, Wash. Alica's perfect planning made for an enjoyable weekend. We went everywhere and did everything. Even the weather cooperated.

2014 - HEART ATTACK

Our 2014 adventures were not over. In early October, Clay decided that he would like to spend a few days playing poker. We drove to Garland, Texas, and visited with our daughter, Alica. On Oct. 8, 2014, we went to the WinStar World Casino and Resort in Thackerville, Okla.

We arrived in time to enjoy the breakfast buffet, and Clay signed up for a spot at the poker table. Until a place became available, we played the slots.

A spot at the poker table opened up, and Clay played Texas Hold 'em for a few hours. When I checked on him about 3 p.m., he said, "I don't feel good. I don't feel good at all!"

We started to leave the Casino, but Clay had difficulty walking. I found a wheelchair, and the Casino medics checked him but didn't find anything wrong.

We had planned to stay in Gainsville, Texas, so we left the Casino and drove south. Clay was never sick. Nothing like this had ever happened before.

He was feeling worse and worse. I didn't know what to do. I stopped at a motel and managed to get him to a room, but his condition continued to worsen.

The young desk clerk called for an ambulance. The Cooke County EMS arrived in a few minutes, and the EMTs transferred Clay to the ambulance. They told me to go to the local hospital to plan for his arrival. I did. Then I waited and waited. The ambulance didn't arrive.

Finally, the hospital phone rang, and the EMTs told the hospital staff that Clay had suffered a "heart issue" in the ambulance and that they were taking him to Denton. As I drove to Denton, I prayed, "Lord, help the doctors to know what to do and help me to be OK, no matter what happens."

Clay had a heart attack. Thankfully, we were at the right place at the right time. The Cook County EMS took him to Texas Health Presbyterian Hospital in Denton, Texas, where they have a rapid response heart center. In only 90 minutes, two stents were inserted, and Clay was out of surgery. It was Wednesday night.

Friday morning, a few minutes after I walked into his room, Clay's heart started beating 260 beats per minute, and he died. He crashed. Code Blue Code Blue was called, and people and equipment appeared from everywhere.

I stood in the hall, and I heard, "Clear . . . zap, zap." and one more time, then, "We've got him. He's back. He's back!" Then I heard, "What is your name? The response was, "Clay Lindsay." The doctor then asked, "When is your birthday?" Clay said, "Aug. 15, 1922". About five minutes had passed, but it seemed longer.

The Casino Guy, which is what they called Clay as he had been at WinStar Casino when he had his heart attack, was the talk of the unit. The doctors and nurses were astonished that I was not falling apart in the hall. I had turned everything over to God as I drove to the hospital. I prayed that the best would happen. I prayed that I would be able to do what I needed to do. My prayers were answered.

Later, more than one nurse told me, "What happened this morning is not what usually happens in the Cardiac Care Unit. Sometimes it takes hours, days, or weeks for a patient brought back to breathe and speak his own. He responded immediately!" You see this on TV, but not here. She shook her head in amazement. A few hours later, she said, "There are many stories about what people see or experience when they are gone. If he remembers anything, please tell me. Him, I would believe."

I spent my nights in a nearby motel, but Clay wanted me at the hospital early every morning. When I arrived Saturday morning, I said, "I didn't know if I should come in or not!" I explained what happened the day before, but he didn't remember anything.

I took a set of dominos with us when we traveled, and I took them to the hospital the following day. My way of testing to see if anything had changed in Clay's memory or mental ability, was to play a game or two. I rolled the tray to his bed and shuffled the dominoes. He chose nine, and we played two games. Thankfully, Clay was OK. He played correctly, counted his scores, and didn't miss a beat.

Alica came to the hospital several times and made sure that we had everything we needed. On Wednesday, Oct. 15, our son, Clay Haley Lindsay, came to Denton from Mason and drove us home. It had been an eventful week.

2014 - THANKSGIVING – LONG REUNION

We were invited to the Long Family Reunion. It was six weeks after his heart attack. Clay was ready to go to another party. The reunion was held at the T Bar M Resort and Conference Center in New Braunfels, Texas.

"Nestled in the Hill Country of Texas sits a spacious 160-acre retreat, T Bar M Ranch. Relax throughout the oak-shaded property or enjoy a variety of indoor and outdoor activities. From high adventure water parks to dancing and dining in Gruene, there's something for everyone in New Braunfels."

We thoroughly enjoyed visiting with everyone.

2015

Thankfully, nothing terrible happened in 2015.

Clay has been able to go out and work a little at a time. It does my heart good to see him going out to his truck and driving off to do what he wants to do. Clay's niece, Sherry from New Zealand, and his nephew, John Clay Lindsay, from Iowa, visited in May. I went to Lubbock for nephew Zeph Bruce's graduation.

Lindsay Davis Trapp, Erin Trisler, and her children, Georgia and Grant, came from Indiana, and David Lindsay came from California. They helped Clay celebrate his 93rd. Birthday Aug. 1st. We met at Nacho's Café. There was plenty of room for us to visit and hang out, and I didn't have to cook, set up, or clean up! I finally got a little wiser!

In September, Fox Sports Southwest came to Mason and filmed the DQ. Game of the Week. Mason was celebrating 100 years of football, and we won! Patricia Beaty made shirts for the Clay's and Garrett showing the year they graduated, 1941, 1995, and would graduate in 2025. Garrett told everyone that his Papa, at 93, was the oldest football player there.

That night, Clay H., Garrett, and their Boy Scout Troop were honored to raise the flag before the football game. These every day, ordinary things happen in our small town. People come together to have fun and do things in the right way.

Clay is still doing well. Cutting brush two hours each morning and then staying in his recliner reading, sleeping, or in front of the TV the rest of the day. He doesn't feel as good as he did when he was 85

He gets aggravated that he can't do as much as he wants to do. I now have a lot more respect for caregivers. Thank you for your prayers.

The wooden deck at the Cabin is no more. Hopefully, we will have a new cement deck next year.

Hunting season won't be the same without the Watson's. Clay will miss breakfast with Janet and Carlton. He enjoyed playing dominoes and Skip-Bo with Angela and David Koonce.

What can we do when so much is happening in our families, communities, country, and world? We can pray to our Lord that His will be done in all things. It is not always easy, but that is what we are told to do.

"Don't be anxious about anything," Jesus said. "But with prayers and supplication, let your requests be made known to God."

I did that last night. Our daughter lives about six blocks from where eight people were killed in Garland, Texas, but she is OK. Our son and family are traveling to Colorado. They spent the night under an awning near Clovis, N. Mex., in a white-out blizzard, but they are all OK this morning.

Thank you, Lord, for taking care of everyone.

2016

We have an elevated cement deck at the Cabin on Comanche Creek.

Clay's friend, Melvin Leifeste, died in April. Melvin was a rancher, a bachelor, and a wonderful man who always had a smile to share and a tale to tell. He and Clay were life-long friends.

Longhorns came to the Lindsay Ranch in June. Clay H. and two friends left early one morning with three trucks and three big cattle trailers going to south Texas to pick up 22 head of longhorn cattle.

If you have never had the word "assume" broken down for you, here it is. When you ASSUME, you make an ASS out of U and ME. Well, Clay assumed that the cattle would be penned and ready to load when they arrived. They were not. They eventually got them loaded, and they were back in Mason a little after midnight.

I took my first ambulance ride at the end of September. I was diagnosed with Atrial Fibrillation or AFib. I was in the hospital in Fredericksburg for three days. So far, so good. My sister, Pamela Bruce, came from Lubbock. She had Clay duty while I was gone. She even cleaned my refrigerator!

Sherry Lindsay arrived in Texas in late September. She and her son, Coby James, came to Mason on Oct. 2. They came through Fredericksburg at the right time to pick me up at the hospital and bring me home. We had a good visit. Sherry was extremely helpful, as always.

I put the Townhouse on the market in November and finished painting the porch. Clay, a man of few words, said, "It looks nice." After working on it off and on since June, I agreed.

2017

This year we remodeled the Cabin on Comanche Creek. It looks wonderful. Thank you, Clay H.

We also planted $800.00 worth of Wilman Lovegrass. Farming and ranching are always a gamble, but if you don't sow, you can't reap.

Jim Long and Susan Cooper visited in the spring. Clay was happy to play Pitch! Pitch is a card game that the Lindsay's always play when they get together. There is usually a lot of yelling and slapping cards down on the table. They had a wonderful time. :)

In April, we drilled a well in the back pasture and hit water! After three dry holes, this was wonderful. Before this, the only water source was the windmill that has been pumping for about 60 years.

Clay H. dug ditches and put water troughs in both pastures. When his dad and I did it, we did everything by hand. What a difference having the right equipment makes.

This year Clay developed an irregular heartbeat that is called Atrial Flutter. The doctor was able to shock his heart back into rhythm. It's incredible what can be done. In 95 years, at 70 beats per minute, Clay's heart has beat 3,495,240,000 times. Most pumps don't work that well.

Approximately 30 guests joined us to wish Clay a happy birthday. He enjoyed the day and played cards until midnight. Not bad for an old guy.

We allow people to come to the Ranch and rock hunt. Topaz, the Texas State Gem, is only found in Mason County. One of our guests was thrilled when he found a 20.32 carat stone.

This fall, Clay H. started selling longhorns. We had too much stock and not enough grass and water. A couple from Hext, a few miles from us, bought two heifer calves and a bull calf. Even though Papa Clay is not in charge of the cattle now, he hates to see the heifers go, but you've gotta do what you've gotta do.

A gentleman from Switzerland owns 90 acres close to Fredericksburg. He needed some Texas Longhorns, so Clay H. delivered three steers. He said there is a large house, a lake, and knee-high grass. Those steers should feel like they are in heaven.

The old hand-dug, rock-lined, well by the old house had been covered for years. It is about 50' deep. When we uncovered it, it had about three feet of water. Clay H. installed a solar pump and put a water trough close by. He installed a switch so his dad could drive his golf cart down and turn it off and on.

After Clay H. installed it, there was no sunshine for a week. Papa Clay went down and checked it every day. He was thrilled when he flipped the switch, and water flowed into the trough. He bragged about what his son had done. We don't always appreciate how intelligent our children are. After his dad's memorial service, someone asked about it. Clay H. said, "I just did it for Dad." Thank you, Clay H., you did a good thing.

Papa Clay has been busy shelling pecans. He enjoyed playing Santa and he gave bags of shelled pecans to Wendy Hudson and Carol Tucker. He keeps busy while he sits by the fire watching TV.

Clay H. and Garrett went to Durango, Colo., to spend a week with the Long's. They always have a good time.

2018

Last year we remodeled the Cabin on Comanche Creek, and this year Mason Mountain Manor has been updated. It's amazing what a good crew can do in a brief time. Thank you, Clay H., for all you do and for knowing who to call.

The new well supplies water for the Manor. Clay H. and his machines did all the work, but Papa Clay went along to supervise and make sure he did it right.

We were saddened by the death of our 12-year-old great-grandnephew, Aiden Hayes, who died Feb. 27, 2018, after a long, hard battle with Aplastic Anemia. Aiden, Oliva's son, and Sherry's grandson lived in New Zealand.

We wonder why things happen as they do. Why is Clay still here at 95? Why is Aiden gone at only 12 years old? There are no answers. Death is as natural as birth, but it hurts not the one who is gone but those of us who remain. In Lessonslearnedinlife.com. Elizabeth Ammons wrote:

"You can shed tears because they are gone, or you can smile because they lived. You can close your eyes and pray that they come back, or you can open your eyes and see all they left for you. Your heart can be empty because you can't see them, or you can be full of the love you shared.

You can turn your back on tomorrow and live for yesterday, or you can be happy for tomorrow because of yesterday. You can only remember that they are gone, or you can cherish their memory and let it live on. You can cry and close your mind and feel empty, or you can do what they would want. Smile, open your heart, love, and go on."

In 2021, on the third anniversary of Aiden's death, his mother, Olivia Lindsay Potter, wrote,

"My heart hurts today as I remember you, Aiden Montgomery Hayes. November 7, 2005 – February 27, 2018. Three years ago, today, our world was shattered into a million pieces; when you left us after an EPIC battle, you fought so bravely!

Aiden, I miss you so much. Among everything else, I miss your cheeky smile, that eye roll you perfected, and of course, your one-liners and witty comebacks.

We took those pieces and created a new life, a better life, a life you would have loved, but it's not the same without you. Your death made us realize that nothing is guaranteed, that life can be so short, and that we must live our dreams NOW.

Not later, NOW. You left us a fantastic legacy. I love you, Aiden. Now and forever."

Clay's nieces Sherry Lindsay, Janet Lindsay, and Janet's granddaughter, August Wooldridge, visited this year. Sherry lives in New Zealand. Janet and August live in Australia. August saw her first deer this afternoon, and she is already rock hunting. August and Clay became instant friends.

Clay had another birthday and another party. When I told Clay that our houses needed to be cleaned because company was coming, he said, "I'll do it." He still has a sense of humor.

Debbie Green and her family came from Canyon. Alica and her friend, Keith Jones, and his daughter Izzie, were here from Dallas. Other guests were Alan and Carroll Johnson from Hurst, Pam and Zeph Bruce from Lubbock, Christie St. Clair from Houston, and Peggy Lindsay from Austin.

There were about 55 people at Nacho's to wish Clay a happy 96th birthday. When it was over, Clay said, "That was nice, wasn't it!" Yes, it was. Of course, he had no idea who and what made it happen.

In October, a foot of rain, yes, 12" fell on the watershed area of the North and South Llano in just a few days. All that water had to go somewhere, and it did. Every river, stream, low spot, and ditch was full of water. The flooding in Junction and Sonora and the surrounding areas was terrible.

In Junction, an RV park on the South Llano flooded. One woman at the RV park was washed into the river. She hung onto debris and rode the river 20 miles; she was rescued in London. There was a lot of damage in the area and two deaths. One body was located close to the Mason County line. The other body was found eight days later on over 100 miles from where she went into the Llano River.

UPDATE: Body Found on Lake LBJ Identified

"The body found in the area of Circle Drive near Kingsland on Lake LBJ in Burnet County on Tuesday, October 16, 2018, has been identified by the Travis County Medical Examiner as Charlotte Moye. Moye went missing during major flooding of the Llano River in Junction in Kimble County on the morning of Monday, October 8, 2018."

People posted videos of the Llano River. It rose from 1.2 feet to 35 feet and changed from a slow stream to a raging river in just eight minutes. The incredible power of the water was unbelievable.

This information from the Llano River Watershed Alliance gives us an idea of how much water flowed toward Austin and beyond.

"Tuesday morning's flood down the Llano was not only a near-record flood peak, but it was also part of the greatest volume of water to pass down the Llano in a given period since records began in 1939.

Since waters from the Columbus Day Flood in Junction began passing through Llano, the 10-day average flow of the Llano has been 28,773 CFS. 1 CFS (cubic foot per second) is equivalent to 448.8 gallons of water flowing per minute. This flow rate over a 10-day period equates to 186 billion gallons of water or 570,000 acre-feet.

That is about 30% of the storage capacity of Lake Travis, or for you longtime Astros fans, this is enough to fill the Astrodome 581 times.

Around the same time, the James River southwest of Mason, crested at 26 feet and 110,000 CFS, considered a 100-year flood event. Rainfall above the Mason gage near the US 87 bridge resulted in a peak of 32 ft (175,000 CFS). The record flood peak for the Mason gage is 46 ft in June of 1935, which also destroyed the bridge at this location."

The Llano bridge was also destroyed then.

Alva Clay Lindsay was 13 years old in 1935. He and his family went to the river, and he watched the bridge as it collapsed and was washed downstream. This year his son Clay Haley Lindsay and grandson, Garrett Clay Lindsay, watched the rising waters. White's Crossing was up over five feet, the James River Crossing and Dos Rios, where the Llano and James Rivers meet, was up at least 10 feet. The water at the bridge across US 87 was up 35 feet. This 100-year flood was something they will never forget.

It is sad that what helps some hurts so many others. The rain we received put water into all our tanks and helped the grass grow. Both branches of Comanche Creek are still running.

The two Clay's, Garrett, and I went to Spring Branch, Texas, to celebrate John Long's 80th birthday. It was a great party. Well done, Ruth. Thank you for inviting us. Not everyone gets to attend his nephew's 80th birthday.

For small towns like Mason, high school football is a big deal. Almost everyone is either related to or knows someone related to at least one player. The Mason

Punchers played at AT&T Stadium in Arlington, and they beat New Deal, 44-6 for the state championship in their division. This was the third time Mason has been to state in the last seven years. We won, then we lost, now we have another win.

Mason's coach, Kade Burns, told a reporter that he had been a Mason supporter all his life. He only lived 100 yards from the school when he was growing up. His Dad, Melvin Burns, was Mason's football coach for several years. He won 101 games. With this win, Coach Kade Burns' teams have won 100 games. The reporter asked Coach Burns, "How do you think your dad would feel today?" With a catch in his voice, Coach Burns replied, "He would be proud. I know he was watching, and he has the best seat in the house."

While doing family research, I found a couple of exciting things. Clay and I were not the first Lindsay–Haley couple to marry. Burkett Battle Lindsay married my 2nd-great-aunt, Margaret Haley, June 16, 1842. After his first wife died, my 2nd-great-grandfather, James Patterson Haley, married Sarah Elizabeth Davis, May 30, 1884. Sarah Davis was a relative of Clay's brother-in-law, Ernest Davis. Ernest Davis was Peggy Lindsay's husband, Mike, and Lindsay Davis's dad. Perhaps I was destined to be part of this family.

Most people don't become interested in family history until the old ones are gone. Spend time with your family, ask questions and listen to the stories the old folks tell. You might learn something.

Our Christmas guests were Coby and Clara James, and Mike and Jennifer Davis. Thank you for coming and donating a few quarters to your uncle.

2019

This year started with Clay watching football. He follows the Texans and the Cowboys. He was happy that the Longhorns, his school, won the Sugar Bowl.

Clay sits by the fire that I started, covered by an electric blanket that I plugged in, drinking a milkshake that I made and took to him. He watches the TV that I turned on and the channels I ordered so that he could watch these games. He's not doing badly.

Garrett placed third at the Junior Robotics Inventions competition in San Angelo. There is no telling what this young man will accomplish.

Two longhorn cows and the bull have a new home at the Boy Scout Retreat near Fort McKavett, Texas. With 200 acres of grass, they will have a good home next door to Herbert H. Mears' Ranch. The Mears were good friends of John and Jesse, and the Lindsay family would spend a week or so visiting them every summer.

Clay, Sherina, Lastani, and C. J. Long from Durango, Colo., came to Texas for Spring Break. It is always nice to have family visits.

Clay H. is clearing land and making major improvements to the Ranch. When he bought the fertilizer, the salesman said, "You realize that you have lost money on the Ranch for the last fifteen years." Last year we only made four bales of hay. Yes, four. Hopefully, this year will be better. Someone said, "What you need to run a ranch is a little grass, a little water, and a whole lot of money." That is not far from the truth. Someone else quipped, "If your ranch ever shows a profit, you have the wrong accountant."

Our nephew, Zephaniah Zane Bruce, graduated from Lubbock Christian University May 11. We are so proud of him. Garrett and Clay H. went to Garner State Park and then to the Boy Scout Retreat at Possum Kingdom. Garrett is learning to play Pitch, and he and his dad stop by to play a few games with Papa Clay. With a look of disgust, he'll say, "I've never seen such luck!" when Garrett gets a good hand and wipes him out.

On July 1, Mr. Barry Davis, from KENS 5 TV San Antonio, came to the Ranch and filmed a rock-hunting feature. You can go to our website www.lindsayranch.net and watch it.

Clay enjoyed another birthday party his year. Thank you for making it a great day. I fell in July. I have a fractured vertebra (L1) in my spine's lumbar region. Looking at the MRI was interesting.

Clay H. has been busy with his business and hauling hay and cattle cubes for the stock. They know the sound of his truck and are happy to hear and see him.

As we come to the end of another year, we realize how quickly time passes. Former, long-time Alabama Coach, Bear Bryant, who passed away in 1982, had a copy of "The Magic Bank Account" in his wallet.

The Magic Bank Account

Imagine that you have won the following "Prize" in a contest. Each morning, a bank would deposit $86,400 in your private account for you to use. However, the prize has rules, which are:

(1) Everything that you did not spend during each day would be taken away from you.

(2) You may not simply transfer money into some other account,

(3) You may only spend it.

(4) Each morning, upon awakening, the bank opens your account with another $86,400 for that day.

(5) The bank can end the game without warning; at any time, it can say, "Game is over." It can close the account, and you will not receive a new one.

If this happened, what would you personally do? You would buy anything and everything you wanted, right? You would buy things not only for yourself but for all the people you love. Even for people you do not know; you could not possibly spend it all on yourself, right? You would try to spend every penny and use it all because you knew it would be replenished in the morning, right?

This game is real. Each of us is already a winner of this "Prize." We just cannot seem to see that. The prize is "Time." Each morning, we awaken to receive 86,400 seconds as a gift of life, and when we go to sleep at night, any remaining time is NOT credited to us because what we have not used up that day is forever lost. After all yesterday is forever gone.

Each morning, the account is refilled, but the bank can dissolve your account any time without warning, so what will you do with your 86,400 seconds?

These seconds are worth so much more than the same amount in dollars. Think about it and remember to enjoy every second of your time because time races by so much quicker than you think. So, take care of yourself, be happy, love deeply, and enjoy life!

John Long wrote, "I have often thought of my daily life in terms of watching a giant hourglass full of sand that has a finite volume in the top that is slowly draining at the waist. Each grain of sand is like the seconds of your life. Once the sand grain drops into the bottom half of the hourglass, that grain (second) is gone forever! Clearly, there is no time to waste. Thanks for reminding me to make each second count." Thank you, John. Well said.

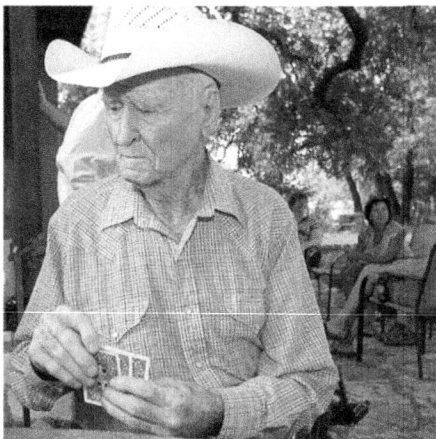

Clay playing Pitch on his 90th birthday.

41
Playing Pitch, Glossary of Insults,
and Other "Terms of Endearment"

James (Jim) Lindsay Long shared this insight into the Lindsay's and their favorite pastime:

Unkie and the Lindsay's are notorious for playing cards - especially pitch. All the Lindsay's thought they were the best pitch players in the land. In the case of Unkie, there is some truth to that.

Unkie was quick to point it out when anyone made a bad play and add some comment about their mental capabilities. In the case of his father, John Alva Lindsay, he may have been the worst pitch player in the land. He piddled away his inheritance playing cards.

Under his stewardship, the Lindsay ranch went from 20,000 acres to 1,000 acres. Fortunately, Unkie was able to buy the last of the Ranch from his father before it was all gone.

Anyway, back to cards.

When John and I were young, up to age 14, we spent the summers at the Lindsay Ranch. The Lindsay men's summer schedule was up at dawn, breakfast, and ride off on horseback to check on the livestock and the Ranch. It was hard, hot work. They were usually done around noon.

Next, a big meal, clean up, get ready to go to town. However, before leaving for town, there was always a big pitch game on the front porch. John and I would watch, and the grownups would play. Mainly Daddy John, Jack, Unkie, Effie, Doris, Peggy (the sisters), and any other adults around who knew how to play.

The games were raucous with lots of shouting and cursing. Jack, (Unkie's brother) was especially vociferous. He would frequently tell his father, Daddy John, "If you had a lick of sense, the Lindsay's would own all of Mason County."

My brother, John, and I would watch diligently, trying to learn more about the game, but we mostly learned how to curse and question everyone's ability at the table. Unkie would usually win, but not always.

He wasn't a good loser. If someone made a really stupid play, he would point it out and sometimes depart, but only when losing, with the words, "If you are going to play like that, I quit!"

Jim provided a list of some oft-heard quotes from the pitch table.

"Quit sitting there like a bottle of water!"
"You can't play a lick!"
"You chump!"
"You nitwit!"
"Why don't you play?" "I'm thinking." "There hasn't been a thought enter your head since you were born!"
"Read 'em and weep!"
"I played what the little boy shot at, game!"
"I can't win for losing!"
"Who played low?" "I did!" "I did!" "I did!" etc.
"Take that!" "And that!" "And that!" (As the cards are slammed one by one on the table.)
"What's trumps?" "Clubs, you moron!"
"Follow suit, half-wit!"
"Who's skunked?" "Pay up, chump!"
"You haven't got a lick of sense!"
"If you are going to play that bad, I quit!"

And still, they couldn't wait to play. Clay could and did play pitch all night. On his 90th birthday, he came in about 8 a.m. with his pockets full of quarters. He was grinning from ear to ear, "I taught them a lesson! I took 'em to the cleaners!"

The last big family pitch game occurred in early March 2020. Clay's nephews and their families came for a visit. John, Ruth, and Brian Long came from Spring Branch, Texas, Jim and Susan Long came from Colorado, and Mike Davis drove up from New Braunfels. Our son, Clay Haley, and grandson Garrett Clay Lindsay drove out to the Ranch from Mason.

The players ranged in age from 97-year-old Alva Clay to his grandson, 12-year-old Garrett Clay Lindsay. Enthusiastic players surrounded the poker table that Coby James and Clay Haley Lindsay gave Alva Clay a few years ago. Cards, money, insults, and light-hearted banter flew around the table all afternoon. Everyone had a good time.

Alva Clay could not hear, and it was apparent that he was frailer than he had been, but his mind was still sharp, and he probably won. He was an excellent winner!

Sherry Lindsay, on Pitch:

Clay, with a predatory gleam in his eye, "Sit down 'LUCKY' and deal 'em up." After not seeing me in a year, "How much money did you bring?!"
"Get in here, Boliver!"
"Throw me some game!"
"Can't you count? Can't you read?"
"You couldn't play darts!"
"What's taking you so long, bottle head?"
"That's pure luck! Even a blind sow can find an acorn once in a while!"

The last pitch game Clay played was with his beautiful daughter, Alica Kay Lindsay. Alica came to visit in May. Of course, he was ready to play pitch.

His eyesight was good, but he couldn't hear, so we wrote notes to him. His mind was sound, but his 97-year-old body was worn out. He had trouble walking, so I rolled his wheelchair out onto the porch and got him situated, but, for the first time, he couldn't hold his cards. I held them for him, and he pointed to the card he wanted to play. My heart broke.

Did Clay win the last pitch game he played? I think he did. Would Alica have LET him win? Probably not. Alica inherited her dad's will to win.

Question: "Clay, who is the best pitch player you know?" Answer: "My daughter, Alica."

* * * * *

PITCH – LINDSAY RULES

Because of the bidding, the game is called Auction Pitch. It is based on a game of English origin and dates from the 17th century. It is still a popular game in the United States. The essential feature has always been the scoring of high, low, jack, and the game. In the Lindsay version, a Joker is added to the deck.

RANK OF CARDS
A (high), K, Q, J, (Joker) 10, 9, 8, 7, 6, 5, 4, 3, 2.

ANTE UP
When Lindsay's play, each person "antes up" a quarter at the beginning of each game. When a bidder does not make his bid, he must put in another quarter. The winner of the game gets the "pot."

THE DEAL
Deal three cards at a time clockwise, beginning with the player to the left until each player has six cards. After each hand, the deal passes to the left.

THE BIDDING
The player on the dealer's left bids first. Each player, in turn, may either bid or pass. The lowest bid is two, and each successive bid must be higher than any preceding bid. You can "Shoot the Moon" and bid five.

Bidding You can bid on the value of your hand. Possible bids are two, three, four, or "Shoot the Moon," which is a bid of five. When you bid two, three, and four, you are bidding how many of the points below you can win.

High: You win the trick, which has the highest available card in the trump suit.
Low: You win the trick, which has the lowest available card in the trump suit.
Jack: You win the trick, which has the jack of the trump suit.
Joker: You win the trick which has the joker in it.
Game: You get the most game points in the round.

All 10s are worth 10, aces are worth 4, kings are worth 3, queens are worth 2, and jacks are worth 1, the joker is worth 1. Other cards aren't worth anything.

Each player in turn bids or passes; bidding always starts at two. Bidding only lasts one round. Each player only gets one chance to bid or pass. If all players pass, the dealer must take the bid for two or throw in his hand and deduct two points from his score.

Note that since not all cards are dealt, ace and two aren't always the high and low card. Sometimes a queen may be the High and a four the Low, for instance. There may not be a jack or joker in any hand since only 24 of 52 cards are dealt in a hand, with four players. With more players, nearly everything may be in play.

THE PLAY

The "Pitcher" (highest bidder) leads first. The suit of the card "pitched" shows the trump suit. On a trump lead, each player must follow suit if possible. On any other lead, a player may either follow suit or he may trump. When unable to follow suit, a player may play any card. The player of the highest trump - or the highest card of the suit led, if the trick contains no trump, wins the trick and leads next.

HOW TO KEEP SCORE

When all six tricks have been played, the points due to each player are tabulated. Usually, a score is kept with a pencil and paper. Each player scores whatever points they make. The bidder must "make his bid," i.e., win points equal to his bid. If the bidder does not "make his bid," the number of points bid is deducted from his score.

Thus, a player may have a net minus score, called being "in the hole." The score for a player in the hole is shown on the score sheet as a number with a ring around it.

The first player to get a plus score of 7 points wins the game. The bidder's score is counted first. If the bidder and another player reach 7 points on the same hand, the bidder wins even if the other player has a higher total score. If two players other than the bidder reach 7 points on the same hand, the points are counted in this order: High, Low, Jack, Joker, Game.

A player who "Shoots the Moon" and makes the bid by winning all 5 points wins the game immediately - unless they were in the hole (in which case they only receive the 5 points).

$$* * * * *$$

John Clabe Long shared his list of other frequently heard terms of endearment:

"You're as dumb as a post."
"You don't have a lick of sense!"
"You ride like a sack of doorknobs."
"You can't run fast enough to scatter your own poop."
"You're as ugly as a mud wall."
"You're so dumb; you couldn't stuff guts to a bear."
"You turned out OK!"

42
My Uncle Clay –
An All 'Round Good Guy

Deborah Dea (Debbie) Dobbs Green shared her memories.

The Horned Toad

One of my favorite Unkie stories occurred in 1963 or 1964 when I was five or six years old. Unkie brought me a big surprise! Actually, it wasn't very big, but it was, sure enough, a big surprise. It was a tiny horned toad.

Unkie told me he went all the way to Mexico to get it for me and that I needed to take good care of it. I did. I was so proud of it that I took it everywhere, even to church.

It couldn't run all over the place at church, so we put it in an old matchbox. In the middle of the service, I would carefully open it, look at that little horned toad and laugh to myself, and smile, remembering how sweet Unkie was to give me that special gift.

A few years ago, I gave him a replica of a horned toad so he would know how much what he did all those years ago meant to me. He kept it with his treasures.

A Special Christmas

We would see him when we went to Mason, either at the Ranch or in Katemcy. One Christmas, many of the family were there. It was one of the biggest Christmas turnouts I remember.

We had all kinds of food, beautiful decorations, and a giant Christmas tree with many presents. It came time for Santa to arrive, so Unkie took all the younger kids upstairs to the guest bedroom with the fireplace; he told us to wait there, then he left.

We were all talking and looking through the windows for Santa. In a little while, we heard noises on the roof, like the prancing and pawing of each little hoof. Right after that, we heard louder noises coming from the chimney.

We took off down the stairs and what should appear but at least three beautiful brand-new bicycles. Mine was gorgeous! It was purple with a silver glitter banana seat and a white basket with flower trim.

We took off on them right out the front door and rode them up and down the dirt ranch road the rest of the holiday. Talk about three happy kids!

I wish I would have asked Unkie about the behind-the-scenes information. Did he throw rocks up there, climb on the roof, put the bikes together, store them, bring them in for us? What was his role in one of my best Christmases ever? I'm sure he played a big part in it.

Visit to White Top

Sometimes we visited him at the liquor store but not often. When he had the store, he gave me several of the cute display items he had. One was a donkey whose head would go back and forth, and another was a cigarette girl.

The Man I Knew and Loved

Clay was an all-around, good guy, the best of the best. His life was a life well-lived. He was content and truly happy. There are very few people like this in the world.

He was a gentleman, respectable, honest, and handsome with a great smile and a twinkle in his eye. He was well dressed. His everyday attire was a cowboy hat, boots, jeans, and a long-sleeved shirt with pearl snaps.

Clay was a hard worker. He wanted to work, to be busy doing something. He had a good business sense and was proud of his accomplishments.

My uncle was a people person and the life of the party. He had a good sense of humor, was fun-loving, and he was a kid at heart. He enjoyed teasing everyone in a good way. No matter what he said, it was all in fun.

Helpful, thoughtful, and kind, he was concerned about others. He also told good stories. Even though he was all these things, he was not loud or boastful. He was a quiet man most of the time.

He was analytical, and he thought things through. He didn't marry until he was 49 years old, and he was a good husband and a proud father. Clay loved his wife and children, his family, and his friends.

Honestly, every word describes my uncle. He was just amazing. There is no bad in his story. He might have gone through some bad tunes in the war, but, in my opinion, he was all good.

When I was little, Unkie made frequent visits to our house. I looked forward to his visits. For me, he couldn't get back soon enough! I wouldn't have minded if he stayed. He was so funny and made life a real party. When he came around, life wasn't so serious.

He always showed up in some different crazy vehicle; it might be a pickup, a car, or an old Rambler station wagon, but whatever it was, it always had some problem, usually a major problem. It would be loaded with clothes for my mom to wash and items he found somewhere along the way.

He always showed up hungry. We'd ask, what do you want to eat? Even though we knew before he said anything because he always wanted the same thing!! He'd say tacus! (We still laugh because Unkie and my mom never called them tacos, it was tacus.) So, mom would make lots and lots of tacus!

If mother needed something from the store, Unkie would take me with him to get it. It was like cruising with Unkie; off we'd go. He either didn't have a functioning air conditioner, or he wouldn't use it. We would roll the windows down, and off we went fast and furious with the wind blowing through the vehicle and the radio playing country music.

He always had plenty of lemon drops, peanut butter, and sweet tea in the car. He was quick to share his lemon drops, and I was ready to eat them! Mother made fudge or chocolate brownies for dessert because they were his favorite. Then we'd all play cards or other games.

For some reason, Unkie made me be his banker. He would give me his money. He told me that I should keep it in a secret place and never tell anyone else where it was. We put it in my playroom, where I kept my toys in a closet that ran under the stairs.

Every time he came back, we would count it to make sure it was all there. It always was, so I guess I was a good banker. One time he needed it; my banking days were over.

Unkie, my mom, Doris, and I went to a carnival in Muleshoe. When it was over, we went back home to find that we were locked out. Unkie to the rescue, he pried open my playroom window and put me through it to unlock the front door.

He liked to talk about the weather. He always looked forward to a good rain. He was happiest when things were green and there was water in the tanks and the creeks. He didn't like it to be dry.

He was funny. When he tried to teach someone how to play a game, if you didn't get it or made stupid moves, he was the first to let you know about it, call you a knucklehead or bottle-head or some other "endearing" name. He didn't go easy on anyone, young or old. He wanted to win all the time!

It meant a lot that he came to my mom's funeral and stayed several days afterward. His birthday parties were fabulous. He liked being the center of attention and visiting with everyone. I have fond memories of those parties. All the guests enjoyed them and looked forward to the next one.

When Unkie turned 90, I wanted to do something exceptional for him. I called the Mason City Office, told the receptionist what I was thinking. She connected me to the mayor. When I told him the story and relayed my request, he laughed.

He said, "Lady, we can't give the keys to the city to someone who is just 90. We have lots of people older than that here, and they haven't been given any special honors like that."

Well, that gift didn't work out, but I had good intentions.

In his later years, he would always ask my daughter, Tiffany, and me if we had a boyfriend or if either one of us had gotten married yet. The answer from both of us was always nope, not yet. He'd give us a questioning look and say, "Well, what's wrong with ya? Tiff and I would look at each other, shake our heads, and say we don't know, and we'd all laugh and laugh.

I was adopted. When we were together, Unkie would look at me and say, "I was there when they brought you home." I was glad that he cared enough to have been there and that he remembered. He always made me feel special.

He was content when he was at the Ranch. It was where he wanted to be more than anywhere else.

The last Thanksgiving, I saw him; he came in and ate and then was off by the fireplace, sipping tea and watching football games, talking about how they "couldn't play a lick."

I remember him standing by the door at the top of the steps, ready to greet everyone, with a hug and a "what took ya so long?" When he became feebler, he would sit in a chair, facing the dirt road that led to the house. He would watch and wait for the next arrival, be it a family member, a visitor, or one of the animals.

As we sat and talked, he'd tell me when someone was coming. I still think of him there, watching and waiting. He will always be the gatekeeper of the Lindsay Ranch. He calls us all there through his spirit and welcomes everyone to enjoy what he most enjoyed in this life.

Thank you, Uncle Clay; you made a difference in my life.

43

More About Clay Lindsay

When we were getting dressed to go to town, Clay would say, "What's taking you so long? I can be ready in five minutes!" He would put on his jeans, shirt, belt, boots, jacket, and hat, and he was ready to go. Clay should have been a model for a Western Wear Clothing manufacturer. He was a natural. He was 6' tall, slim, and everything looked good on him. As his niece, Sherry Lindsay said about a recent photograph; he looked very dapper. He might have looked out of place on the streets of New York or San Francisco, but not in Texas.

What sizes did he wear? 32x34 jeans, 15 ½ x 34 shirts, 40 long jackets, 9 ½ or 10 boots, depending on the brand. His hats were size 7 ¼ or 7 3/8 long oval. For many years, we owned and operated the Lindsay Country Story. Clay got his clothes at a discount.

Clay always wore a hat. He wore a straw hat in the summer and a felt hat in the winter. He never discarded a hat. When they were too stained and misshaped to wear to town, they became work hats. He didn't care what he wore when working on the Ranch, but it was different when he dressed to go to town.

He would look through all the hat boxes until he found the right one. He would wipe off the dust, check for stains and make sure the crease, the band, and the feather were just right.

When you go to church or out to eat, everyone hangs their hat on the hat rack. However, many of them look alike, same brand, same color; someone might pick up the wrong hat by mistake. Many hat manufactures made a tag that fit inside the band. The one in Clay's best hat read, "Like hell it's yours! This hat belongs to Clay Lindsay."

Clay also had several pairs of boots. His dress boots were often hand-made. He had a high instep, and there were times when he slept in his boots because he couldn't get them off.

Old boots became work boots. Clay would take them to the boot shop to have them half-soled, have new heel caps put on, or have the sole resewn when the stitching came loose. You didn't waste money; you fixed what you had. A bootjack, boot polish, shoeshine kit, and shaving kit went with him when he traveled.

Clay was good at nearly everything he did. He was a good horseman, cattleman, rancher, roper, dancer, businessman, husband, and father.

He was a lover of many things. He loved family, friends, animals, children, lemon drops, brownies, milkshakes, sweet tea, music, dominoes, Texas Hold 'em, and games of all kinds. He especially loved Pitch, peanut butter, Pepsi Cola, and Patsy Cline.

Clay was a collector. He collected stamps, first-day covers, coins, and bottles. He owned the White Top Package Store for nearly twenty-five years, and he collected every "Jim Beam and Wild Turkey Collector's Edition" bottle that came through the store.

It is amazing how many people he knew and loved and how many loved him in return. It's also noteworthy that these special friendships lasted all his life. A few that come to mind are the Auld, Nutter, and other families from Mountain Home, Texas. The Larimore, Parker, Beam, Bailey, and Hudson families in Mason. The Winkler family in Kalgary. Numerous people in Spur, Crosbyton, and Post, Texas. The Cross and the Weaver families from Lubbock.

He remained friends with many families who hunted with him. These include the Watson, Koonce, Hall, Eaves, and Wells families from Center, Texas plus, the Broussard, Murphy, and Krenek families from Pearland, League City, Texas City, and the Canion's from Longview.

Clay worked and played with these families. He enjoyed everyone, the men, women, and children, and they were happy to see him when he walked through their door.

Clay made a lasting impression. Clay befriended two young boys who were living in Mountain Home, Texas. Clay took them to Garven's store and bought them ice-cold Pepsi Cola's and candy. On several occasions, Joe Dickey stopped by the Ranch to visit with Clay. He told Clay how much his kindness meant to him and his brother.

Clay was a keeper. He kept cards, letters, thank you notes, photographs, and bank statements, some from the 1940s. Their words describe the man they knew and the influence he had on their lives.

I have so many fond memories of Clay growing up. Clay was part "second Dad" and part big brother and friend. He was always a part of the family - always.

Nan Winkler McCloy, Kalgary, Texas.

February 18, 2015.

Hi

I was with a group called Casa Royale Hunt Club that leased Clay's land to hunt on in the mid-'70s. I killed my first buck there. I loved that place, and I always looked forward to coming there.

I remember that Clay had an old orange Chevy truck that he used to drive me around at night to shoot rabbits. He was a great guy that I always enjoyed being around. I am curious to know if Clay is still alive, and if so, how he is doing? He would have to be in his upper 80's now.

I live in Oklahoma now, and I never get anywhere near Mason anymore. Still, I would love nothing more than to see that land again and to have those great memories come back to me.

If Clay is still with us, please say hello for me and tell him that some of my greatest memories came from hunting at that Ranch and being around him.

Thanks,

Marc

Life lesson: Be yourself but be aware that someone may remember what you do.

Clay and the Cross family were close friends for over fifty years and through four generations. Lana Cross wrote "88 Reasons We Love Clay Lindsay" and gave it to him for his 88th birthday. Lana, and her 10-year-old granddaughter, Emerson, recently added to the list.

100 REASONS WE LOVE CLAY LINDSAY
by LANA CROSS

1. HE'S CLAY LINDSAY
2. HE MADE CUT OFF JEAN SHORTS WITH BOOTS COOL
3. ALWAYS HAS LEMON DROPS TO SHARE
4. LOVES TO SHARE YOUR PUDDING CUPS AND OREOS
5. ALWAYS HAS A PEPSI OR MUG OF ICED TEA (WITH A LITTLE SUGAR)
6. HAS A WIDE VARIETY OF COWBOY HATS
7. HE HAS THE COOLEST KINDS OF BELT BUCKLES THAT YOU CAN'T FIND ANYWHERE ELSE
8. HAS A FEW SETS OF DOMINOES
9. ALWAYS WANTS TO KNOW WHAT TAKES YOU SO LONG TO PLAY A DOMINOE
10. DAD GUM!! IS THE WORST CUSS WORD HE SAYS PLAYING DOMINOES
11. LOVES TO GO SHOPPING IN FREDERICKSBURG
12. TEACHES YOU HOW TO TRAP TURTLES
13. ALWAYS HAPPY TO LET YOU OPEN THE GATES
14. MAKES GREAT SWIMMING POOLS IN BARRELS IN THE BACK OF HIS PICKUP (CAN ALSO BE USED TO WATER THE DONKEYS)
15. LOVES PARADES – ESPECIALLY BEATING THE KIDS TO PICK UP THE CANDY THAT IS THROWN FROM THE FLOATS
16. LOOKS GREAT IN PEARL SNAPS & COWBOY HATS!
17. KNOWS THE WORDS TO ALL OF PATSY CLINE'S GREATEST HITS
18. HAS A GREAT MILKSHAKE; MALT MAKER
19. KEEPS HEB IN BUSINESS BUYING PEANUT BUTTER
20. MAKES A MEAN HOMEMADE PIMENTO CHEESE SANDWICH WITH LOTS OF PIMENTOS
21. LOVES THE LORD
22. LOVES HIS WIFE OF 48 YEARS
23. DIDN'T MARRY UNTIL HE WAS 49

24. INTRODUCED US TO LLANO RIVER STATE PARK IN JUNCTION, TEXAS
25. LET'S US PULL HIM BACK UPSTREAM ON HIS INNERTUBE!
26. HIS FAVORITE VOICE MAILS TO LEAVE ARE "WHAD R YA DOIN' SLEEPIN'?"
27. HAS BURNT ORANGE BLOOD
28. WENT TO SCHOOL AT "THE UNIVERSITY OF TEXAS!"
29. LOVES TO ROOT FOR THE LONGHORNS!
30. CAN NAME ALL OF THE WILDFLOWERS ON THE RANCH
31. LOVES TO TELL STORIES ABOUT GARRETT "HE'S SOMETHING ELSE!"
32. HAS THE SMARTEST GRANDSON IN MASON COUNTY
33. LEARNED THE HARD WAY NOT TO PARK HIS PICKUP AND TRAILER ON A HILL IN MASON. (Clay parked on the highway and went into Donop's Feed Store. Someone came in and said, "Hey, Clay, your truck is rolling down the road." It stopped when it ran into the back of a parked truck in front of Mason Gas Company. Thankfully no one was hurt.)
34. HAS A GREAT COLLECTION OF HOOPIES (SOME EVEN STILL RUN)
35. GOOD AT TEACHING YOU HOW TO FIX HIS FLATS!
36. CAN KIND OF PLAY SKIP-BO
37. GOES TO OUT OF TOWN WEDDINGS, GRADUATIONS & BIRTHDAY PARTIES
38. ALWAYS CONCERNED & ASKS ABOUT SOMEONE
39. PRAYS FOR LOTS OF PEOPLE
40. NAMES HIS CATTLE AFTER YOU
41. LET'S YOU RIDE HIS "TAME" DONKEYS
42. TAKES YOU TO EAT AT ALL THE HOT SPOTS IN TOWN, ZAVALA'S & WILLOW CREEK
43. WAITRESS HAVE TO REFILL THE SUGAR DISPENSER AFTER HE LEAVES
44. STANDS IN LINE FOR HOURS AT THE DOSS LABOR DAY WEEKEND FISH FRY
45. GETS ICE COLD BEERS FOR FRIENDS WAITING IN LINE

46. LOVES TO SIT AND WATCH THE HUMMINGBIRDS THAT DEE KEEPS FED

47. HAS GREAT FISHING TANKS AND EVEN DUG A NEW ONE

48. KEEPS THE FISH FED AND HAPPY

49. HAS A SECRET RECIPE FRUIT SALAD THAT HE MAKES AT THANKSGIVING – DELICIOUS!

50. KNOWS WHERE THE BEST BBQ JOINTS ARE

51. WOULD GIVE YOU THE SHIRT OFF HIS BACK

52. ALWAYS TOLD HIS HUNTERS HE DIDN'T HAVE ANY GOATS ON THE RANCH. THOSE 100 HEAD MUST HAVE SLIPPED THRU McMillan's FENCE

53. CLAY IS THE ONLY PERSON WE KNOW WHO CAN LOAD UP HIS GOATS IN THE TRAILER, HEAD TO JUNCTION FOR THE SALE AND END UP WITH NO GOATS WHEN HE GETS THERE. (He backed the trailer up to the loading shoot at the sale barn in Junction and the workman asked, "What are you trying to sell? The trailer is empty!" Clay looked all along the highway for loose and/or dead goats on the way back to the Ranch, but he didn't find any. When he got to the back creek, there was the end gate. It had bounced off when he drove over the creek. The goats were in the pasture, waiting for him.)

54. HAS READ EVERY LOUIS LAMOUR BOOK SEVERAL TIMES

55. WILL CALL YOU AND TELL YOU HE'S JUST SITTIN HERE BY THE FIRE (GUESS WHO CARRIED ALL THE WOOD IN AND STARTED THE FIRE). DHL

56. HAS A BAD HABIT OF PICKING UP PEOPLES' CAR KEYS, TOYS, ETC. (For safekeeping, of course)

57. RODE A HORSE TO BEHRENS SCHOOLHOUSE

58. LOVES HIS FAMILY MEMORIES

59. HAS FRIENDS FROM 2 TO 102

60. CAN PARTY (OR PLAY CARDS) TIL THE COWS COME HOME

61. KNOWS EACH COW BY NAME

62. HE DOES NOT LIKE TO LOSE…AND HE VERY SELDOM DOES!

63. HE LETS DEE WIN EVERY ONCE IN A WHILE, SO SHE'LL STILL PLAY WITH HIM

64. HAS GONE THRU SEVERAL CHAINSAWS CUT LOTS AND LOTS OF BRUSH ON THE RANCH
65. DOESN'T HAVE A SCRATCH OR DENT ON HIS RANCH TRUCKS 😊
66. HAS NEVER EVER CLEANED OUT A PICKUP
67. HAS XRAY VISION AND KNOWS EVERYONE'S DOMINOE HAND
68. TELLS YOU WHAT DOMINOE TO PLAY BEFORE ITS EVEN YOUR TURN
69. HAS TIME JUST TO SIT AND TALK ABOUT ANYTHING WITH YOU
70. GREAT STORYTELLER, AND HAS LOTS TO TELL
71. WATCHED HIM RIDE A BIKE AT THE HILL COUNTRY INN PARKING LOT AT 80 YEARS YOUNG
72. LOVES TO PUSH PEOPLE IN AND HELP THEM COOL OFF AT THE HILL COUNTRY INN POOL
73. CAN EAT ANYTHING AND NOT GAIN A POUND (OH WAIT, THAT'S WHY WE DON'T LIKE HIMJ)
74. THINKS THE AGGIES ARE A CULT
75. KNOWS LOTS OF PEOPLE AND THEY'RE USUALLY GLAD TO SEE HIM
76. LOVES, LOVES KIDS! (BECAUSE HE IS ONE)
77. HAS A HARDY LAUGH!!
78. LOVES PEOPLE UNCONDITIONALLY
79. THINKS THE OUTSIDE STRIPE ON THE HIGHWAY IS THE CENTER LANE TO DRIVE DOWN
80. DOESN'T NEED BRAKES, REVERSE, ETC. ON HIS PICKUPS (JUST BACK UP TILL YOU HIT IT!)
81. TREATS EVERYONE LIKE YOU'RE HIS FAMILY
82. HAS "SELECTIVE HEARING!!"
83. USES THINGS AND LOVES PEOPLE...NOT THE OTHER WAY AROUND
84. LOVES AND TAKES GREAT CARE OF THE LAND
85. LOVES EVERY SINGLE DROP OF RAIN THAT FALLS IN HIS GAGE

86. LIKES TO CALL YOU AND GIVE YOU A WEATHER REPORT FOR MASON COUNTY &TELL YOU HOW PRETTY IT IS THERE!
87. KNOWS ALL THE BEST SWIMMIN' HOLES IN THE HILL COUNTRY & HAS ONE AT THE RANCH!
88. REFER BACK TO #1 "BECAUSE HE'S CLAY LINDSAY!! 😊
89. LOVES A GOOD SOFT TACO WITH MASON COUNTY TOMATOES
90. CAN HAVE A KID IN A LEG LOCK OR PINNED DOWN WITH HIS KNEE IN ONE MINUTE FLAT
91. KNOWS HOW TO PLAY MASON PUNCHER TENNIS!
92. GIVES YOU THREE HAPPY THINGS IN LIFE- -SOMEONE TO LOVE, SOMETHING TO LOOK FORWARD TO, AND SOMETHING TO DO
93. WE DIDN'T KNOW WHAT TRUE FRIENDSHIP MEANT UNTIL WE MET YOU
94. NEVER HAD A MOBILE PHONE BUT ALWAYS KEPT IN TOUCH
95. ALWAYS HAD A FEW EXTRA PIECES OF CORN IN HIS POCKET AFTER FILLING DEER FEEDERS, WHICH HE USED TO START A FIGHT.
96. WHEN WE LEFT THE LINDSAY RANCH MEMORIES WOULD SNEAK OUT OF OUR EYES AND ROLL DOWN OUR CHEEKS
97. HE WILL ALWAYS BE REMEMBERED AS "THE GEM" OF MASON COUNTY
98. YOU HAVE NO IDEA THE AMOUNT OF LOVE AND HAPPINESS YOU BROUGHT TO SO MANY LIVES
99. HE'S IN EVERY GAME OF SKIP-BO AND DOMINOES WE STILL PLAY
100. WE WISHED HE WOULD HAVE MADE IT TO 100.

Emerson and I played several games of Skip-Bo yesterday! We laughed and said, "Dad Gum," a lot. We said, "I'm going to help you out," (famous last words Clay would say as he played the card you needed to play to get rid of your stockpile).

Emerson, age 10, said, "I met him on his 97th birthday. He was so much fun! I felt like I had known him all my life. I wish I would have met him sooner; I've heard so many stories about him from you, my dad, and Cody and all the fun y'all had with him."

I loved Clay's dry wit and his sense of humor. Before we married, I watched as Clay threw all his socks and underwear into a drawer. I asked, "How do you ever find two socks that match?" He said, "Oh, it doesn't matter. I wear boots, and you can't see your socks when you have boots on. Besides, this way, I can tell my right foot from my left foot." He always made me laugh.

Clay and I married Oct. 30, 1971. My dad, Vernon Lawrence Haley, died a week later, Nov. 6, 1971. We didn't realize that she was ill, but my stepmother, Madelynne Speights Johnson Haley, died Feb. 20, 1972. My older half-sister, Melody, was seventeen and my younger half-sister, Pamela, was only eleven years old.

Pam remembers that Clay stayed with her at the funerals. She never forgot his kindness to her. I lived in Lubbock for another year. I worked at AT&T and lived with my sisters. Clay and I saw each other on the weekends. Did this situation have a detrimental effect on our marriage? Not at all. We were both adults, and we did what needed to be done.

Time passed, and things changed. Melody married, and Pam went to live with a foster family. Clay and I traveled between Mason to Post each week. The extended family decided that Pam would live with a foster family to have a permanent address and attend school. In hindsight, this was not the best decision, but it seemed right at the time.

In his last days, Clay said, "I don't have to worry about Clay H. or Alica. They'll be OK. I don't have to worry about Pam or Zeph, (Pam's son that Clay always called "Jeff,") either, but if they ever need anything, be sure you help them." His last thoughts were not of himself but of the people he loved.

44
Zeph's Memories of Clay

Clay had a dozen nieces and nephews for most of his life, and you have read stories from many of them. On Nov. 4, 1996, another nephew joined the family. Zephaniah Zane Bruce was born to my sister, Pamela Sue Haley Bruce, and Dale Russell Bruce.

Now instead of twelve nieces and nephews, there were thirteen, a baker's dozen. Clay and I were fortunate to be a part of this now 24-year-old man's life. Of course, Clay never called Zeph by his name. When he wasn't commenting on his ability, or lack thereof, to count or to play dominos, or Skip-Bo, Clay called him "Jeff."

Zeph, your Uncle Clay loved you and was very proud of you, even though you couldn't count! I think it is appropriate that you have "the last word." Thank you for sharing your memories.

* * * * *

Memories with Uncle Clay

Heading to the Ranch, I knew I could always find Lemon Drops, Peanut Butter, Sweet Tea, and Pepsi, and Uncle Clay would always be waiting on the porch with a warm welcome.

I have one memory that I don't think many others have. When I first started driving, there were a few times where Uncle Clay would ride Shotgun and open the gates for me. I found this very amusing since I was so used to being the designated gate opener.

I remember going with him to play Skip-Bo with the Watson's in the back Manor. He always enjoyed winning.

There is one thing that I'll never

Clay opening the gate.

forget. Every time we would head back to the ranch house, right before we would walk in the door, he would turn around, give me a twenty-dollar bill and tell me to take care of my mom.

I will be forever grateful for my trips to the Ranch. I learned a lot of things like how to change a tire and life lessons from Aunt Dee. I will never forget that at the Lindsay Ranch, I was loved and cherished by Aunt Dee and Uncle Clay.

Zeph

45
The Final Days
2020 & 2021

2020

On the Ranch, life goes on. Clay H. plowed, raked, and planted several acres in permanent grass. He and Mendy also decorated Mason Mountain Manor. It looks wonderful.

In March, John, Ruth, Jim and Bryan Long, Susan Cooper, and Mike Davis came to Mason. The card table was surrounded by enthusiastic Pitch players from 12-year-old Garrett to 97-year-old Alva Clay. It was evident that Clay was physically weaker, but he enjoyed playing and visiting with everyone.

Clay was always so active that it was difficult for him to understand that he needed help standing and walking, He fell more than once, and when I asked, "Why didn't you call me?" He said, "I didn't think I would fall." Thankfully, there were no broken bones.

On Sunday, May 10, I had to ask Clay H. to help his dad get in and out of the bathroom. How degrading was that? What does that do to a proud man? That feeling of helplessness was devastating. The following day Clay H. called and said, "Mom, I think you need to call this number." I was doing everything I could to help Clay, but I was so involved with the day-to-day things that I couldn't see the bigger picture. I didn't realize that we both needed professional help.

May 11 - I called the number Clay H. gave me. It was the number for Ave Maria Hospice in Fredericksburg. Two people came that afternoon, and they assessed our situation.

May 13 - Mr. James Bennett came from Hospice and said that Clay had been accepted. We completed the paperwork, and Clay was evaluated. The nurse found that he wasn't sick; he was just old.

May 15 - A hospital bed and other items were delivered. Mr. Bennett gave me three phone numbers. He said, "We want you to be able to contact someone night or day if you have any concerns or questions."

Clay is weaker physically, but he knows what's going on, and he doesn't mind telling me when there is something he doesn't like.

May 16 - A hospice nurse came yesterday and brought five medications that we might need in the future. Thank you for your prayers and offers of help.

May 18 - I wrote this in "Hill Country Happenings," a weekly update that I email to family and friends.

"Last week was quite eventful. I am thankful for all I learned and for the support I received.

Clay cannot get out of bed by himself. He can only stand for a minute or two and only then with help. His mind is sound, he is not in pain, and he doesn't mind letting me know if he needs another blanket or if his water is not cold enough.

If you even think you might need the help of Hospice, please give them a call. They are staffed with wonderful, caring people, and they have access to all kinds of resources. I called Ave Maria Hospice in Fredericksburg last Monday. Since then, four nurses have seen and evaluated Clay, and we have received equipment and medications. These people not only care about the one who is ill but the family as well. They are there to serve. Many of you have been concerned about me. I am doing well."

May 20 - An article I read listed nine things that happen when a body is shutting down, and Clay checks off every box. Does not falling apart mean that you don't care? No, not everyone reacts to life and death issues in the same way. I have learned to be content. That doesn't mean that I'm happy. It means that I have learned to let God take care of things that I can't control. All I must do is get up every day and do my best. In Matthew 6:34, Jesus said, "Therefore do not worry about tomorrow, for tomorrow will worry about itself. Each day has enough trouble of its own." Thank you for all your support. Today we are OK.

Saturday, May 23 - Hill Country Happenings.

I want you to know what has gone on in the last two weeks. Clay's 97-year-old body is getting weaker each day. Sometimes when you are in the middle of a situation, it becomes normal. That is what happened to me. I didn't realize that both he and I needed help.

I am so thankful that Clay H. found Ave Maria Hospice in Fredericksburg. They asked if I had contacted someone about the final arrangements. I knew that Clay wanted to be cremated and that he wanted his ashes scattered on Mason Mountain, but I hadn't thought about who to call to arrange it.

Again, Clay H. had the right suggestion. I called Mason Funeral Home and talked to Randy Beckman. He took our information and assured me that he would take care of everything. When the time comes, I only need to make two phone calls. First, I call Hospice, and then I call Randy. They will take care of everything. I also learned that I don't have to be in a hurry to make those calls. I can take my time.

I'm not telling you this to get sympathy or to have you feel sad. I want to pass on what I've learned so that you won't hesitate to make the calls if you are ever in a similar situation,

One thing is sure; we are all going to die. That is normal. We start dying the moment we are born. We all have an expiration date, and the Lord knows that date; we don't. We have been blessed with caring friends and family and now Hospice. Clay is not in pain; his body is just slowing down.

Most of you know that I have a weird sense of humor. I told the Chaplain, Dan McGookey, that I had considered using the King David comfort method with Clay, but I couldn't find any qualified applicants. He didn't know what that was. Do you? Read 1 Kings 1:1-4.

God is in control, and His timing is perfect.

May 28 - James Bennett, an RN with Hospice, came yesterday. He gave me some helpful hints on how to move Clay without hurting him or myself and other tips on helping Clay be more comfortable.

May 29 - Clay will not get better. He is slowly getting weaker. After the first two or three weeks of rapid changes, they are happing more slowly, but they are coming. I am resigned. Yes, that is the word I intended to use; resigned - having accepted something unpleasant that one cannot do anything about. That says it all. Winston Churchill is quoted as saying, "It's not good enough that we do our best. Sometimes we must do what is required." I am officially an RN, a Resident Nurse. So far, my patient is receiving good care.

The article "And Then it is Winter" by an unknown author explains how quickly our lives change:

"It seems like yesterday that I was young. I wonder where all those years went. The winter of my life catches me by surprise. How did I get here so fast? Where did my youth go? Now I see an older person in myself, and I am unprepared for the aches and pains and the loss of strength and ability to go and do things that I used to do. Don't put things off too long! Do what you can today; we are not promised tomorrow."

Thank you for the calls, texts, and emails.

May 31 - We are in a holding pattern. No matter what the situation, God's word is true, and we can trust His timing. One of my favorite Bible passages is Philippians 4:6-7, "Be anxious for nothing, but in everything, by prayer and petition, with thanksgiving, present your requests to God. And the peace of God, which surpasses all understanding, will guard your hearts and your minds in Christ Jesus." When we rely on God, we can have that peace, no matter what. God is good.

June 1 - Yesterday and last night were not good. Clay was very restless all day, and by the afternoon and night, he couldn't swallow any liquid without coughing. I started giving him Ativan. Hospice said to use this for anxiety, breathing, and coughing problems. It is a relaxant that calms things down. It worked.

The Hospice nurse verified that I did the right thing. She said that the restlessness was another sign of the body slowing down, and she suggested that I give him a small amount of morphine at bedtime so that we both can sleep. With her help, we changed the bed, etc., and Clay has been peaceful all day. I'm glad that I did the right thing. God works things out on his timeline. We can trust Him, and that gives us peace.

June 3 - Clay is slowly dying. That may sound like a harsh way of putting it, but that is what's happening. There is no way that he will get better. After 97 years, his body is slowing down. Hospice has been with us for three weeks. Alica met Mr. Bennett when she came for a quick visit to check on us. He assured us that we are doing all that we can do to make Clay comfortable, which is the objective.

Clay sleeps most of the time, and he cannot swallow liquids, except for a few sips at a time, without choking. He is most awake and aware late in the afternoon. He knew Alica and Clay H. yesterday. He asked Clay H. a question he often asked, "When is it going to rain?"

Now we wait. Alica, Clay H., and I are prepared for the end. We have seen Clay declining more rapidly in the last few weeks. For us, it will be a relief when it is over. That is not being callous; that is being realistic. It is tough to see their dad and my husband in his current condition. We have had years to process the changes in Clay's health and his recent rapid decline. When he leaves this world, he will not be dead. He will be changed, and he will go to the next world to live again.

In some ways, his death will be harder on you, his nieces, nephews, and friends than on us because we have had time to process everything as we go through the day-to-day changes. What you remember and see in your mind's eye is the Clay that used to be. That is a good thing. Thank you for your support. We will continue to keep him comfortable and to keep you informed.

The poem "Gone from My Sight" by Henry Van Dyke, is designed to help people understand the normal, natural way death occurs from disease or old age. It describes what will happen in a beautiful way:

"I am standing upon the seashore. A ship at my side spreads her white sails to the moving breeze and starts for the blue ocean. She is an object of beauty and strength. I stand and watch her until, at length, she hangs like a speck of white cloud just where the sea and sky come to mingle with each other. Then, someone at my side says, "There, she is gone."

Gone where?

Gone from my sight. That is all. She is just as large in mast, hull, and spar as she was when she left my side. And she is just as able to bear her load of living freight to her destined port. Her diminished size is in me -- not in her. And, just at the moment when someone says, "There, she is gone." There are other eyes watching her coming and other voices ready to take up the glad shout, "Here she comes!"

And that is dying.

June 4 - Clay is still with us, but each day I wonder if it will be the last. There have been changes, and the Hospice nurses tell me that these are part of the normal process of a body shutting down.

Clay is not in pain, and he has me to wait on him hand and foot, 24/7; what more could he want? Some wonder how I can smile. That's easy. I'm doing all I can, and I let God take care of the rest. He is doing a good job. We have support from friends and family like you. All will be well.

June 5 - I am reminded of a joke I heard long ago, "Lord, give me patience. . . and give it to me RIGHT NOW." I know that God is in control, that His timing is perfect, and that things will happen when they are supposed to . . . but . . .

June 6 - Some have wondered why I'm not falling apart. There are several reasons. For one thing, that is not how I react. I'm not made that way. But the main reason is that I have learned to accept the things I cannot change.

Clay had not spoken clearly in several days, but he started talking, in a loud, clear voice, this afternoon about a party he attended when he was nine or ten years old. The first thing he said was, "I remember all that water; you've never seen so much water! It was as blue as could be." For the next 30 minutes, he told me about a week-long engagement party for Dorothy Schwartz that he and his family attended at Balmorhea, Texas.

Balmorhea is called "A Cool Oasis in the High Desert." More than 15 million gallons of water flow through the pool each day, gushing from the San Solomon Springs. The pool is up to 25 feet deep, covers 1.3 acres, and holds 3.5 million gallons of water. The water temperature stays at 72 to 76 degrees year-round. I recently learned that the Splittgerber family had owned part of that property. Tommy Splittgerber and Clay were good friends.

The hospice people told me that, toward the end, Clay might tell some wild stories, so I questioned him to see if this story was real or imagined. I asked, "Who was there"?

He said, "I don't remember everyone, but it was a really big party; there were a lot of people. We stayed a week. The grass was green, the water was blue, and it was really pretty. Mr. Schwartz was a big man with a long black beard. His son was named Dan. Dorothy was a beautiful woman, but those other girls weren't good lookin' at all!" Clay always had an eye for the ladies. He wondered if any of them might still be alive. Then he said, "No, probably not, I was just a kid, and that was over 90 years ago."

He also talked about a man who drowned while he was fishing. He said, "I don't remember his name, but he went fishing by the creek, and he couldn't swim. There was a flash flood; the water came down, and it filled his boots. That was the end of him." I enjoyed listening to Clay talk about old times. These were the last stories he told.

June 7 - This afternoon, I was sitting beside Clay's bed. Out of the blue, in his normal voice, he asked, "Are you sleepy?" When I said, "Yes," he said, "Well, go take a nap!" Those were the last words he spoke. When I am tired, I remember his words, and I smile. He cared about me.

June 8 - Clay is weaker every day. Lord, help him to have a peaceful passing! I've prayed that I would be able to care for Clay as long as he needed me, and I have been able to do that. No matter what, God is good.

June 9 - We show our love for others by what we do. Yes, Clay and I love each other. We care for and take care of each other. I am doing the best I can to care for him. "Do to others as you would have them do to you." Luke 6:31

Our son called to check on his dad. He said that he was awakened at 5:30 a.m. by a dream about him. I also dreamed about Clay this morning. I am praying for a peaceful passing and for it to happen quickly. I know the Lord is in control, but perhaps I can encourage Him a little.

June 11 - How am I doing? I'm tired.

The hospital bed was delivered a month ago. As rapidly as Clay had been declining, I couldn't see how he could live longer than a few more days. I never thought he would be in that bed for four weeks. Now I wonder, how many more? The Hospice nurses have been telling me that it could take a long time for him to die, but I haven't wanted to believe it. Not because I want him gone but because I know that he can't get better.

I've done my best to take good care of Clay, but some things are out of my control. His body is breaking down at pressure points, spine, hip bones, shoulders, ankles, etc. He may develop bedsores. It breaks my heart. We have an air mattress, and I turn Clay every few hours, but that will not be enough if this goes on much longer. It is not my place to question God, but I can't help but ask, "Why?" Why so long, Lord?

Sorry. I had a bad morning, and here I am, dumping it all on you. Thank you for all you do to help us. I know that the Lord is gracious and good and that everything happens at the proper time. I just want that time to be soon, very soon.

I apologize for this morning's "rant." What got to me was the feeling of helplessness. I can't "fix" anything. I can't make it better. I know that God will take care of both Clay and me, but it is hard. I am better now, thanks to a nap and your prayers and calls.

June 12 - I am back in my watch and wait role now. Of course, I am still asking, "What is taking so long?" But I am OK with waiting—most of the time. Yes, Lord, give me patience.

June 13 - Another Saturday, and I wonder what will happen today. Every Saturday, for the last six weeks, something unusual has happened. We'll see what today brings. I didn't turn Clay today. He looked so peaceful and pain-free that I decided to leave things alone. He is not eating or drinking anything. Clay has not been awake since the nurse left. I gave him his medication about midnight. When I awoke at 6:00 AM, his body was there, but he had been gone for several hours.

June 14 - Hill Country Happenings.

I am writing to ask you to be happy for Clay and for me. I am crying, but not because I am sad. I am crying because I am relieved, and I am thankful. Clay was not in pain. He was at home, on the Ranch, where he wanted to be when he died early this morning. I prayed that Clay would have a peaceful passing, and God answered my prayer.

Who was Alva Clay Lindsay? He was the last of his generation, and he was many things to many people. He was a brother, uncle, husband, father, and friend to many. Those who knew him well knew the man with the wicked wit, the kind heart, the mischievous nature. The fun-loving, people-loving, children-loving, blonde-loving gentle man that he was. I want you to remember that man. I want you to remember the good times, the fun times, the happy times, and even the sad times you shared.

I had a vivid dream about Clay five days ago. In my dream, I was sitting at the end of a large room. From where I sat, I could see down a long hall, and there were doors on both sides of the hallway.

As I watched, a door open and Clay walked into the hall. He was fully dressed in his hat, jeans, western shirt, boots, and belt. I was amazed. I thought, "How did you do that? You haven't been able to dress yourself in weeks?"

Without hesitation and without looking right or left, he walked briskly across the room and through the open outer door. I could see a car parked there. Clay walked to the car, leaned down, and talked to the driver through his open window.

Then the scene changed. Alica and I were standing by the dirt road that goes past our house. We heard a noise, and there came Clay driving his old brown truck up the road. He had his hat cocked back; he was looking straight ahead, and he was driving as fast as the truck would go. Clay only had one speed, wide open. Through the gate, up the dirt road, and over the hill, he went. All we could see was a cloud of dust. I'm not sure how you get to heaven. Perhaps one way is by driving up a dusty road.

June 14 - I made two phone calls. Ave Maria Hospice and the Mason Funeral Home took care of everything. Clay H. told Mr. Bennett that his dad always said he just wanted to fall over in the pasture but being at home in his room was perfect since that didn't happen.

After everyone left, Clay H. said, "Well, I'm glad it's over!" I replied, "So am I." Clay H. and I took a nice drive to the back part of the Ranch. The grass he planted was growing, and the pastures were beautiful and green. He said, "I wish Dad had been able to stay around long enough to see it."

June 16 - When Clay was getting more and more feeble, my prayer was, "Lord, help me know what to do. Help me to help him." Even when I complained to the Lord and asked, "How long? What are you waiting for?" He didn't quit listening to me. I was able to do what was needed until it was time for Clay to go.

You prayed for both of us, and now you are praying for me. How am I doing? Because of your prayers and that "peace that passes all understanding," I am doing well, and I can do what needs to be done.

"The Dash," by Linda Ellis

A man stood to speak at the funeral of a friend. He referred to the dates on the tombstone from the beginning to the end. He noted that first came the date of birth and spoke of the following date with tears, but he said what mattered most was the dash between those years. For that dash represents all the time they spent alive on earth, and now only those who loved them know what that little line is worth.

2021

Since Clay's death, I have been writing about him and the people, places, and events that shaped his life. This book, "Good Times," is my way of sharing the man I knew with you. Clay wanted to be cremated, and he wanted his ashes scattered on Mason Mountain. In a private ceremony, the immediate family went to the top of Mason Mountain on Sunday, Mar. 28, 2021, and Alica and Clay H. fulfilled their dad's wish. The celebration of Clay's life is described in the next chapter.

Alva Clay Lindsay was loved, he is missed, and he will always be remembered.

46
Celebrating the Life of Alva Clay Lindsay

Alva Clay Lindsay, the son of John Alva Lindsay and Jesse Gamel Lindsay, was born Aug. 15, 1922, on the Lindsay Ranch in Mason, Texas. After living 97 years and ten months, that is where he died June 14, 2020.

Clay's roots ran deep in Texas and Mason County. His maternal grandfather, John William Gamel, was one of the men who gave land for Mason's town square. His great-grandfather, Franz (Francis) Kettner, came to Texas from Germany in 1848.

His paternal 2nd-great-grandfathers, James Buchanan Lindsay and Thomas S. Milligan, were both in Texas in 1836. They got to Mason as soon as they could. One of his relatives, Sterling C. Robertson, signed the Texas Declaration of Independence.

Clay and his sisters, Doris, and Peggy attended the Behrens School in Mason County. They rode horses or drove a team and wagon five miles each way every school day. Some called Behrens the Jackass School because the students rode their donkeys, horses, and mules to school.

The end-of-school party and picnic always included a goat roping contest, and Clay won more often than he lost. Stella Gipson Polk was one of Clay's teachers.

He attended high school in Mason and then went to the University of Texas in Austin. His time at UT was cut short by WWII. Clay and several other young men went from Mason to San Antonio to enlist. Clay didn't remember how it happened, but he enlisted in the United States Merchant Marine Corps Nov. 20, 1942. This twenty-year-old young man lived an entirely different life for the next few years.

Clay was preceded in death by his parents, brother Jack and his sisters Effie, Doris, and Peggy. His nephew Tom Lindsay, who lived in Australia, his great-great-nephew Aiden Hayes, who lived in New Zealand, and many close friends.

Clay is survived by his wife Deloris, his daughter, Alica Kay Lindsay of Garland, Texas, his son Clay Haley Lindsay, daughter-in-law Mendy Beaty Lindsay and grandson Garrett Clay Lindsay, all of Mason, Texas, and many nieces and nephews.

Our prayers were answered Sunday morning, June 14, 2020, when Alva Clay Lindsay left this earth. He was not in pain. He was at home on the Ranch where he wanted to be, and he had a peaceful passing.

If you didn't know him well, let me tell you a little about him. Clay enjoyed playing games of all kinds. He started playing dominoes with the old men on the square when he was seven years old.

One time, Clay pointed to a picture in the courthouse and said, "I used to play dominoes with that man." The young man, whose office we were in, said, "Oh, no, you couldn't have. That was my grandfather, and he's been dead for a long time!" Clay replied, "Well, he was really old, and I was really young, but I played with him."

He remembered this gentleman so well because he would give Clay a dime every week and have him go downstairs to the drugstore to buy them each an ice cream cone. A seven-year-old would never forget a man like that.

Clay also enjoyed dancing, parties, and music, especially Patsy Cline. He never smoked nor drank, except for sweet tea and Pepsi-Cola, and he didn't run around with wild women until he met the "cheerful, young, divorcee" that he married.

Clay was extremely competitive, a great winner, and a terrible loser. He never "let" anyone, young or old, win. When he did lose, he didn't like it very much.

Clay was many things to many people. He was a son, brother, uncle, husband, father, grandfather, and friend to many. Those who knew him well knew the hard-working man with a quick wit, who always had a comeback.

Clay was a generous man with a kind heart and a mischievous nature who enjoyed life. He loved his family, children, and blondes. He was a gentleman and a gentle man in every sense of the word.

On the day he died, his daughter, Alica Kay Lindsay, wrote:

My Dad passed away peacefully early this morning with my mom by his side. The last few months were tough on all of us, and I'm glad I got to visit with him multiple times, as did my brother. My mom was always there.

He knew I was there the last few visits, but that isn't the dad I am going to remember. I'm going to remember the dad that always took care of me and wanted me to be happy and healthy. The dad who helped me whenever I needed it, the dad who taught me to play Pitch, to love road trips, and never to settle. We will miss him dearly. We are glad he is at peace, in a better place, and got to leave this world at his Ranch.

THE FINAL PARTY – MARCH 26-27, 2021

Alva Clay Lindsay enjoyed people and parties. The first big birthday party was his 80th in 2002. Since then, each year, he would ask, "Are we going to have another party?" Sometimes they were big parties; sometimes they were just gatherings of a few friends and family members, but he enjoyed them all.

Visiting, riding around the Ranch, playing Pitch, dominoes, Skip-Bo, Crazy Eights, or Old Maid with the little ones, Clay always had a good time. When the party was over, he would say, "That was really nice, wasn't it?"

Clay would sit on the porch and watch the road. When guests didn't arrive as soon as he thought they should, he would say, "I don't know what's taking them so long! If I was going somewhere, I'd get up and get off!" When the company finally arrived, Clay would meet them at the door and ask, "What took you so long?"

Clay died June 14, 2020. He wanted to be cremated, and he wanted his ashes scattered on Mason Mountain. We chose March 26-27, 2021, as the time when we would invite family and friends to come to Mason to fulfill his wish and to say our final goodbyes.

Clay H. plowed, planted, and cleared mesquite for several months. Mendy, Garrett, and Clay H. worked for weeks clearing and getting the Ranch and the top of Mason Mountain ready for company. What they accomplished was amazing.

Using eight-inch channel iron, his plasma cutter, his skill, and his artistic talent, Clay H. designed, fabricated, and installed an eight-foot-tall cross on the southern end of Mason Mountain to honor his dad. He placed the granite VA marker, inscribed with his dad's birth and death dates and the words, "He Loved This Land," at the foot of the cross.

The only word to describe the cross is "perfection." The placement is such that it is visible when you drive to the Manor and from the Manor itself. One guest commented, "It is inspirational."

The weekend activities began on Friday, March 26th, at Nacho's Café. After good food and conversation, everyone did their own thing. Of course, there was a Pitch game. In any Lindsay family gathering of more than two people, someone will say, "Let's play Pitch."

When I sent out the invitations for Clay's Celebration, many replied, "Let me know if I can help." Don't tell me that if you don't mean it! Everyone I asked did everything I asked them to do, and they did it well. Clay's party was a success, and everyone had a wonderful time.

First, I want to thank Clay H., Mendy, and Garrett Lindsay. They worked tirelessly to make sure that everything was ready. On Saturday morning, they oversaw everything that was happening on top of Mason Mountain, from the placement of the chairs to the arrangement of Clay's boots, hat, and photograph at the foot of the cross.

A special thank you to Zeph Bruce and Robert Johnston ensuring that the chairs were in place when and where needed. Pam Haley Bruce and Jennifer Porter-Davis registered the guests and gave everyone a package of Clay's favorite lemon drops, a red envelope containing a few quotes from this book, and a name tag. Well done, ladies.

Karla Schmidt and Rhonda Thomas picked up breakfast tacos, and Kerry and Robert Johnston brought doughnuts to Mason Mountain Manor for the guests to enjoy. Bing and Michaelle Canion and Jason Wells and Carrie Welch, our dear deer hunters, served as hosts at Mason Mountain Manor. Thank you, thank you. I couldn't have had a better crew. Everyone was impressed.

More than 60 people came to the Lindsay Ranch on Saturday, March 27, 2021. They came from twenty-four cities in Texas, Colorado, California, and Connecticut to celebrate Alva Clay Lindsay's life. Even though he was not physically here for his final party, I know that he watched everyone as they arrived, and he was happy to see them.

After visiting at the Manor, we went to the top of Mason Mountain for the formal ceremony. However, since it was a Lindsay gathering, it wasn't precisely formal.

At the proper time, some drove their vehicles, some walked. Bing and Jason transported many of the ladies to the top of Mason Mountain in their "buggies," or as I call them, their fabulous four-wheelers. Everyone enjoyed the experience. Most of the guests had never been to the top of Mason Mountain before; they were impressed. The cross was majestic, and the view was magnificent.

I was the designated MC. I have been known to say a word or two, so I didn't mind fulfilling that role. The ceremony began with a prayer by Mr. Dan. McGookey, a Chaplain with Ave Maria Hospice in Fredericksburg, TX.

When I asked if anyone would like to speak to the group, a couple of people wrote what they wanted to convey and asked me to read their words. My sister, Pamela Haley Bruce, wrote:

Clay,

Although you are no longer physically with us, you will forever remain in our hearts and your spirit and will always be felt. You touched so many different people in so many ways, friends and family.

It was indeed an honor to know you. I met you when I was ten years old when you married my sister. I always felt so special whenever you and Dee would come to Lubbock and take me to dinner when I lived with my foster family. You never left my side at Melody's wedding. That meant the world to me.

Fast forward several years. Thank you for being a great influence on my son, Zeph. He learned life lessons from you and Dee. You were always there for me through the good, the bad, and the ugly. I can't wait to hear you say, "What took you so long?" when I get to heaven.

Your favorite sister-in-law, Pam."

Clay's nephew, John Clabe Long, wrote:

Unkie,

Every family needs uncles and aunts. My Uncle Clay's influence on my life is profound, as was yours, Dee. The first thing he taught me as a nine-year-old was how to save money. Saving every dime or quarter is important. If you save money every day, you can become well to do.

Wealth is not important for buying toys. Having a little cash gives you "freedom." Savings give you the "independence" to live your life, with the blessings of God, the way you want to! You can be who you want to be. Thanks, Unkie; I have never forgotten what you taught me.

John Clabe Long.

William Alan Johnson told the crowd about his first meeting with Clay at one of the Haley Family Reunions. Clay said, "Hello." and that was it. Later, when Alan visited the Ranch, Clay took him for a ride. They drove and drove, and Clay talked the entire time. He was an entirely different man in his environment.

Alan also told a few stories about riding with Clay. Most could relate to riding in the truck with Clay and living to talk about it. Everyone thought that they were the "official gate openers." It depended upon who was riding in the right-hand seat at any given moment. A few remembered being left at the gate after they opened it.

Nephew Mike Davis shared stories of traveling with his uncle. He has never forgotten how to change tires. He recalled the good food they ate while they were "on the road," peanut butter, crackers, Zagnut candy bars, and Pepsi-Cola's, some of the time. Sleeping in the Rambler was also a treat.

Janet Lee (Dolly) Long Hannon told the group how appreciative she was that Clay looked after her mother, Effie, when she was ill. She also reminisced about her visit with Clay at Alica's wedding reception in Dallas.

Diane Kettner Esquell's husband, James, told the story of a domino game between Clay and Diane's Dad, Henry Kettner. James said, "They were both good players. After a few plays, Clay said, "Play that deuce-trey, Henry." Henry said, "I've got other plays." A few minutes later, Clay again said, "Play that deuce-trey, Henry. That's the only play you've got!" Henry reluctantly laid it in. Then Clay said, "Now, tell me how much count I get!"

The stories brought nods of agreement, a lot of laughter, and occasional tears to everyone's eyes. The ceremony ended with Mendy Beaty Lindsay playing Taps. That haunting melody, floating across the land, was beautiful. Thank you, Mendy.

Our nephew, Coby James, owner of Gulf Coast Imaging Studios, a full-service photographic studio located in Texas City, Texas, specializing in studio and location portraiture, brought his equipment to the Ranch and photographed the event. Garrett Clay Lindsay and Diego Silvas assisted him.

Coby, your photographs and videos captured memories that will live longer than most of us. They will be passed down for generations. Thank you is not enough to convey my gratitude for all you did.

After the ceremony on Mason Mountain, some went to Willow Creek for lunch. The next scheduled event was a get-together at Lea Lou Co-Op Saturday night. Everyone enjoyed the outdoor venue.

Sunday morning, after a brief worship service, the immediate family drove to Mason Mountain and scattered Clay's ashes. Alica and Clay H. walked to the southern tip of Mason Mountain. The wind started blowing. Clay's ashes formed a cloud, and his remains floated out over the land he loved. It was the perfect ending.

We returned to the house, where the party continued Sunday afternoon and evening with more Pitch playing, family visits, and storytelling. Thank you for coming and thank you for everything you did to make Clay's final party a true celebration of his extraordinary life. Remember the good times you shared with Alva Clay Lindsay. He loved you all.

EPILOGUE

After Clay's death, I asked friends and relatives to share some of their memories of him. Their words describe the man they knew and how he influenced their lives. I included family history because those people, places, and events shaped his life. I planned to create a handout for family and friends attending his memorial service; however, the project grew and grew. This book is the result.

Why did Clay marry after being single for 49 years? What was so special about me? I was fourteen years younger than Clay. I was not bad-looking, I was independent, and I was not looking for a husband.

When he asked me to marry him, I didn't say yes. I said, "I have been married, and I don't know if I want to go through that again!" He replied, "Well, I'm not him. Let me know if you change your mind."

In the fall of 1971, Clay decided to clean out the earth tanks on the ranch. It had not rained in a long time, and the tank was dry. He had an old 1940-1950 model Farmall tricycle frontend tractor with a bucket on the front of it.

He scooped up a load of dirt from the middle of the earth tank, drove up the bank, and dumped the dirt over the edge. He overloaded the bucket, lifted it too high, and the tractor, bucket, and dirt flipped over backward.

Clay jumped off. He wasn't pinned under the tractor, but he could have been. He wasn't injured or killed, but he could have been. Those thoughts went through my mind when he told me the story.

He was working by himself. There was no one around to know or help if he was injured. That scared me. I started thinking of all the "what-ifs." I realized that he could have been killed and that I didn't want to live my life without him.

Being the romantic that I am, I called Clay and said, "I've decided. We are getting married. Go get your blood test." In the United States, premarital blood laws were enacted during the 1930s and 1940s when syphilis was considered a potential public health concern. The blood tests were to ensure the infected person got treated prior to infecting his or her partner or child. We got our marriage license.

On Saturday, Oct. 30, 1971, we drove to Leakey, Texas. Clay's grandparents lived in Leakey. His father, John Alva Lindsay, was born there, and his grandmother was buried there. It was not far from Mountain Home, Texas, where Clay lived after WWII. He knew the area, but I had never been to that part of the state.

We located a preacher and were married in his living room with his wife as our witness. After the wedding ceremony, we drove to Del Rio, Texas, and then across the border to Ciudad Acuna, Mexico.

We stayed at Ma Crosby's, the Internationally Famous Café & Hotel, previously owned by Mrs. Esther Otamendi Crosby, one of Clay's distant relatives. He had fond memories of the many times he and his family stayed there. It was very elegant.

I hope you have enjoyed getting to know Alva Clay Lindsay, the officer, and gentleman that so many people loved.

When I asked Clay, "Why haven't you married before now?" He said, "I guess I was just waiting for you!" I'm glad you waited for me, Clay.

Thank you for the "Good Times."

47
Photos

ome stories are best told in pictures. Each image represents a snapshot of a point in time and place; so, if a picture is worth a thousand words, then this may be the longest chapter in the book!

Lindsay Ranch home after remodel and installation of rock wall in 1936.

John Alva Lindsay (Daddy John), Mason parade c. 1939.

Jesse Presnall Gamel Lindsay, Mason parade c. 1939.

A boy and his dog, Alva Clay Lindsay.

Alva Clay Lindsay with nephews John Clabe and James Lindsay Long. Clay was on leave for his Grandmother Alice Kettner Gamel's funeral.

Alva Clay Lindsay (left, in both photos) with unknown friend. WWII Merchant Marine.

*Jesse Presnall Lindsay and granddaughter
Deborah (Debbie) Dea Dobbs Green.*

Clay and great-niece Olivia in San Antonio.

Niece Sherry Lindsay & Uncle Clay

Clay Haley Lindsay and Mendy Beaty
Wedding Buggy

Lindsay family – Alica Kay, Clay Haley, Deloris
& Alva Clay Lindsay

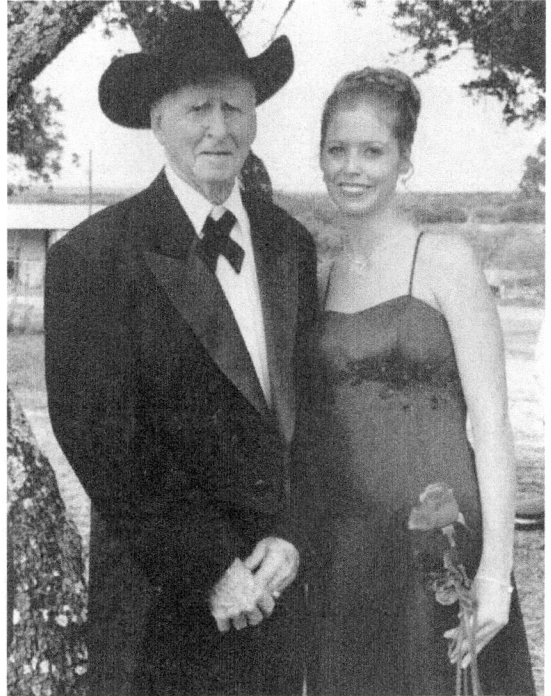

Alva Clay Lindsay and his daughter,
Alica Kay Lindsay

*Clay supervising. Watching Clay H. build
the new entrance,90th birthday.*

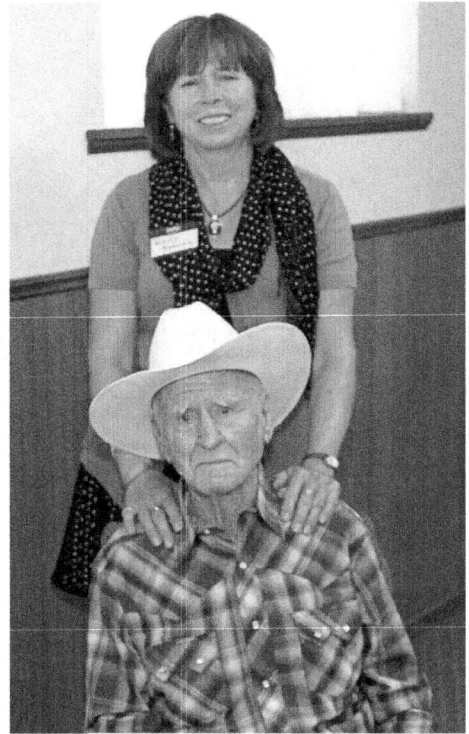

*Clay & Janet Lee (Dolly) Hannon
90th birthday.*

*Garrett Clay Lindsay and his Papa Clay wearing football
jerseys with their graduation year:
Garrett 2025, Papa Clay 1941.*

*Alica Kay Lindsay & her Dad,
Alva Clay Lindsay,
90th birthday.*

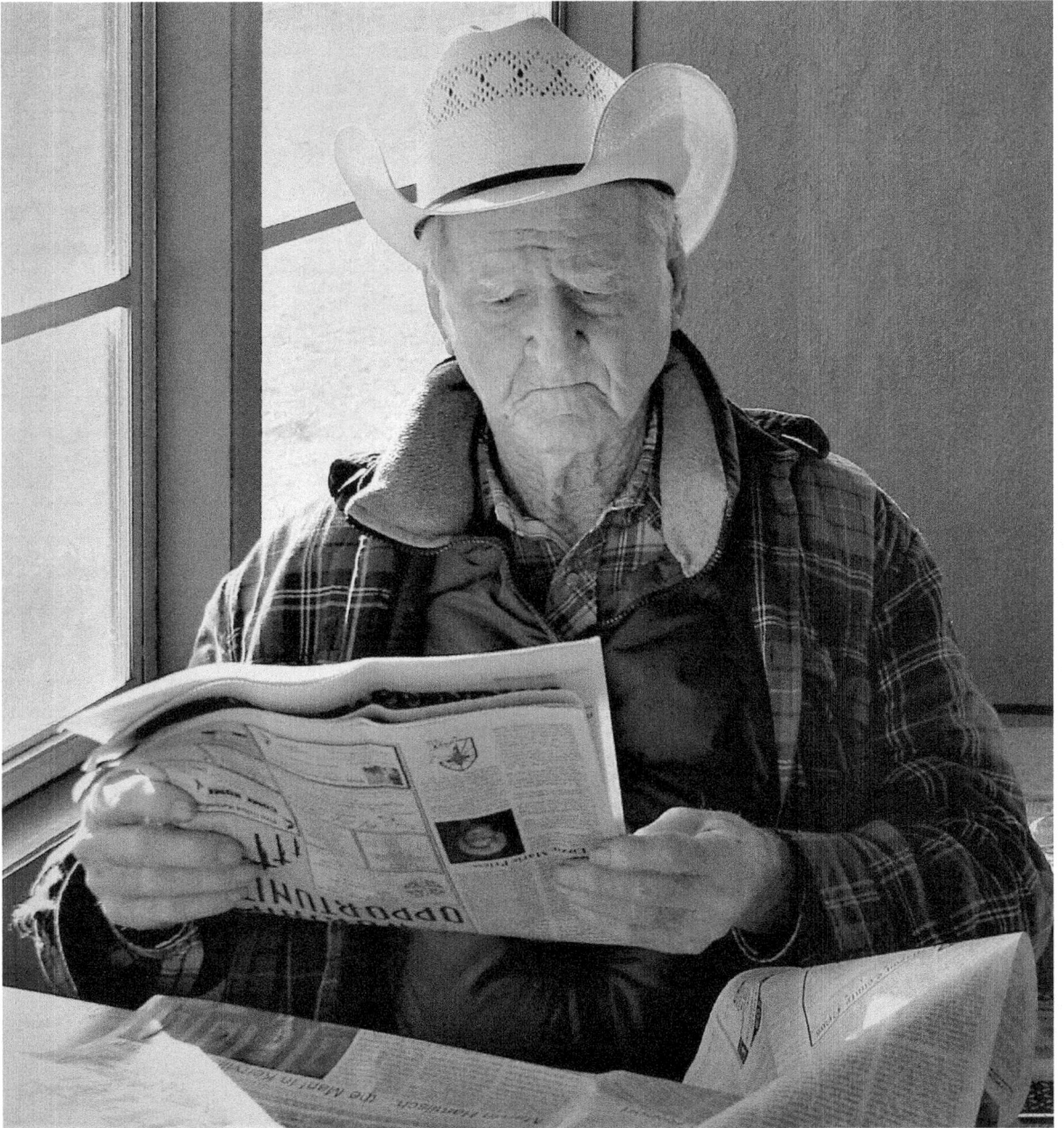

Clay & newspaper. "There's not a thing in here!"

32 John Lindsay

16 James Buchanan Lindsay
b: 29 Mar 1813
d: 1874

33 Martha Ledford

8 John Allen Lindsay
b: 22 Jul 1836
p: Jackson County, AL
m: 1858
p: Mason TX
d: 1 Oct 1891
p: Mason TX

17 Martha ?
b:
d:

34

35

36 George Milligan

18 Thomas Stanley Milligan
b: 1819
d: 19 Feb 1860

37

4 Alva James Lindsay
b: 21 Apr 1863
p: Mason TX
m: 28 Jun 1883
p: Mason TX
d: 2 Nov 1926
p: Mason TX

9 Matilda Ellen Milligan
b: 10 Sep 1842
p: Titus County TX
d: 22 Dec 1934
p: Schleicher County TX

19 Mahayla Allen
b: 1825
d: 4 May 1890

38 Hugh Joseph Allen Sr.

39 Caroline Matilda Frazier

2 John Alva Lindsay
b: 13 Mar 1887
p: Mason TX
m: 12 Sep 1914
p: Mason TX
d: 30 Mar 1974
p: Mason TX

40

20
b:
d:

41

42

21
b:
d:

43

10 George Turner
b: 1848
p:
m:
p:
d: 1910
p:

5 Mary Ellen Turner
b: 7 Sep 1865
p: Arkansas
d: 12 May 1890
p: Leakey TX

22 John Sanford Rainwater
b: 1819
d: 1899

44

45

11 Mary Ellen Rainwater
b: 1847
p:
d: 1925
p:

23 Lucinda Shehan
b: 1822
d: 1850

46

47

1 Alva Clay Lindsay
b: 15 Aug 1922
p: Mason, Mason Co. TX.
m: 30 Oct 1971
p: Leakey, Texas
d: 14 Jun 2020
p: Mason, Mason Co. TX.

sp: Myrtis Deloris Haley

24 Israel Gamel
b: 1788
d: 1828

48

49

12 William Thomas Gamel
b: 10 Jan 1822
p: Alabama ?
m:
p:
d: 1906
p: Mason County, Texas

25 Nancy Smith
b: 1790
d: 1844

50

51

6 John William Gamel
b: 16 Aug 1844
p: Georgia
m: 15 Sep 1881
p: Mason TX
d: 21 Mar 1917
p: Mason TX

26 William Tucker
b: 1795
d: 1866

52

53

13 Catherine Tucker
b: 12 Apr
p:
d:
p: Mason County, Texas

27 Rebecca Reynolds
b: 1808
d: 1890

54

55

3 Jesse Presnall Gamel
b: 23 Oct 1897
p: Mason TX
d: 23 Mar 1987
p: Mason TX

28 Franz Lambert Kettner
b: 1793
d: 1875

56

57

14 Francis (Franz) Kettner
b: 23 Oct 1826
p: Oberkirck, Germany
m: 3 Sep 1857
p: Texas, United States
d: 8 Sep 1907
p: Texas, United States

29 Maria Clara Strickfaden
b: 1802
d: 1869

58

59

7 Alice Kettner
b: 4 Jun 1863
p:
d: 29 May 1942
p: Mason TX

30 Johann P. Kahler
b: 1802
d: 1872

60

61

15 Catherina Keller
b: 1839
p:
d: 1913
p:

31 Anna Maria Mohr
b: 1817
d: 1907

62

63

Pedigree Chart, Alva Clay Lindsay.

ABOUT THE AUTHOR

Deloris Haley Lindsay was born in a small, rural community close to Abernathy, Texas. Growing up during the Depression and WWII wasn't easy. Still, the Haley family of four, living on an 80-acre farm, managed very well, even though their two-room house didn't have electricity or running water.

Deloris and her brother had chores to do each day. Taking care of the animals, the garden, and the orchard was hard work, but the family enjoyed fresh milk, cream, butter, and eggs every day and fried chicken on Sunday. A Saturday afternoon trip to town in the old Ford provided the things they couldn't raise on the farm.

Deloris attended school in Abernathy and Lubbock, Texas. She graduated from Lubbock High School and married the same year. Shortly after, she moved to Pueblo, Colorado, where she lived for many years. After her divorce, Deloris returned to Texas. A few years later, she met and married a 49-year-old bachelor, Alva Clay Lindsay. Their marriage was blessed with a daughter, a son, and a grandson.

The Historic Lindsay Ranch, established in 1858, is in Mason, Texas, in the northern part of the Texas Hill Country. The family Ranch was Clay's lifelong home, and it was there he died June 14, 2020.

Deloris still resides on the Ranch. She manages two guesthouses, the Cabin on Comanche Creek and Mason Mountain Manor, and maintains the Ranch's website www.lindsayranch.net.

Deloris shares a daily "Thought for Today" and a weekly "Hill Country Happenings" article with friends and family.

An amateur photographer, Deloris sees beauty in everyday things such as sunsets, wildflowers, green grass, blue skies, and water in the creek. Through her photographs, Deloris Haley Lindsay shares that beauty with others.

Made in the USA
Coppell, TX
10 July 2021